ZIK

A SELECTION
FROM THE SPEECHES OF
NNAMDI AZIKIWE

Governor-General of the Federation of Nigeria
formerly President of the Nigerian Senate
formerly Premier of the Eastern Region of Nigeria

CAMBRIDGE
AT THE UNIVERSITY PRESS
1961

PUBLISHED BY

THE SYNDICS OF THE CAMBRIDGE UNIVERSITY PRESS

Bentley House, 200 Euston Road, London, N.W.1

American Branch: 32 East 57th Street, New York, 22, N.Y.

West African Manager: P.O. Box 33, Ibadan, Nigeria

©

CAMBRIDGE UNIVERSITY PRESS

1961

PRINTED AND BOUND IN ENGLAND BY
HAZELL WATSON AND VINEY LTD
AYLESBURY AND SLOUGH

CONTENTS

PREFACE

Many well-wishers have urged me to arrange for publication the speeches which I have delivered over a number of years. With the help of Mr Alphonso Okolo, Secretary of the Zik Enterprises Limited, and of Mrs Beryl Glew, Confidential Secretary to the Premier of the Eastern Region, I gathered together a large number of my speeches; Mr Philip Harris has now made a selection from these papers arranged in a series of chapters each dealing with a particular topic.

It is my hope that the publication of this selection from my speeches will enable critics to appraise more intelligently the rôle which I have played in many spheres of activity over three decades. It will, I hope, enable my compatriots to appreciate my unrelenting stand on issues of fundamental importance. It will, I am sure, provide a source of information for those who are interested in the study of Nigerian development.

It has been suggested that it would be helpful if I were to knit this collection of speeches together with a short biographical sketch. I was born in Zungeru in Northern Nigeria in 1904, where my father was serving as a clerk in the Nigeria Regiment. I attended mission schools in Onitsha, Lagos and Calabar before travelling to Lagos for further education in 1921. After a period as a government clerk in the Treasury office in Lagos, I sailed for the United States in 1925. Here I enrolled in Storer College, but soon transferred to Lincoln University and subsequently to Howard University in Washington, D.C. After securing my degree I lectured in political science at Lincoln University and while there obtained postgraduate degrees at Columbia University and the University of Pennsylvania. I returned to Nigeria at the end of 1934, but soon moved on to Accra, where in 1935 I became editor of the Accra *African Morning Post*. In 1938 I returned to Nigeria, where I established the newspaper *West African Pilot*. After a period of political activity in the Nigerian Youth Movement, I combined

vii

with the late Herbert Macaulay to found the National Council of Nigeria and the Cameroons. From that time, through journalism and through political leadership, I have fought consistently for the greatness of Africa and for her citizens everywhere. In particular I have constantly striven for the freedom and unity of Nigeria. I led the NCNC delegation at the 1953 London Conference on the Nigerian Constitution and again in 1957.

From 1954–59 I was Premier of the Eastern Region of Nigeria. In December 1959 I resigned from that office and was in January 1960 elected President of the Senate. From November 16 1960 I shall continue to serve my people in the post of Governor-General of the Federation of Nigeria.

As a young man, I saw visions: visions of Nigeria becoming a great country in the emerging continent of Africa; visions of Nigeria offering freedom to those in bondage, and securing the democratic way of life to those who had been lulled into an illusion of security under colonial rule. Many of these visions have now been fulfilled. The reader of this book who knows the present Nigerian scene will quickly be made aware of the rapid rate of change. Racial segregation and discrimination which featured in the social life of Nigeria in the thirties and forties are now things of the past. The senior ranks in the army, which were then a European preserve, today contain many fine Nigerian officers.

My most consistent theme has been that there must, in Nigeria, be an end to colonial bureaucracy. Today Nigeria is free from colonialism, free to work out her own great destiny and free to show the light to the peoples of Africa, everywhere.

As a young man, I saw visions. I do not doubt that as an old man, I shall dream dreams. Some of the dreams must be of my relentless struggle for the peoples of Africa, and for the cause of Nigerian freedom and unity. I trust that I shall dream my dreams amid the peace and ever-increasing prosperity of the people of my native Nigeria. The motto of the independent Federation of Nigeria is 'Unity and Faith'. I pray that we may guard our unity and keep our faith.

Summer, 1960, London   NNAMDI AZIKIWE

CHAPTER 1

ZIK IN AMERICA

From a speech delivered when proposing the toast 'To the High School Department of Storer College' at the Young Men's Annual Party which was held in the Anthony Memorial Hall, at Storer College, Harpers Ferry, West Virginia, in May 1927.

I am proud to have graduated from the High School Department of Storer in May last year. Since my experience of life is limited, all I can advise the upper class men and women is to remind them that this college stands for high ideals. It stands for purity of youth; it stands for the advancement of coloured youth; it stands for all that is good, noble and lofty in life.

Those of you who are on the threshold of graduating from this intellectual shrine should henceforth fashion your lives to the highest principles and ideals, so that when you depart from here to take your places in life, as men and women of our race, you will be worthy of emulation by posterity.

From what we have been told by our fathers and teachers, the ocean of life is tempestuous and it is filled with hidden rocks and shoals. However, we are encouraged to know that only lion-hearted men and women can endure and survive life's problems successfully. That being the case, it is my hope that high school graduates will gird their loins for the struggle and remember that in the final analysis, they are the captains of their fate and the masters of their destiny.

*From Ƶik's eulogy on the late Hogan Edem Ani-Okokon delivered
in the Rankin Memorial Chapel, at Howard University, Washington, D.C., on May 10, 1928.*

Okokon was patriotic, but he was not parochially so. Although
he loved Africa, he realized that America had a lot to offer Africans
by showing them the way to real freedom and true democracy.
He admired and respected the ideals and traditions which
animated the founding of this great republic. He had visions of
Nigeria becoming a great country, emerging from the continent of
Africa, offering freedom to those in bondage, and securing the
democratic way of life to those who have been lulled into a false
sense of security under colonial rule.

It is my fervent prayer that God may sanctify the life of this
young African so that we, his survivors, will not forget the sacrifice
made by this pioneer of freedom in Africa. If God spares me to
return home alive, I pledge that I will join crusaders for human
freedom anywhere in the world and we shall intensify the struggle
for democracy in Africa.

I will never forget to remind my fellow crusaders in Africa that,
in the spring of 1928, we buried him in Washington, and that the
spirit of Okokon stands guard over his grave which is now a landmark in our journey from the world of darkness to the world of
light. May the body and soul of Hogan Edem Ani-Okokon rest in
peace, and may his memory be an inspiration to Nigerian posterity.

*From an address delivered in the Abyssinian Baptist Church, New
York, on November 10, 1931, during the annual meeting of the
Association for the Study of Negro Life and History.*

The eyes of the world are on Liberia. Men without appreciation
for the contribution of the Negro to modern statesmanship are
content to criticize this African Republic without deep thought on
the onerous duty of statecraft. Greedy nations are lurking and
watching Liberia like hawks. In this her hour of despair and
universal condemnation, Liberia needs to take seriously the political philosophy of that great Cuban Negro, Senor Rafael Serra,

who warned that it is necessary for the government to exercise more urbane and equal treatment and less oppression, so as to safeguard the security and liberty of the individual and the nation itself.

Ladies and gentlemen, I submit that eighty-four years of political autonomy are not sufficient to pass a final judgment on the political incapacity of the Liberian Negro. Dr Woodson states that Liberia's first century compares favourably with that of the colony of Virginia. While Liberia encouraged education and social uplift, Governor William Berkeley was narrow enough to 'thank God that there were no free schools or printing presses in the province.'

Let it be remembered also that it took Great Britain fourteen hundred years after the conquest of Boadicea to draft the Magna Carta. It took her several centuries more to pave the way for the English Revolution which established a constitutional democracy. It took France eighteen hundred years after Caesar's conquests in Gaul to dream up and effect the French Revolution, thereby founding a government of the people, for the people, by their accredited representatives. Even the United States of America spent one hundred and fifty-six years, after the landing of the Pilgrim Fathers, in political tutelage as a vassal of an alien colonial power. As Judge T. M. Stewart pointed out, the United States was heir to generations of civilization and experience in government. Her builders were fresh from the schools and universities of Europe. British brains and capital laid the foundation of the American commonwealth of nations.

In spite of this unequal handicap, Liberia is still keeping pace. Commander A. H. Foote states the case for Liberia more tersely: 'Let then the black men be judged fairly, and not presumed to have become all at once and by miracle, of a higher order than old historic nations through many generations of whom the political organization of the world has been slowly developing itself.' Even acknowledged authorities in the field of politics and government recognize the evolutional nature of modern democracies. Liberia should not, therefore, be hastily condemned.

3

I come from a part of the world called Nigeria, in West Africa. When the foundations of democracy were rocked, during the World War II, my country played an honourable part in order to preserve this political philosophy from extinction. We sent our sons and daughters to the various theatres of war and we shed our blood in order to make the world safe for the democratic way of life. Side by side we fought and died with the American soldier, sailor and aviator; hoping, trusting and believing that, jointly, we should defeat the common enemy and that, side by side, we should win the peace. I and my inarticulate people hope that these gallant heroes and heroines have not died in vain.

I bring to you goodwill from across the Atlantic. We are thirty million. We have our own traditions and heritage which go back to ancient Egypt. Some of us are literate, articulate and able to adapt ourselves to the contradictory conditions of contemporary world society; but not all of us are literate and sufficiently advanced to appreciate the import and significance of the material and social techniques of modern industrial civilization. Nevertheless, we have the breeding and native intelligence to appreciate good neighbourliness in a world that is gradually becoming one through the magic wands of twentieth-century science and invention.

Twenty years ago, whenever I visited New York City on a short trip from my university, and found it uneconomic to seek for a house to pass the night, I learned from experience how to pass a comfortable night in the subways, so generously placed at the disposal of guests and residents of the city, for the nominal charge of a nickel! In those days, I was also acquainted with the methods of some employment agencies at Sixth Avenue where, on the payment of five dollars, one can be hired today and fired tomorrow; and on payment of another five dollars to the same agency, one can be re-hired by the same employer the following day. Naturally, such recollections are inspiring, for apart from helping me to

4

cultivate a sense of humour, they strengthen my faith in American democracy, because, in spite of handicaps of yesteryears, I have forged ahead, I have realized my dreams, and I have learned to love America as 'God's Country'!

From a response to a toast made in his honour at the dinner arranged jointly by the Lincoln University Alumni Association and the African Academy in the Hotel Pennsylvania, New York, on June 27, 1947.

I wish to speak to you tonight on the subject of co-operation between the United States and dependent territories in West Africa. . . . As I see the issue, it is one of human contacts. The minds of men and women must be liberated from those social forces which foster intolerance and ignorance. The more we know each other, the more we will appreciate the oneness of humanity, and the more we will cultivate the urge to create goodwill, fellow-ship and mutual understanding. Let us recognize and emphasize at once that such a task cannot be restricted to one continent alone. It must be a two-way traffic. This implies bridgeheads in Africa and America, in order to make co-operation worthwhile. . . .

At present, the United States have many universities at their disposal and West Africans have none. But the idea of exchange implies equality of a basic nature. Here is where I think American educators and those interested in building up goodwill between the two countries can be of immense aid. The granting of scholar-ships to African students to study has its advantage. So too good-will tours to West Africa by Americans. But to broaden the base of operations and make this two-way traffic much more efficacious we have to make university education accessible to the Africans as well. By the establishment of a university in West Africa, organized and administered by the American and African peoples concerned and their friends, we should succeed in creating good-will centres where teachers and students from America can spend sabbatical leaves. Surely, if we can have 'Yale University in China', 'American University in Turkey' and 'American University in Beirut' I can see no reason why we should not have 'Lincoln

5

University' or 'Howard University' in Nigeria. I trust that all who are interested in this project of adjusting human relations will bear in mind this idea of establishing a university in West Africa in order to make the bridge-head in Africa more secure and more valuable to the cause of understanding, goodwill and fellowship with the United States.

From an address delivered at the Banneker High School Auditorium, Washington, D.C., on December 27, 1949, at the 35th Anniversary of the Phi Beta Sigma Fraternity.

I have travelled 8,500 miles in order to be present on this momentous occasion. It took me less than 40 hours to make the trip by aeroplane, in two stages, thanks to modern scientific knowledge. I bring you greetings from Sigma men who are scattered over the continent of Africa. In concert with their comrades-in-arms they are playing their part in the great awakening which has gripped that continent of everlasting spring, having been imbued with the idea of 'Culture for service and service for humanity'.

What is the nature of the struggle for national freedom in contemporary Africa? What are the forces at work to intensify that struggle? What is the reaction of the African people towards national realization? What is the role of the United States in this attempt of the African towards national self-determination? These are some of the issues I shall attempt to clarify within the limited time at my disposal. Throughout Black Africa, a struggle for national freedom is in the offing, because factors of imperialism have stultified the normal growth of Africans in the community of nations. Consequently, our indigenous people present a sorry spectacle of degraded humanity. Politically, they are dominated by alien races and are denied the basic human rights. Socially, the African has been made to witness discrimination of different kinds against him in his own native land. Economically, the African has been subjected to exploitation of a most heinous type, whilst he vegetates below the minimum subsistence level of existence. . . . Yet, in spite of his plight he has become self-assertive and he is demanding a place in the sun.

6

What forces have been at work to intensify this struggle of the African for self-determination? Let me take the liberty of referring to comments made by Mrs Eleanor Roosevelt during the World War II, when it appeared that certain sections of American society were diffident in participating wholeheartedly in the war. She said: 'We are fighting a war today so that individuals all over the world may have freedom. This means an equal chance for every man to have food and shelter and a minimum of such things as spell happiness to that particular human personality. If we believe firmly that peace cannot come to the world unless this is true for men all over the world, then we must know in our nation that every man, regardless of race and religion, has this chance. Otherwise we fight for nothing of real value. . . . If the future holds only a repetition of the past, if in each nation there are to be real slaves, even though they do not exist in name, then the boys who say they do not know why they fight have a right to say so. There would be no world worth fighting for and the only men who would have any reason for fighting would be the professional soldiers who fight for the love of fighting.'

That was precisely what happened to the African. He was persuaded to fight in order to free European nations. His reward was denial of freedom and the tightening of the chains of servitude. Due to the forces of intolerance, prejudice, ignorance, pride, and superstition, those whose homes were bombed by the V1 and V2 bombs, those who had suffered the humiliation of the concentration camp—refugees, displaced persons, kings without kingdoms, 'Governments' without countries—these ungrateful Europeans continued the enslavement of their former comrades-in-arms, after winning the war. Thus they have failed to win the peace. Today, man is still a wolf to man, and the teeming millions of Africans have been denied the heritage of democracy, despite their sacrifices in two world wars for its attainment.

. . . I think that the Government and the people of the United States can play a creditable role in the attempt of the African to achieve freedom in his life-time. Emerging from World War II not only as an arsenal but a bastion of democracy, the United States has been presented by history with an opportunity for constructive statesmanship on the continent of Africa. Having been educated in the United States, I could be expected to be steeped in the traditions of Jeffersonian democracy. But that cannot make me blind to any situation which might stunt the natural development of my people towards an independent national existence. At times, I am perplexed at the role of the United States on the African continent. Is this great nation buttressing the forces of European reaction so as to manacle the people of Africa and thwart their legitimate aspirations towards nationhood?

It is obvious that the United States Government is assuming some responsibility for the development of the under-developed areas of the world. We who live in some of these under-developed areas are profoundly gratified that such a great nation should realize the urgent need for this economic step. The proposal of the Point Four Programme by President Harry S. Truman is indicative that this part of the world feels that its economic life is affected by the conditions which have caused stagnation in under-developed areas, comprising more than half the people of the world. Perhaps it is fitting at this moment to interject an old adage familiar to all of you, that no economic chain can be stronger than its weakest link. From the fact that more than half the chain is weak, it follows that the economic mooring of the world is not too secure.

It is commendable that at this moment in the course of world history, when cold war propaganda has such an unnerving effect on the more highly developed nations, President Truman should propose something that should lighten the tension of this ideological warfare. Such a project is ripe with possibilities that may save the world from a war more devastating than the two struggles that most of us have witnessed in our life-time. The crux of this programme seems to me in a large measure to be the solution of the problem with which we are confronted in West Africa. Moreover, it is a denunciation of the old imperialistic policies based on exploitation of less fortunate people, that has heretofore set the world asunder. It means that the people of the western world may look forward to a more bountiful life; that they may feel that they can enter more freely in the competitive struggle to

8

satisfy their human wants. The effect on the people of Africa can be better imagined.

But is there a deeper economic significance to the Point Four Programme? Is it possible that the under-developed areas contain raw materials which the United States must have because the stock-pile reserves are getting dangerously low? To an African who has been conditioned to expect many strange behaviour patterns in international relations, in so far as these patterns have affected Africa, the questions seem to cast the twin shadows of doubt and fear. I am optimistic enough to believe that President Truman must have fully realized that in spite of the urgent need for replenishing the stock-pile of priority materials, such as cocoa, tin, columbite, bauxite, palm products, uranium and so on, which abound in my country, all under-developed areas must be invited to participate in a programme that has the potential ingredient for establishing more firmly the four freedoms so essential to a free world.

One feels that the President had rightly put the aims and objectives of his country first. It follows that all advantages for that country must be considered. That, again, is as it should be for the best interest of this country. But we who live on the other side of the world could derive many benefits from these co-operative efforts. Naturally, our aim would be to work vigorously for the success of such a programme. In it we can visualize a turn of events which can lead ultimately to our independence.

However, the general nature of the President's Point Four Programme has elicited different interpretations from various interests. Big business in America, for instance, sees it as a new avenue for private ventures and from all appearances suggests that the Government guarantees security of operation against risk. While, on the other hand, the British authorities have interpreted the Point Four Programme as a new device for bridging Britain's dollar gap. In the light of this latter interpretation, which is very vital to the struggle we are making for freedom, it is heartening to know that the United States is not necessarily in accord with Britain on this score. This may suggest the reason for the Kennan Report's recommendation of an on-the-spot study of the African situation. It may hasten the day when the United States and Britain must re-orientate their policies in respect of future relations with Africa as an under-developed area.

From an address delivered in the Abyssinian Baptist Church, Harlem, New York, on January 15, 1950, with Congressman Adam Clayton Powell as Chairman.

The importance of Africa in contemporary world politics is becoming clearer, thanks to the emergence of certain forces which have affected the existence of Europe and America. Whether we like it or not, Africa is destined to become the continent of the present century. What happens there today must be material to the future course of world history. Without exposing myself to the righteous indignation of well-meaning critics, may I be permitted to say that Nigeria is a key to the solution of the African problem. Every sixth African is a Nigerian. With its raw materials, Nigeria enjoys prestige in the forefront of African nations. In spite of the impact of Western culture, its institutions are basically African. The future of Nigeria is thus intertwined with the future of Africa, nay, the Negro race.

Two main problems have projected Nigerian affairs on the screen of world opinion : the demand for independence and the shooting of Nigerian coal miners. To have an intelligent grasp of these problems, you are entitled to be well-informed about their setting. This should enable you to pass a fair judgment on the crusades we have embarked upon for the emancipation of Nigeria in the life-time of those crusaders who have made this a life mission.

Nigeria is partly a Crown Colony, partly a Protectorate, and partly a Trust Territory. With a population of thirty million and an area of 372,000 square miles, it is easily the most important dependency in the British colonial system. By virtue of a Treaty of Cession negotiated in 1861, the sovereignty of Lagos and certain areas was ceded to Britain for ever. By virtue of over 400 treaties, the main areas of Nigeria were placed under British protection. Cameroons became a trust territory following the change from the mandate system. In spite of the well-defined status clarified above, Britain has ruled Nigeria as a British possession, thus embittering Anglo-Nigerian relations and leading to a demand for complete independence.

Protectorate status was established as a result of treaties which took the following pattern : the Nigerian signatories, in return for British protection against external aggression, agreed

to help in the suppression of the slave trade;
to abolish human sacrifice;
to co-operate in establishing British trade in the country;
to facilitate the activities of British missionaries;
to protect British subjects and their property.

Britain also guaranteed not to interfere in native law and custom, excepting where they were repugnant to conscience. In other words, the treaties creating such protectorate status reserved to the Nigerians the right to internal sovereignty, and conceded to the British the exercise of external sovereignty. The paradox of this situation is that the British, in spite of their solemn treaty obligations, have exercised both the internal and external sovereignty, without due regard to the objections of the Nigerians and contrary to the decisions of the British and international courts on protectorate status. Since it is obvious that our forefathers did not cede the Protectorate of Nigeria to Britain, we are determined to regain our territories in order to take our rightful place in the world community of nations.

The economic background of our problems is one of life and death. In spite of our natural wealth we are regarded as a 'backward', 'under-developed', and 'undeveloped', or 'non-self-governing' area. Our oil, coal, lignite, tin, iron, lead and uranium-233 deposits have not been utilized to transform Nigeria into an industrial and manufacturing country. Our agricultural resources are used to buttress the domestic economy of Britain. There is a restricted market for our raw materials, so that the world has no free access to them, contrary to the Atlantic Charter. The British have established a regime of monopoly in the commercial, shipping, banking, and mining enterprises of that country. Through their pools and chambers of commerce and mines they dictate the price to be paid to the Nigerian producer for his raw materials, and also dictate what price the Nigerian consumer must pay for imported and manufactured goods.

Taxation is both arbitrary and oppressive; although the necessary amenities for business and tax-payers are not provided, business and individuals are taxed almost at the rate obtaining in the United Kingdom. The cost of living is high owing partly to artificial scarcities created by the monopolies and combines in the essential supplies and necessities, and partly to the concentration of the farmers on economic crops which find a ready market, rather than food crops, with their price deteriorations. The wages-index has been erratic in that certain discriminatory practices have established bi-racialism in the domain of labour. The currency is controlled by Britain and Nigerians have no voice in determining its value; the present devaluation of sterling has brought hardship to the Nigerian economy against which we have no remedy. Naturally, these economic factors have had an adverse effect on the standard of living of the people, most of whom may be said to be living below the minimum subsistence level. To the outside observer, it is clear that such a challenging situation can exist only in a country which is in political bondage. That is true.

An address delivered during the banquet arranged by the Board of Trustees of Howard University to honour the recipients of honorary degrees of that university, on June 4, 1954.

Mr President, distinguished guests, it is with humility and respect that I rise to place on record my gratitude and appreciation of the distinction which Howard University has conferred upon me today. In making me one of the recipients of your doctorate in Law, you have honoured my people and the Government of Eastern Nigeria, of which I have the honour to be Leader and Minister of State charged with the portfolio of Local Government.

12

As a crusader in the cause of human freedom in Africa, I am very grateful to Howard University for helping to mould my outlook at the formative stage of my intellectual and physical development. Here at the Hilltop, I learned the rudiments of the humanities, the anatomy of the social sciences, and the grammar of politics. Tunnell, Locke, Harris, Bunche and Hansberry were among my teachers. They gave me an insight into the complex problems of human nature.

My body was made beautiful as a temple to house the intellectual currents to be generated after my college days. Your athletic field and gymnasium gave me opportunity for rehearsing the battle of life, thanks to the skilful guidance of Watson, Pendleton, and Burr. That was twenty-five years ago.

Having been armed mentally and physically, I was ready to take my place in the romance called life. The academic background served as a weapon to challenge cant and hypocrisy, to sift the chaff from the wheat, and to cultivate objectivity in assessing human situations and problems. The training in physical education provided poise and the spirit of *noblesse oblige*.

For twenty years now, I have been comrade-in-arms with others in the crusade for human freedom in Africa. It has been an arduous struggle—long, tough, bitter and excruciating. Sometimes, one is tempted to surrender, especially when allies of yesterday become enemies of today. Sometimes one feels like a motherless child, hoping against hope to be transported to Nirvana, where it is hoped there will be no more sufferings, no more disappointments, and no more sorrow. Then out of nowhere will come the faint echo of the Spiritual : 'I will go, I shall go, to see what the end will be.'

The goal is now in sight. The Pharaoh of yesterday, who knew not Joseph, has now known him and found in him attributes of statesmanship. The lion and the palm tree have found much in common to make life worthwhile. It is no longer a question of might being right. The issue now resolves itself into what is right for humanity. Dr Johnson, it is with happiness that I announce that a few months from now, your humble servant will become Premier of Eastern Nigeria, an autonomous Government within the Federation of Nigeria, whose cabinet of twelve ministries will formulate policy for the maintenance of law and order for the eight million inhabitants living within its jurisdiction. Her Majesty the Queen will sign the constitutional instrument by an Order-in-Council which will be promulgated immediately. In other words, the 32 million inhabitants of Nigeria are now on the threshold of independence; other things being equal, by 1956, the world will witness the emergence of a new State in the family of nations.

I have outlined the course of our national struggle because I want to emphasize the point that, in spite of its magnitude and the length of time involved, not a drop of blood has been shed towards winning our freedom. We were provoked beyond description perennially—some of us were jailed, fined heavily, exiled temporarily, and some of us died in the course of the struggle. But we did not allow ourselves to be deflected from our goal, nor did we lose our heads, in spite of handicaps. Rather, we inched along patiently, tactfully, confidently.

I can never forget the opportunity which Howard University offered me to be of service to humanity. I fought the fight as a member of a team, obeying the rules of the game, yielding ground gracefully when I must, making no excuses, and being noble without ostentation even in the finest hour of victory.

From an address delivered in the Harold Fetter Grim Gymnasium, Lincoln University, Pennsylvania, at the Banquet of the General Alumni Association, on June 6, 1954.

Fellow *alumni*, I am very proud to be a Lincoln man because I know what Lincoln has done for me. This great institution gave me an opportunity to develop my personality in an environment which tested my character almost to the limit of human endurance. Claude McKay said that although United States fed him with bread of bitterness and sank into his flesh its tiger's tooth, yet he loved this 'cultured hell'. Many times I have often felt that way too, but I have faith in this country as a bastion of democracy. However, I must warn that times are changing and we must not only evaluate the present in terms of the past, but we must bear in mind what the future holds in store for humanity at large.

Lincoln University has equipped me for the great task ahead by making me appreciate that although the continent of Africa is rather late in the race for progress and advancement in the world, yet handicaps were made to be overcome and barriers to be hurdled. I am, therefore, ready for this glorious task. I have faith in humanity. I have the vision and the imagination to appreciate the need to dedicate myself selflessly to this romance of nation-building in Africa.

At this stage, I would like to say that the struggle for national self-determination with which I have been actively associated in the last twenty years has not been without its toll of penalties. Provocations were many, not to speak of the numerous persecutions, prosecutions, victimizations, ostracizations or the galaxy of fines inflicted on my business enterprises in order to crush my spirit. Need I remind you of the numbers of my comrades in arms who were imprisoned or those who died while furthering this noble cause? Nevertheless, we have fought the good fight without shedding one drop of blood, without violence, without bitterness, and we have gained a grand and glorious victory. Today, the lion and the palm tree have cultivated mutual respect. Having understood each other, they now realize that the world is big enough to contain them, and they have decided to co-operate to mutual advantage.

An address delivered at the celebration of the fiftieth anniversary of the National Association for the Advancement of Coloured People, held on the Polo Grounds, New York City, July 19, 1959.

I am greatly indebted to the National Association for the Advancement of Coloured People for the invitation to speak on this occasion of the celebration of its fiftieth anniversary. For five decades, this organization has been in the vanguard of the struggle for human freedom in America. Its objective has been the attainment of equal rights for people of African descent and other peoples of colour who are citizens of this great bastion of democracy.

In the thoughts of Abraham Lincoln, this country was conceived in liberty of the individual and it was dedicated to the idea that democracy as a way of life can only be meaningful not only to its inhabitants but to the rest of the world if all facets of its society respect human dignity in the noble attempt to create equality of opportunity for all.

For 183 years, the people of the United States have been involved in a historic experiment to determine whether democracy can survive as an ideology which places a high premium on the value of the individual in a society which is heterogeneous. Throughout this period, this great country has been the cynosure of the world. Every little mistake in human relations has been magnified out of its proportions. Every error of judgement in the relations of the races has been critically analysed. And every act of injustice based on such extraneous factors as race, colour, creed or station in life has been subjected to the most severe strictures.

Such a negative attitude has not been due to any inveterate hatred of the United States per se (although we must admit that those with axes to grind cannot but make capital out of such slips), but the main reason is the universal respect which the world has for this country. Because of this high esteem, the outside world expects the United States, like Caesar's wife, to be beyond reproach, so far as respect for human dignity is concerned, bearing in mind 'the spirit of 1776'.

As students of human relations we know the fundamental social problems which confront those who are privileged to rule others. We also realize the impossibility of changing human nature in particular areas of social activities. But any Government which makes the slightest pretension to be democratic must prove itself equal to its responsibility by ensuring the application of the rule of law in the maintenance of order in a stable society, and by guaranteeing to its citizens the enforcement of fundamental rights.

What are these fundamental rights? They are the window display by which democracy advertises itself as a way of life. They are the yardstick by which the success or failure of democracy as an ideology can be most accurately assessed. These imply the exercise of freedom of speech, the freedom of peaceful assembly, the

16

freedom of association, the freedom of movement, the freedom of private property, the freedom of public trial, the freedom from want and the other essential human freedoms which are enumerated in the Universal Declaration of Human Rights.

For fifty years the NAACP has weathered the storm in the challenging situation of the American scene, which finds American citizens of colour in the ironical position of constantly reminding certain segments of American society, through the due process of law, that American democracy must be a living reality in American society. That this point of view has been stressed with all constitutional means at their disposal is very commendable indeed because it demonstrates their implicit faith in and unalloyed loyalty to the American way of life.

The NAACP has been an inspiration to me and to my colleagues who have struggled in these past years in order to strengthen the cause of democracy and revive the stature of man in my country. As a student in this country from 1925–1934, I had the opportunity of being fed with my American cousins what Claude McKay called the 'bread of bitterness'. But I have also had the unique honour of sharing with these under-privileged God's own children the challenge to conquer man-made barriers and to forge ahead to the stars, 'in spite of handicaps'.

This spirit of the American Negro, as exemplified in the constitutional struggles of the NAACP, has borne fruits of victory in the course of the years. It has given the United States a fair chance of reconciling the theory of democracy with its practice in America. It has also fired the imagination of the sleeping African giant, who is now waking up and taking his rightful place in the comity of Nations. What a glorious victory for the American Negro!

Since the historic decision of the United States Federal Supreme Court in 1954, the Government and people of this country have been alive to their duty to the people of America and to the world. They have worked assiduously to enforce the constitutional guarantees of the fundamental rights of the citizen within the territorial limits of this country. And they have proved their genuine desire to improve race relations in this great country.

17

It is true that the NAACP, as one of the watch-dogs of the less privileged people, is still on the warpath; nevertheless history has provided the answer to the question whether the American Government believes in and practises democracy. Any serious student of race relations in America must admit that there have been radical changes for the better in the last quarter of a century. Only Governments which believe in democracy are capable of allowing themselves to be influenced by organized public opinion, and this is a credit to the present Government, in spite of what its critics may honestly choose to add to the other side of its balance sheet.

In Africa, the NAACP spirit of active resistance to the forces which are inconsistent with democratic principles has fired our imagination. We have relentlessly fought any attempt to foist upon us the horrible stigma of racial inferiority. We have successfully challenged cant and hypocrisy among those who pay lip service to democracy. And we have severed for ever the chains of autocracy in many African countries where millions of Africans were held in political bondage. We are proud that today Egypt, Ethiopia, Ghana, Liberia, Libya, Morocco, Sudan and Tunisia are free, sovereign and independent States; and we look forward with joy to the celebration of the independence of French Cameroons, Nigeria, Somalia and French Togoland in 1960.

Since I come from Nigeria, it may be pertinent for me to say a few words about my country and our plans for the future. Nigeria is a country which, in area, population and potential, can stand comparison with all but the largest countries in the world today.

Our population is estimated between 34 and 40 million. This is three times the population of the Union of South Africa and 10 million more than the population of Egypt. We are the largest populated country in Africa and the thirteenth in the world. In size, we are thrice as large as Great Britain and larger than any country in Europe except Soviet Russia.

Our mineral resources include large reserves of coal, iron ore, tin, lead, zinc, limestone, petroleum and natural gas; and our agricultural resources include palm oil and kernels, cocoa, rubber, groundnuts, cotton, timber, hides, and skins. Ours is an expanding economy. We have had a favourable balance of trade for many years now and, judged by our sterling balances aboard, not only is our currency very stable but our public finances are viable.

It is true that our languages are multifarious and give the impression to the outside world that Nigeria is a mere geographical expression because the British are said to be the only cement which holds Nigeria together. But the fact remains that Nigeria is also a historical reality, since social forces have caused the people to live together and to become integrated as a nation in the last fifty years. Factors which led to the building of America, Canada, Switzerland, and other nations, in spite of their racial, cultural and linguistic differences, are also at work in Nigeria, and we are optimistic that, other things being equal, our similarities are bound to outweigh our dissimilarities in the long run.

I therefore appeal to the Press and journalists, particularly of the Western democracies, to display statesmanship and be more objective in analysing our internal problems and not to exaggerate them, since these differences are not unique or peculiar to us but also exist among peoples of other continents who have ultimately resolved them and forged themselves into one nation. I have been obliged to mention the Press and journalists of the Western democracies, because, to my knowledge, the Press and journalists of the Soviet bloc have neither exploited our differences to their advantage nor used them in order to mislead the outside world or to knock our heads together as the former had done and are still doing.

Our people are essentially democratic and our major political parties are working hard to establish parliamentary democracy in Nigeria. Having experienced the tutelage of British rule, we have learnt to appreciate the traditions of constitutional government, and we are all geared to continue the rule of law and respect for human dignity, on the attainment of independence in Nigeria, next year, as we are successfully doing today.

As far as I and my Party are concerned, we shall continue the difficult task of inculcating a sense of one-ness in our people so as to crystallize common nationality. We believe in the creation of one country and we will always eschew the idea of breaking

Nigeria permanently into three or more divided and weak units, which would be innocuous as a factor to be reckoned with either in Africa or in the community of free nations. I speak in this vein because, like many other Nigerians, I have lasting connections with all the three Regions which now form the Federation of Nigeria.

I was born in Northern Nigeria, where the boundaries of the country lie on the verges of the Sahara Desert, and where the majority of the inhabitants worship God according to the tenets of Islam, and where the camel caravans still ply to and fro in their various missions across the desert to the Middle East.

I was educated in Lagos, the capital of Nigeria and a great seaport, where the ships of various nations anchor to trade with us. When the Ministerial system of government was introduced into Nigeria, I represented Lagos in the Legislature of Western Nigeria, where I still reside, in spite of my temporary absence in Eastern Nigeria.

My parents are natives of Eastern Nigeria, the arsenal of republicanism in Nigeria. Although I am Ibo, yet I speak Yoruba and I have a smattering of Hausa. I am now Premier of Eastern Nigeria, the land of my fathers, which lies five hundred miles from Lagos and almost a thousand miles from the place of my birth in Zungeru, in Northern Nigeria. Each of our three Regions is vastly different in many respects, but each has this in common : that, despite variety of languages and custom or difference in climate, all form part of one country which has existed as a political and social entity for fifty years. That is why we believe that the political union of Nigeria is destined to be perpetual and indestructible.

This, then, is the Nigeria which in fifteen months' time will become a free, sovereign and independent State. It will be, by a very large margin, the biggest State in Africa. It will be no vassal State depending for its existence on the sufferance of other Powers. It will formulate its foreign policy in its national interest, but it will not be neutral on any issue which effects either the destiny of peoples of African descent anywhere on this planet or the peace of the world. Sustained by its connection with the democratic world, and powerful through the number of its inhabitants and the extent of its resources, Nigeria will be a country of consequence and, I am convinced, a force in world affairs.

Let me also emphasize that it will be a democratic country. In recent years great efforts have been directed actively towards building the institutions of democracy, and the fruits of these endeavours, together with the essentially democratic character of indigenous African society, give hope that Nigeria will be a country where the rights of the citizen will be respected, and where freedom under the law will be guaranteed to all. In Nigeria, we are building a country of which the whole black race can be justly proud. We have entrenched in our Constitution such fundamental human rights as civil liberties and freedom from discrimination of any kind.

Although Nigeria enters a future rich in promise, problems remain in plenty. The greatest of these is to raise the standard of living of our people, and it is in this connection, in particular, that we of Africa seek the co-operation of citizens of African descent in the United States. As I have shown earlier on, we have vast human, vegetable, animal and mineral resources awaiting development. All we need is capital investment, technical and managerial skills before these resources can be put to their fullest uses for the benefit of the people of my country and the investors.

You can help us by ensuring that this great country of America expands its existing trade relations with Nigeria. You can encourage our endeavours not only by opening the doors of your seats of learning to students from Africa, but by giving us the desired technical, technological and managerial co-operation in the development of our natural resources.

At this Convention today, we look back over the fifty years since the NAACP was founded. That period has seen great strides made in the struggle for justice for peoples of African descent, both here and in Africa. Today, we in Nigeria stand on the threshold of great events and we enter a future bright with promise.

I am convinced that developments in my native land will do much to enhance the prestige of peoples of African descent who are scattered all over the world. Your kindness in inviting me to speak today underlines the basic community of feeling between coloured Americans and their brothers in Africa. We struggle towards the same ultimate objective : to revive the stature of man so that man's inhumanity to man shall cease. Your success shall be our success and your failure shall be our failure. In this basic unity lies the promise of great advancement for the black race throughout the entire world.

CHAPTER 2

ZIK ON EDUCATION

From a speech delivered at the Methodist Boys' High School, Lagos, in November, 1934, on his return from the United States en route to Onitsha, his home-town.

I postulated at the outset that scholarship is coterminous with social progress. It is the scholar who makes or unmakes society. He may not be appreciated by his generation, or even by generations after him. But time offers reward to scholars who lay foundations for the society of tomorrow, by immortalizing them in human history.

The African should go beyond the veneer of knowledge. Ability to quote Shakespeare or Byron or Chaucer does not indicate original scholarship. The capacity to know what is the periphrastic conjunction, or to solve the Pythagorean problem, or to understand the principles of heat, light and sound, or to translate Aramaic, or to know all the important dates of British history, does not indicate true academic scholarship. These are the superficialities of a decadent educational system. These do not make for a dynamic social order. They are by-products of the imitative complex which Gabriel Tarde expounds excellently in one of his books.

Originality is the essence of true scholarship. Creativity is the soul of the true scholar. Initiative, emulation, and the urge to be intellectually honest are the earmarks of research and academic freedom. Heirs and heiresses of the New Africa must now consecrate themselves for scholarly research into all the aspects of world society in general and African society in particular.

Herodotus said that Africans ruled Egypt but that does not necessarily mean that it is true. That Professor Bonehead taught that the African race have not shown any capacity for civilization, and therefore could not have ruled Egypt, except in the mythology of the Greeks, does not mean that this view need be accepted. The true scholar studies Herodotean literature and the writings of his contemporaries, analytically examines the archaeological remains of the pertinent period in history, judiciously observes and critically studies the reports of archaeological expeditions together with the data, hypotheses, theses, and *obiter dicta* connected with other evidences adduced, validates them in the accepted style of scientific research, and then formulates his conclusions. If he is competent, and if his contributions are accepted by the confraternity of scholars, then his opinions are just as valid and acceptable as those of his colleagues.

Africans need to be scholars. We need to be creative. We must emulate and not imitate. In the end, we shall find that there is joy in scholarship.

From a speech made in the Legislative Council at Kaduna on March 3, 1948, supporting a motion to adopt the Memorandum on Education Policy in Nigeria.

I do not agree with the sentiments expressed by the honourable member who thinks that educational progress has made our children become a social problem. It is true that people coming to this particular part of the world, not understanding our philosophy and psychology, may misunderstand us and feel that we constitute a problem. It is a misunderstanding of social attitudes.

I do not agree with my honourable friends who feel that, today, education is making our children rebel against authority. This attitude is not peculiar to Nigeria; it is so in all parts of the world. I know that if some of our honourable members were to visit England or the United States they would be shocked at the manners of some of the children of these countries. They speak to their fathers without calling them 'Sir', and they do not kneel before them, as we do. Although the average African would be shocked at this behaviour, yet that does not mean that English and American children are necessarily rebellious; they have been educated to realize the practical workings of democracy.

As an instrument of change, this Memorandum is welcome. The average African child should be educated to appreciate that the *status quo* is not the best of all possible worlds. He should realize that his opposite number in other parts of the world is also seeking knowledge for a richer and fuller life. I feel, therefore, that the philosophy of the memorandum is worthy of commendation. I do not think that we should cherish the return of the good old days when we would have to go back to the villages and our children would have to content themselves with the chores of the home and merely bow to their parents. I agree that it is essential to have training in domestic matters but that is not the exclusive job of the schools, and I do not think that the honourable the Director of Education should be taken to task on this; after all, it is really the function of the home. The parents should see to it that their children receive moral training and are taught to respect their elders. Schools should merely act as a supplementary agency.

A speech delivered as President of the Amateur Athletic Association of Nigeria at the close of the Sixth International Athletic Meeting between Nigeria and the Gold Coast, on April 18, 1953, on the Police Sports Ground, Obalende, Lagos, under the patronage of His Excellency the Governor, Sir John Macpherson, G.C.M.G.

Your Excellency, Lady Macpherson, Distinguished Visitors, Ladies and Gentlemen : We have just concluded the Sixth International Athletic Meeting between Nigeria and the Gold Coast, and I hope that all have had an enjoyable time as the athletes representing the two great countries vied for honours in their various specialities. May I take this opportunity to thank Your Excellency for your presence this evening in spite of your multifarious engagements as Governor of this territory. We heartily welcome Lady Macpherson, our distinguished visitors, and the officials and athletes from the Gold Coast. We are delighted to associate with our friends from the Gold Coast in one common comradeship and fraternity in the realm of sport. We wish them a pleasant stay among us and trust that when they leave, they will carry with them pleasant memories of friendships made and acquaintances renewed.

International meetings of this nature enable us to realize the importance of sports in the character training of our youth, because in the field of sport there are no barriers of race, nationality, religion or any other extraneous factor. Here we have the practicalization of real democracy, because each athlete has an equal opportunity and participates according to his ability according to the highest traditions of sportsmanship. Such traditions are based on high ethical conceptions, which remind me of a saying of that great sportsman, Baron de Coubertin, father of the modern Olympic Games, who emphasized that 'The important thing in the Olympic Games is not winning but taking part; the essential thing in life is not conquering but fighting well.'

Therefore, in offering my congratulations to the winners and losers, I trust that, like thoroughbreds, they will be noble in victory and graceful in defeat. I cherish the hope that the high ethical conceptions which animate athletic competitions of this nature will influence their conduct and way of life after their athletic days are over and they have taken their places in the arena of life. . . .

Finally, may I, on behalf of the Amateur Athletic Association of Nigeria, express our gratitude and appreciation of their cooperation to all who have given of their skill, energy, time, and resources, either in the capacity of officials or patrons or supporters of this year's meeting. As you see the officials, black and white, commingled with the athletes. Theirs is not the thought of personal gain, but of service to humanity. May their breed continue to multiply so as to help these two countries to take their rightful places among the sports-loving nations of the world.

From a Presidential address to the Sixth Annual Convention of the National Council of Nigeria and the Cameroons held at Dayspring Hotel, Enugu, on January 6, 1954.

We are not happy at the way our education is administered. While we realize the great contributions made by those who have operated this important department of State in the past, yet we have decided to take positive measures towards working out a new educational programme in the future. The idea of 'approving', 'recognizing', 'assisting', and 'aiding' certain schools to the exclusion of others must have been well-conceived but it has out-lived its usefulness as a result of the tremendous strides in the field of education in Nigeria in the last two decades. Consequently, we shall abolish all forms of discrimination, whether intentional or not, and we shall establish a State system of certification for the elementary and secondary schools of the Region. The possession of a duly authenticated State certificate in elementary or secondary education, following a State-wide examination, conducted under State auspices in all the schools of the Region, will gain real value because it will be based on merit and not on any extraneous factor. Any school will then have a fair chance to play its role in the education of our children. Equality of opportunity of this nature can bring untold blessings to the Region; our education law will be subsequently amended with this object primarily in view. We must reiterate that our education must emphasize the principle of *what is right* as distinct from *who is right* in the interplay of social forces. A system such as is envisaged will establish minimum standards for all schools in the Region and no official barriers will be placed in the way of any person or agency in the establishment of new schools, provided such minimum standards are met and maintained.

A speech accepting honorary membership of the Ibadan University Students' Union, delivered at a meeting held in Hall No. 2, University College, Ibadan, on April 2, 1954.

It is with humility that I accept the honour you have conferred upon me tonight, by inducting me as an honorary member of your Students' Union. When I recall that 21 years ago last February, I received the degree of Master of Science at the University of Pennsylvania, in Philadelphia, tonight's ceremony revives happy memories of academic life. University life is a sacred privilege which must not be underrated. The pastoral atmosphere of campus life, the life-long friendships and acquaintances made, the training of the mind to be detached and objective in approaching problems—these, among others, offer students an opportunity for service to humanity.

The idea of a students' union is an admission of the constructive role students are destined to play in the evolution of universities. It shows that university administrators realize that one way of providing opportunity for leadership-training is student self-government. In the Victorian days, it would have been impossible for university students to participate in the government of the universities, owing to the ethos of that era; today, no progressive university excludes its students from the exercise of this form of autonomy.

Student self-government develops leadership and followership. Leadership is infused into the elected ones with the native ability and inculcates in them a sense of duty and responsibility. Student leaders are thus co-opted in making and enforcing bye-laws of the university, which enable them to gain rich experience from the interplay of social forces which prevail in their miniature world. On the other hand, through followership students learn to appreciate what obedience, loyalty, faithfulness, reliability and other forms of social co-operation connote in the conflict of emotions which animates human activities. Thus equipped, they leave the precincts of the university to take their places in the arena of life as future leaders, since it becomes patent that it is only a good follower who ultimately develops into a good leader.

Naturally, sportsmanship enters into the activities of student self-government. With the equality of opportunity which sports offer to the university student, he is educated to win nobly without indulging in vain boasting to boost his ego. If he loses, he is taught not to make excuses to explain why he lost, but to lose gracefully and, above all, to congratulate his opponent on his good fortune.

As a laboratory of leadership, student self-government must encourage the cultivation of the spirit of sportsmanship because through it the university student will better appreciate the practical meaning attached to the expression, *noblesse oblige*. Translated into the hurly burly of life, a training of this nature enables one to play the game of life according to the highest traditions of sportsmanship.

You have honoured me by making me an honorary member of your Union not because I possess any extraordinary gifts, but because you realize that I am only a member of a great team working co-operatively to achieve a goal which will bring blessing to our people. If the team wins, it is the result of team work, and members of the team should be proud of victory so collectively won. One should be regarded as a victim of vanity if one regarded oneself as an indispensable star which must so shine as to eclipse other stars. Training in sportsmanship must destroy such an illusion.

I am, therefore, grateful to you for giving me the exclusive privilege of coming back to university and re-living the life I was used to, barely 21 years ago. It is the greatest chance in a life-time to join forces with intellectually alert youth, male and female, working for a brighter and better tomorrow. I hope that I will prove myself worthy of this honour and I trust that your confidence in me will not be in vain.

Finally, let me remind you that the greatest task facing our generation is the salvaging of our people from the thraldom of intolerance, prejudice and superstition, which stems from ignorance and poverty. Let university training and experience in student self-government equip us to destroy these forces and enable us to break these chains of psychological slavery.

An address delivered as President of the Amateur Athletic Association of Nigeria after the All-Nigeria Athletic Championships held in the University College Sports Ground, Ibadan, on Saturday, April 3, 1954.

Your Honour, Ladies and Gentlemen, I count it a privilege to be able to join with this distinguished concourse of sports lovers to witness our annual athletic championships. From all parts of the country—north, east and west—our athletes have congregated, having passed through the crucible of eliminating contests either at the provincial or regional levels. From your reactions, it is obvious that you have been impressed by the way the cream of the nation's manhood demonstrated their skill, speed, stamina and strength for the eighth time in the history of the Amateur Athletic Association of Nigeria. As spectators, we have enjoyed the sight of handsome runners, jumpers and throwers with beautiful bodies in symmetrical form.

In the sprints, where runners of African descent had excelled the world's best, from the days of Howard Drew, Pollard, Eddie Tolan, Jack London, Ralph Metcalfe to the reigns of Robinson, Bragg, Macdonald Bailey and Andy Stanfield, Nigerians have not lagged too far behind. Although we have not broken world records, we are certainly within the privileged circle of the world's most creditable performers in consideration of the records of Adeola, Eneli, Erinle, Oluwa, Ajado and Omagbemi.

In the middle distance events, which produced such black world champions as Phil Edwards, Herb McKenley, Jimmy Lu-Valle, Woodruff, Mal Whitfield and Arthur Wint, we are slowly but surely developing our quarter-milers and half-milers to find a place in this division of world athletics. Our own Jack Awashere, Nwigwe, Amu, Hassan, Okeyodun, Arogundale, Adamolekun and Dangaruwa have shown great possibilities.

In the long distance events, where speed and stamina are basic, it would appear as if our tropical climate had heavily weighed upon us, so that we are still on the outer fringe of the narrow circle of celebrities such as Paavo Nurmi, Willie Ritola, Emil Zatopek, Gordon Pirie, Jim Peters, Barthel, Wes Santee, Ashenfelter, Landy and Bannister. But our Kannike, Baptist, Sho-Silva, Akran, Anujue, Tarfa, Oduguwa and Pinda Biu have shown potentialities.

It is in the high and long jumps that, in addition to our natural ability, we have found scope for improvement in technique as we have grown in experience. The late Cornelius Johnson, Al Britton, Mel Walker and Ed Burke—all Negroes—dominated the high jump at the period of the Berlin Olympics. DeHart Hubbard, Ned Gourdin, Jessie Owens, Silva Cato and William Steele shone brilliantly in the Olympic long jump in their heyday. Naturally, we are proud of our own Garrick, Adedoyin, Osagie, Majekodunmi, Odobo, Crigbolu and Guobadia in the former event, and S. O.

Williams, Olowu, Towesho, Engo, Esiri and Buraimoh in the latter. They have been consistent performers.

In the hurdles, where Lord Burghley, Pollard, Dick Attlesey, Bones Dillard and Milton Campbell have been the rage of the world, we have not failed to produce our own excellent performers even on a modest scale!—Ekperigin, Ekwensi, Igbinogun, Kadiri, Ezizia and Obi. In other words, Nigeria has athletes with talent which is at the moment only latent, but with proper coaching under ideal conditions, our running, jumping and throwing can be improved to make us attract the attention of the world.

After attending the last Olympic Games at Helsinki, and basing my judgement on observation of the Nigerian participants there, I felt proud that, although Nigeria did not win any medals, yet in this competition against the best athletes in the world we were not the worst performers, and we had gained supreme confidence in ourselves. Other things being equal, I venture to predict that, in the immediate future, Nigerians can still make history in the realm of athletics. In my humble opinion, Nigeria can realize this dream provided certain essential prerequisites are satisfied. I have in mind the provision of properly-graded and marked running tracks and the availability of coaches in the various events. If these imperative needs are met, supplemented with the supply of serious athletes who will undergo systematic training in the techniques of track and field athletics, we should improve our standards to lift us up from a position of apparent obscurity to world class.

We are grateful to those who arranged for this year's championship to take place in this beautiful stadium. The Ibadan University College has earned fame as the site of the best running track in the country. Not only is it well graded, rolled and marked, but the allocation of space for the various events measures up to the highest standards of international athletics; and the accommodation for spectators is simply superb.

Within two months, Nigerian athletes will proceed to Canada in order to take part in the Commonwealth Games scheduled to be held in Vancouver. I hope that all who are interested in making athletics popular in Nigeria will give this venture their blessing and support. In these days of much misunderstanding among human beings in the world, athletes have a unique chance to become ambassadors of goodwill between their country and the outside world.

The very essence of athletics—its competitive nature, its code of honour, and its equality of opportunity—gives impetus for human beings to strive with gusto to attain victory, by giving of their best, even if that is not good enough to win a prize. Therein lies a great lesson in the game of life. It means that success cannot be measured only in terms of conquests and defeats, but also on a plane of spiritual satisfaction. I may not be the fastest runner in my team, nor its most cagey miler, nor its most nimble hurdler, nor its most classical jumper, nor its strongest performer in the throwing events; but it is certain that I can be the most obedient, the most loyal, the most faithful, and the most friendly member of my team, by not seeking by word or deed to gain an unfair advantage over my team-mates.

In this respect, sportsmanship is coterminous with character-building. A good sportsman will always be a person of exemplary character on and off the field of sport. In the battle of life, where the combative and competitive instincts are given free play, a good sportsman will not resort to foul tactics, no matter how tempting, in order to gain success which, in the final analysis, is bound to be ephemeral. Rather than make a false start by beating the gun so as to win life's race, we should restrain our passion and accept the starter's penalty even if that means hardship or ultimate defeat. That is the spirit of sportsmanship which, among other lessons of life, athletes absorb in youth to make their beautiful bodies a hallowed temple for beautiful minds to inhabit.

On behalf of the Amateur Athletic Association of Nigeria, may I take this opportunity to express gratitude to the officials of to-day's championships and to the Principal and staff of the University College. Their co-operation in officiating and allowing the use of this splendid ground have helped to make this year's competition a success. I wish also to express my thanks to the officers and members of our beloved Association throughout the country. I appreciate their loyalty and co-operation in making this Association a living force in the lives of our youth and of the people who live in this country. Their continued interest in the encouragement and promotion of amateur athletics and their zeal to improve the management of athletic meetings, wherever they may live, have been an inspiration to many. They work for the love of sport in the true amateur spirit. When the social history of this country is fully written, and the historian chronicles the development of physical education as a foundation of character-building in Nigeria, these social engineers will not be forgotten.

Finally, may I offer my congratulations to the new athletic champions of Nigeria and remind them that championship implies nobility of spirit and character. May I also comfort those who failed to win a prize by adding that the glory in sport is the joy of participating and gaining spiritual satisfaction.

From a speech delivered in the House of Representatives on August 23, 1954.

My humble opinion is that University College Ibadan is becoming a million-dollar baby. Every time the baby cries he is given a kiss worth one million pounds, and so the baby has found out that it pays to cry, and crying has become his pastime. I feel that it is time the legislature applied the brake to this tendency towards squandermania. Those who control the College's finances must be told in plain language that the tax-payers of this country can no longer afford to pay super-scale salaries to the senior staff of the university, and cannot afford the most expensive luxury of giving them and their wives and children a vacation to Europe every year with first-class passages paid in and out. If the scale of salaries were reasonable and the tour of duty of the staff increased to two years, instead of one, then there would be no need for the heavy deficits which characterize the finances of the University College.

We respect the principle of academic freedom and we expect the university to relate its curricula to the immediate needs of the country. We have faith in the present administration of the University College and we hope that the new University Council will not be a rubber stamp as the Provisional Council obviously was. We trust that members of the new University Council will have the courage of their convictions and wield the axe where necessary in the expenditures of the university. What this country sorely needs today is a first-class institution of learning and not a first-class exhibition of streamlined buildings.

As I see the problems of the University College, four solutions appear inevitable : firstly, the university must not bar external students; secondly, prefabricated houses must be built for the senior and junior staff; thirdly, education and other subjects, instead of having separate faculties created for them, should be included in the liberal arts curriculum for the time being; finally, the university must submit its annual report to this legislature, temporarily, until it is able to demonstrate its financial responsibility.

There is no intrinsic value in restricting the students of the university to residents. Very few modern universities of the world adopt this rather restrictive and archaic practice of limiting university education to a select few. The tendency nowadays is to accept residential and non-residential students. If the university authorities were disposed to change their attitude in this respect, the institution would attract more students, who would live either in approved hostels or wherever was convenient to them. The effect of this would be to increase the revenue of the university in respect of tuition fees and reduce costs for building halls of residence to the barest minimum.

The sum of £225,000 out of the required £648,000 for new works is for building senior and junior staff quarters. It would be less expensive to construct prefabricated houses of different types. In certain countries in Europe which I had the pleasure of visiting in recent months, the technique of prefabricated housing has improved so considerably that less than one-third of the amount estimated would provide the university with at least one hundred comfortable houses for its senior and junior staff. A saving of £150,000 is definitely worthwhile.

There has been agitation for some time now for the university to establish new faculties of education and economics. Whilst it is true that to satisfy public demand more money should be provided, yet it is obvious that, within the framework of the Faculty

34

of Arts, subjects in the fields of education and economics can be taught. It would only cost the university the salaries and perquisites of the teachers, plus some additional books in these fields in the library, together with a small sum for other contingencies.

Legislative control of universities, whether general or financial, is usually looked upon with suspicion and distrust. But when the Government makes grants-in-aid to institutions of higher learning, it must retain an element of control in order to ensure financial responsibility. I will not advocate the type of control which we have insisted on for statutory corporations, although if I did so I would be perfectly justified, in view of the way this country has been let down by the Provisional Council. In order to avoid the recurrence of financial irresponsibility I am of the considered opinion that the time has come when the annual report of the University College should be tabled by the Minister of Education in this House for debate. By throwing a searchlight on to its activities, and not necessarily seeking to control it, we may persuade the university authorities to behave more responsibly in the administration of their finances.

Mr President, it is with diffidence and reluctance that I have to take a stand on this Motion, simply because I would not like to throw a monkey-wrench into the works of the administration and management of our beloved University College. Other things being equal, I hope that those concerned will take into serious consideration the observations which I have made in good faith. I have nothing personal against any of the officials of the University College, but I feel that on its merit, the request contained in the White Paper deserves constructive criticism.

Sir, I support the Motion.

From an address which was broadcast over the national programme of the Nigerian Broadcasting Service on March 9, 1957, at Lagos, Enugu, Ibadan and Kaduna in connection with the general elections to the Eastern House of Assembly.

My fourth argument in seeking for the endorsement of the NCNC by the electorate is that we have formulated and are implementing a bold education policy which is dedicated to the emancipation of our people from the darkness of ignorance and from the blight of superstition. When we took over the Government in 1954, there were 566,000 children attending schools in the Region. Today, this figure has increased to 1,300,000 and it is the greatest number of children at school in any country in Tropical Africa. Before 1954, the previous Government had built 205 new schools; the following year this was increased to 700. Today, 1,780 new schools have been built. In order to enable our children to have a sound education we have introduced the Universal Primary Education Scheme which is recognized by educationists to be the most comprehensive and extensive in the whole continent of Africa. There are now 6,500 schools under this scheme, of which 5,000 are run by the voluntary agencies and the rest by local Government Councils.

In implementing our education policy, my Government did take pains to express appreciation of the constructive role of Missionaries in the education of our people. These pioneers have played a commendable part in this respect and the NCNC feels proud to join with them in a great partnership to emancipate the minds of our children from ignorance and superstition. As an earnest of our sincerity of purpose this Government has spent over £3 million in order to encourage education in this Region. To be factual, the following expenditures have been made : total grants (excluding the £500,000 earmarked to assist Local Government bodies in building their own schools) £2·3 million. Out of this sum the Roman Catholic Mission received £1·1 million; the combined Protestant Missions (which include the Church Missionary Society, Niger Delta Pastorate, Methodist Mission, Church of Scotland Mission, Qua Iboe Mission, and Salvation Army) received £940,000; Local Government bodies received £146,000; other voluntary agencies received £120,420.

Let me give in more details, the picture of the grants-in-aid which the NCNC Government had made so as to foster education in Eastern Nigeria. The sum of £1·1 million was distributed for payment of teachers' salaries in primary schools as follows: Catholics £543,000, combined Protestants £542,000, Local

Government bodies £49,000; other voluntary agencies £107,000. Another sum of £264,000 was distributed as grants for teacher-training institutions as follows: Catholics £153,000, combined Protestants £110,000, nil for Local Government bodies and other voluntary agencies. The sum of £178,000 was distributed for secondary schools as follows: Catholics £106,000, combined Protestants £61,000, Local Government bodies £4,700. Another sum of £194,000 was distributed as grants for the expansion of teacher-training as follows: combined Protestants £71,000, Local Government bodies £65,000, Catholics £51,000, other voluntary agencies £8,000. For the development of secondary schools we gave grants totalling as follows: combined Protestants £42,000, Local Government bodies £28,000, Catholics £20,000, other voluntary agencies £5,000. In addition, the Ministry of Education has spent the sum of £428,000 under the Colonial Welfare and Development Scheme as grants as follows: Catholics £226,000, combined Protestants £202,000. The above figures do not include all other grants made to certain private schools, but these figures are publicized in order that the electorate should appreciate that this Government does not discriminate against any religious organization or denomination, as some people seem to imagine, judging by recent happenings in this Region.

... It is true that the working of the Universal Primary Education Scheme has presented some embarrassment to the Government, as a result of the activities of the Catholic Council, but it is equally true that wise statesmanship on the part of His Grace Archbishop Heerey and some spokesmen of our Government averted a misunderstanding which could have developed out of proportion. As far as I know the complaints of the Catholics have been fully investigated and given immediate attention by me and I hope that no candidate at this election will introduce religion as an issue because that would not help the cause of Catholicism in this part of the country. The problem created by our education policy is neither religious nor theological and any attempt to be-cloud the issue, as the UNIP has amateurishly done in its Manifesto, is to encourage religious squabbles in a Region which is famous as a haven of religious freedom.

Consistent with this view, the Government of the Eastern Regions has made it clear in unmistakable terms that although it intends to introduce a State system of education yet this must be realized on a co-operative basis with the Missionaries and other voluntary agencies. To this end we have guaranteed religious freedom in respecting the fundamental right of parents to choose schools which their children should attend, from a purely religious point of view. Although there was a slight misunderstanding between the Catholic authorities and the Government in implementing our education policy, I am happy to report that this has been resolved and the two parties are now working hand in hand in order to make this scheme a success.

In the field of secondary education the NCNC Government has been able to increase the number of students in secondary schools from 8,200 pupils in 1954, when we took office, to 11,000 today. We have also increased the number of secondary grammar schools in the Region from 50 to 70, and we have eliminated the element of discrimination in making grants to secondary schools so that practically all the secondary schools which operate in this Region receive grants-in-aid. When the University of Nigeria begins to function, these secondary schools will serve as a feeder to enable the University to play a constructive role in producing leaders for the various spheres of endeavour in this country. Of the sum of £5 million voted for this scheme, £1,500,000 is available and it is proposed that work on our own University will start in the immediate future.

With reference to scholarships, the Government has been very realistic indeed. Whereas less than 200 scholarships were awarded by the Eyo Ita Government, we can claim to have made 622 University awards and 423 secondary awards by the end of 1956. We propose to make more awards this year. Any Government which can achieve so much in the field of education within a space of three years deserves the support of the people and I am not lacking modesty when I ask the voters of this Region to judge us on our past performances in this respect and return us to office.

An address delivered at the University College Sports Ground, Ibadan, on April 13, 1957, before the March Past for the International Athletic Championships between Nigeria, Ghana and Sierra Leone.

Your Excellency, Lady Rankine, Mr Premier, Ladies and Gentlemen, on behalf of the Amateur Athletic Association of Nigeria, I welcome the visiting athletes from Ghana and Sierra Leone, and the Nigerian athletes who are congregated here today from different sections of this great country. It is also refreshing to observe the increasing number of female athletes who are participating in our little Olympiad.

To an extent, sports is a unifying factor in human relations because its competitive nature has enabled an ethical code to evolve and to influence the behaviour patterns of society. In obeying the strict rules of athletics, competitors are restrained from taking an unfair advantage so that they all have equal opportunity to display their prowess.

This athletic code of honour has affected the formation of character in the youth of the world and has so influenced the ethics of society that we now place enough emphasis on such abstract notions as fair play and equity as to give them concrete form in our social conventions.

I wish all the contestants success in their endeavours and hope that this year's competition will provide them with an anvil on which to forge lasting friendship and goodwill so that when it becomes their fortune to lead their communities in any sphere, they will bring into play the code of honour they have learned in the world of sport.

A message delivered at the annual convention of the Nigeria Union of Teachers which was held at the Dennis Memorial Grammar School, Onitsha, on January 7, 1958.

On behalf of the people and Government of the Eastern Region, I welcome the officers and members of the Nigeria Union of Teachers who have done us honour by holding their annual convention today in our historic riverine community. I regret my inability to be present in person in view of the fact that the Minorities Commission has just begun its sittings here, but I can assure you of the goodwill of my Government and we wish you success in your deliberations.

Those who are engaged in the profession of teaching in the whole Federation deserve the gratitude of the parents and guardians of the school-going children of Nigeria for three reasons: in spite of alleged adverse conditions of service, teachers have been loyal to their noble profession; because of the industry of teachers and their devotion to duty, the country has been able to satisfy the demand made on its human resources so as to make our experiment in parliamentary government successful; with the active co-operation of the teaching profession two Regional Governments and the Federal Government have made universal primary education a reality.

The Government of the Eastern Region appreciates the difficulties confronting teachers in respect of the variegated conditions of their service in the Federation, but my Government has given them incentive and security by assuming responsibility for the payment of the salaries and perquisites of all registered and qualified teachers of this Region as an earnest of our good faith. I can assure you the fullest co-operation of my Government in the effort of your Union to obtain a uniform scale throughout the Federation and we shall do all we can to support this move when it is considered by the National Council on Establishments.

Since the year 1952, five Governments have been created in the Federation of Nigeria. This has meant a drain on our man-power, since our legislatures and cabinets must be manned by the products of our schools. Whilst it is true that inroads were made into the reserves of other professions, I think it is fair to admit that your profession was called upon to bear the brunt of the sacrifice. In spite of the exodus it entailed, I am happy to observe that the profession is still growing from strength to strength, for which you deserve the gratitude of the Nation.

Universal primary education is now an accomplished fact in the Western and Eastern Regions, as well as in the Federal Territory of Lagos. It required years of planning and heavy inroads into the exchequers of the Governments concerned to make it a success. Buildings had to be erected, and teachers had to be trained, some of whom had to undergo privations in order to qualify at the first possible moment for the introduction of this most desirable form of social service. Your profession deserves to be praised because the introduction of universal primary education has increased the number of our primary schools, the population of our school-going children, and the number of our teacher-training institutions. These achievements have enabled Nigeria not only to lead every other country in the whole continent of Africa, but also to be among the leading nations of the world in these respects.

My Government is keen on relating the education of our people to their daily needs. The teaching profession should not be satisfied only with raising academic standards in its methods of imparting knowledge, but it should also realize that political advancement has brought in its train certain social and economic problems which can be resolved succesfully by correct perspectives in education. The products of our schools are holding their own so far as the classics and the humanities are concerned; but as a Government, we are being confronted with administrative problems which can be handled successfully only if we have the men and women with technical know-how.

We appreciate that contemporary philosophy of education has given the teachers and the taught definite objectives, to wit: accumulation of knowledge, transmission of knowledge, training of character, development of the creative faculties, control of the emotions, inculcation of spiritual values, etc. But we are faced with practical problems which must be solved in a practical manner, hence we now visualize the need for broadening the curricula of our schools so as to make them more practical in their content.

We hope that in the forthcoming financial year, it will be possible for the Government of this Region not only to introduce vocational guidance in our schools in order to save our children from blind-alley employment, but to encourage vocational education so as to give our sons and daughters opportunity to acquire skills in the various occupations and thus make them employable. In this connection we shall require the active co-operation of your Union because vocational education must be supplemented by physical and religious education so that the products of our schools will be able to adapt themselves to our contemporary life.

Your task will be very important indeed, for not only are you now called upon to impart knowledge to our children in order to make them proficient in the classical disciplines but our development as a country has made it incumbent on teachers as well as Governments to encourage other disciplines of a utilitarian nature in order to provide avenues for honest living among the products of our schools.

Revolutionary changes must therefore be envisaged in the purpose, content, organization and methods of education in our country. That being the case, we have every right to expect revolutionary changes to take place in the training of our teachers. I hope that my Government can count on your Union to co-operate in accelerating those reforms which are inevitable if we are to take our place in the comity of nations without being apologetic for our backwardness in technological education.

I cannot essay a cut and dried solution to the imminent problem of your fraternity. Unless we improve substantially the quality of the teaching force, and above all see that only men and women fitted by temperament, character, intelligence, and aptitude for teaching are allowed to become teachers, we may look, but we shall look in vain, for any reform in education, however much we may improve the organization, plant, and amenities of the public system of education.

Once more, I welcome you to the Eastern Region and trust that this year's meeting will add to the stature of the Nigeria Union of Teachers. The Government of the Eastern Region will co-operate on any reasonable basis in order to safeguard the interests of the teaching profession in Nigeria. I have outlined to you the basic problem confronting all Governments today in making it possible for our children to acquire skills for adaption in a technological civilization. I hope that I can count on your Union for advice, help and support. Yours is a heritage accumulated from the experience of by-gone years. But you are now teachers of a new Nigerian society. Let us work together to face new problems in such a way as to transform this historic heritage into an imperishable legacy.

From a speech delivered in the Eastern House of Assembly on February 13, 1958, in support of the need to modify the Universal Primary Education Scheme.

Mr Speaker, I submit that a case has been made for the modification of the Universal Primary Education on lines which would enable the communities concerned to assume local responsibility for education. I and my colleagues are advised that if we continue this policy of making the Government bear the full brunt of the capital and recurrent costs of primary education, it is bound to have an adverse effect on the finances of the Region. We are told that it would cost this Region £6,950,000 in 1958–59, £8,264,000 in 1959–60, £9,603,000 in 1960–61, £10,985,000 in 1961–62, and £12,425,000 in 1962–63. These increases are astronomical and they are certainly beyond the financial capacity of a territory of this size with its limited resources and stunted economic development.

Certain accusations have been made against the Government in respect of this scheme. It has been alleged that there was inadequate consultation with the people. It has been hinted that the people were not told the truth about the implications of the scheme. It has been said that the Government has yet to explore all sources of revenue in order to cope with the demands of this scheme. We plead 'not guilty' on all these points.

The Hon. Minister of Education consulted the representatives of voluntary agencies, Local Government Associations and the Board of Education before coming to the decision to divide the cost of primary education between the Regional Government funds and those of Local Government bodies. It is unfair to imply that the people were not made to appreciate the magnitude of this obligation. When His Excellency delivered the Speech from the

Throne in March 1957, he gave indications of the upward trend of the cost of education and called the attention of the House to the fact that to vote 42% of the budget for education is a 'heavy responsibility which reflects not only popular demand but my Government's faith in the expansion of the educational system as a main road to progressive prosperity and as such a road along which the Region shall move as rapidly and as far as financial resources permit.' Clearly, here was a warning in unmistakable terms.

We have explored all sources of revenue and we have almost reached the end of the possibilities. We introduced a purchase tax on beer, stout, brandy, schnapps and spirituous liquors, but the people who are now complaining of the reintroduction of school fees commuted to Asaba in order to evade taxation. Then we introduced purchase tax on petrol and increased the motor licences. Again, they used their nefarious art of evading taxation by obtaining their motor car licences from the Northern and Western Regions, where they are cheaper. We amended the First Schedule to the Finance Law, so that the incidence of taxation should fall less on the lower income group and more on the higher income group. They changed tactics and not only failed to give a true declaration of their income but encouraged fraudulent under-assessment of their true incomes.

The Government has tried legitimately to find money with which to give the children of this Region universal primary education, but the greed and avarice and lack of public spirit on the part of tax-evaders have almost made this noble scheme come to grief. Therefore, the only practicable way is that suggested by the honourable mover of this Motion, and I support it because it is fair and equitable.

I commend this timely Motion to the House and I trust that in spite of what may be your misgivings about the circumstances which forced the Government to seek to modify the scheme, you will give it your blessing. That is the manly and courageous way of facing the realities of our education policy. Mr S. Milburn, a former Education Officer in this country, said in a publication

44

entitled *The Growing Cost of Education,* 'A Minister of Education must be something of a prophet if he is to inspire the people, something of a disciplinarian if he is to control a team, something of a diplomat if he is to guide that team along a road accepted by themselves, at a pace that will satisfy the people of the country and the citizens of the world. He must, in addition, be something of a wizard if he is to do what is expected of him on the money provided by those of us who know little of income tax and who often demand higher education and lower taxation in the same breath.'

A message broadcast over the Eastern Regional Programme of the Nigerian Broadcasting Corporation on the occasion of Youth-Day, on March 27, 1958.

Today is one of dedication to the youth of the land. We have proclaimed it a public holiday and called it Youth Day. Henceforth, this day shall be reserved as one set apart to glorify the daring and enterprise of Youth—that stage in the physical growth of man which is known as the spring of life.

As a fitting tribute to youth, we have planned to stage a series of athletic events throughout the Eastern Region in order to give scope to the physical prowess of youth. There will be running events so that youth may exhibit its speed and endurance. There will be jumping and throwing events so that youth may demonstrate its skill and technique.

We are giving our youth the opportunity to develop the body beautiful. We want them to worship their bodies and to preserve them as a symbol of perfection, because only in such a healthy temple can a healthy mind thrive successfully.

As one who has been intimately connected with sports for a greater part of his life, I feel it is an honour and privilege to speak to the youth of the land today. They may be far away from Enugu now, but the wonders of modern science have made it possible for them to hear me wherever they may live. I implore them to appreciate the importance of sports not only in the symmetrical development of their bodies but also in the constructive formation of their character as individuals.

45

Athletic competition is the anvil on which our personality may be forged. The shorter running events enable us to be more expeditious and determined in what we do. The longer running events make it possible for us to develop our stamina and a spirit which knows no defeat. The jumping events perfect our skill in making judgments, and the throwing events engender in us a competitive spirit which always seeks to surpass the attainment of yesterday. These are necessary ingredients of success in life's great struggle for existence.

May I give a word or two of advice to those athletes who will have the distinction to compete in today's contests. Remember that you are as good as the other fellow; do not be discouraged because of his stature or because of his previous achievements in sports; it is true that not all fingers are equal, but it is equally true that if a man is determined to succeed and will make the necessary sacrifices, success is bound to crown his efforts.

So many young people give up so easily in life's tough battle, because they have no faith in themselves. The spirit of sportsmanship means studied resistance to the bitter end. It implies nobility in victory and gracefulness in defeat. If one should emerge a victor after an athletic contest, he should appreciate that, in other conditions, his opponents could equally well have been victorious. Therefore, one should be humble even in victory. If one fails to win one's contest, one should give credit to the victor and accept defeat without excuses. The greatest athletes of the world are modest and humble.

At the end of the competitions prizes are usually awarded to the winners in appreciation of their prowess; but that does not mean that those who failed to win a prize must be blamed or disgraced. It is true that the victors deserve praise to enable them to aim higher, but it is also true that the vanquished deserve commendation to enable them to improve on their past performance. This is one reason why the founder of the modern Olympic Games explained that it is not so much joy in winning as joy in participating in the Olympiad that distinguishes the true athlete from all others.

In conclusion, I congratulate the youth of the land on this first day in which we celebrate Youth Day. Let it be a challenge to our youth to dedicate their lives to the service of their country, and let them learn to be good citizens by being good sports-men and -women so that, in victory or in defeat, they may be more determined to make the world a better place than they found it.

CHAPTER 3

ZIK ON LIBERTY

From a statement made to a group of supporters in the precincts of the Supreme Court at Accra, Gold Coast, on January 11, 1937, after his conviction for seditious libel.

The fight for liberty has just begun in Africa. Only those who are prepared to face odds with a will that knows no defeat—having Right as their armour, and the Sword of Truth as their weapon—must follow the thorny road which was trodden by Socrates, Jesus of Nazareth, Paul of Tarsus, Saint Peter, Thomas More and other immortals of history.

My destiny is not affected by the question of whether I have been convicted or not; I know that I am not the first person, and I will not be the last person, to be convicted because of his ideals. The problem is whether the spirit which motivates me is capable of being deflected from its course by the vicissitudes of human life.

As far as I am concerned I am prepared for the inevitable if through this oblation Africa will speed on its way towards redemption and self-determination.

From a speech delivered at a rally held at Trafalgar Square, London, on December 4, 1949, under the auspices of the West African Students Union of Great Britain and Ireland and associated organizations.

In the United Kingdom, there were formal 'debates' in the House of Commons about the shootings. What interested some of the Members of Parliament was the effect of the disturbances on the shipment of groundnuts to Britain. Some Africans lobbied them, not realizing that the debate on this subject had closed fifteen minutes before the lobby. In the House of Lords, dyed-in-the-wool imperialists took the opportunity of advertising that they were not politically dead but were passing through a stage of suspended animation so far as colonial affairs are concerned. They gave the impression of being less interested in the killing of mere natives than in the audacity of the United Nations in meddling with what they termed the domestic affairs of Great Britain. Said Lord Listowel, who hitherto had been regarded by some misguided Africans as a friend of the 'colonials' when he was a Labour back-bencher back in the days of Churchill: 'We have sole responsibility for formulating the policy pursued in these territories and for choosing the right method of putting our policy into effect. We cannot allow any outside authority to usurp a function which we regard as essential to sound and progressive administration. It is our duty, in judging policy, to consider first the welfare of the indigenous inhabitants and to reject the counsel of the United Nations Assembly when in our opinion it conflicts with their interest. . . . Indeed it would be a dereliction of our duty to the peoples of the Colonies if we were to offer to share our present responsibility with the representatives of other countries. . . . Our reasons for not wishing to throw the colonies into the arena of debate at Lake Success are that criticism there is often warped by anti-British or anti-Colonial prejudice and too infrequently directed to serving the genuine interests of colonial peoples.'

The reaction from abroad has been very enlightening. Two hundred thousand workers in Eastern Germany protested against the shooting. Three million Czech trade unionists registered protests against this evidence of man's inhumanity to man. The National Union of Furnishing Trade Operators demanded the resignation of those responsible for the shooting. British Guiana workers were prevented from holding a rally to register their protest. A delegate from Poland at Friday's meeting of the United Nations General Assembly at Flushing Meadow, demonstrated that the statement of Lord Listowel was far-fetched and that it was necessary that the 'colonial idol' should be destroyed in view of the 'awakening of dependent peoples' and the 'bloody disturbances in Nigeria.'

It is a tragedy that a country which produced Thomas Clarkson and William Wilberforce is now telling the world that it is not prepared to be accountable to a world organization for its colonial administration, because in the words of its delegate at the United Nations it would mean 'to put back the hands of the clock by committing colonial peoples to policies in the formulation of which they have no say and which the United Kingdom regards as misguided.' Since when, may I ask, has the British Government consulted us or respected our opinion in the formulation of colonial policy? What a brazen piece of smug hypocrisy! If it were left to the average Nigerian, we would rather have the United Nations exercising trusteeship over us if Britain thinks that shooting down our workers in cold blood is the correct way of exercising a protectorate over our people. . . .

The people of Nigeria cannot continue to accept as their destiny the denial of human rights. We, too, have a right to live, to enjoy freedom, and to pursue happiness like other human beings. Let us reinforce our rank and file in the fight for freedom, no longer suffering in silence and whining like a helpless dog, but striking back with all the force at our command when we are struck, preferring to suffer the consequences of pressing forward our claim to a legacy of freedom, than to surrender our heritage to despoilers and usurpers. Be of good cheer, my compatriots. The struggle for African fredom may be long and gloomy, but behind the cloud of suffering and disappointment loom the rays of hope and success on the distant horizon. So long as we are undaunted and are determined to be a free people, the fire of freedom shall not be extinguished from our hearths, we shall march forward towards our national emancipation. So long as we refuse to believe that we are doomed to be the serfs and peons of others, our continent shall be redeemed, and we shall have a new life and enjoy it abundantly.

We have friends in unexpected places: genuine and sincere friends. Freedom is within our grasp. Shall we let it slip away? Shall we relapse into the dungeon of fear and the servitude of hesitation? Let us no longer quake or doubt about our capacity to enter into our rightful heritage. Why not deal one blow in a gamble for national liberty? Let there be no mistake about our future. We are determined to discard the yoke of oppression. We shall be free. History is on our side. In this hour of national peril, Nigeria expects every patriot to stand firm in the cause of justice and righteousness. God knows we hate none but we love our country. Long live Nigeria and the Cameroons.

Excerpts from a speech delivered at the Legislative Council at Enugu on March 9, 1950.

Our youths are in revolt against the cant and hypocrisy of contemporary times. So far as I know, they are not antagonistic towards any particular race, and they do not necessarily loathe any particular nation. So far as I have been able to ascertain, our youths do not hate any particular person and they do not dislike any particular official; but they have a highly developed sense of justice, hence they are averse to exploitation and oppression; and they want to be free. Edmund Burke said, 'Tell me what are the prevailing sentiments that occupy the mind of your young men, and I will tell you what is to be the character of the next generation.'

Why, then, should some of us, members of a generation which has had its opportunity and failed to usher in freedom in its lifetime, have the audacity to misinterpret the yearnings and desires of our youth? If we prefer to remain slaves, what right have we to sentence the generation which follows us to slavery? Only confirmed slaves would tighten the chains of slavery round their necks and those of their children. I am not a slave and I have no desire to commit my children to slavery; but if I were a slave, and preferred to have my children follow in my footsteps, then it were better that I had never been born. Edmund Spenser in his *Faerie Queene* said, 'A fool I do him firmly hold that loves his fetters, though they were of gold.'

A statement made on the National Day of Mourning, July 4, 1950, in memory of twenty-one miners who were slain at Enugu on November 18, 1949, at the order of a British Police Officer.

On this historic occasion when we mourn the death of our departed compatriots, let every Nigerian be optimistic as to the outcome of our struggle for self-government. Let us remember that at one time when the workers of England attempted to effect a change in their way of life, they and their leader, John Ball, were executed; yet, today, England is a paradise for workers, compared to Nigeria.

Many of us salute the Union Jack, but do we appreciate the sacrifice in blood, toil, tears and sweat which gave birth to it as the national banner of Britain? It took the blood of St George, the cross of St Andrew, and the toil and sweat of St Patrick to give Britain this symbol of her unity and liberty; yet George and Andrew were executed by Rome because they dared to ask for the exercise of the right of conscience, the right of free speech and the right of peaceful assembly.

Our kith and kin have been slain in the cause of Nigeria. It is for us, the living, to show that their blood shall not have been shed in vain; rather, it shall hallow the ground on which it fell. Even the blood of the two innocent children who were shot at Onitsha shall fertilize the barren soil of Nigerian nationalism, and there shall arise a breed of Nigerians with love of freedom in their sinews, and they shall not take a backward step once they are on the march for freedom.

Let there be no mistake about our future; we are determined to be free, and history is on our side. It is not whether Nigeria is right or Britain is right; it is what is right for Nigeria. In these days of struggle for national survival, let us not be bitter; let us bear no malice; let us be charitable and stand firm in the cause of justice and righteousness. God knows we hate none on account of race or colour, but we love our country, and we want our country to be free, and we shall be free.

From an address delivered before the NCNC Members of the Eastern House of Assembly and executive officers of the NCNC in Owerri Hall, Enugu, January 3, 1952.

Comrades-in-arms and Assemblymen of the Eastern Region, for many years we have sought sanctuary in freedom; for many years that magic word and condition of life have eluded us. Now, we meet so as to shape the course of our country's history, and lo, we are free to make our choice—limited as it is—without outside interference. Indeed, it is a remarkable progress and a great opportunity.

Our brilliant success at the polls has resounded throughout the world where free men live and worship the tradition of freedom. This historic victory has guaranteed liberty in the Eastern Region and the Cameroons under United Kingdom Trusteeship, and has been written in indelible and ineffaceable characters of gold. But it took the toil and sweat of countless unknown soldiers to win this freedom. 'Timid men prefer the calm of despotism to the boisterous sea of liberty.' So said a sage, one and a half centuries ago ; but you have proved yourselves fearless and courageous, hence the struggle for national freedom must continue to its logical conclusion.

Here you are today, placed in an exalted position to express the yearnings and hopes and aspirations of our people. Here you are, leaders in your own right—from the cold and temperate plains of Awgu and Nsukka, to the mountainous terrain of Buea and Bamenda; from the jagged and rugged littoral of Brass and Calabar, to the undulating plains of Okigwi and Wum; from the shining serpentine course of the lordly Niger, to the muffled and winding trails of the Cross River. The joy of it is that you were elected by your compeers to sound the death-knell of autocracy and resuscitate the heritage of democracy conceived by our ancestors and preserved for us through the centuries.

The continent of Europe set a pattern for bloodshed in the attainment of liberty. Hence Charles Dickens could exclaim : 'The libation of freedom must sometimes be quaffed in blood.' But we in forgotten and neglected Africa know better. We are so steeped in religiosity and humanitarianism, and are so cultured and civi-

53

lized that we have often trodden the path to freedom bloodlessly, as our victory at the polls indicates. Are we not now poised to enjoy the blessings of freedom, without bloodshed?

This glorious victory of ours has emboldened me to dare to engage in plain talk with you. Did we participate in the struggle because of the spoils of war and the swag of victory? Did we enlist in the colours of our Army of Liberation in order to advance our selfish interests? or did we fight in order to safeguard for our children a free country?

A statement broadcast over the National Broadcasting Service on September 10, 1954, following an announcement that the Leader of the Action Group would visit the Eastern Region in order to lead a campaign for the Federal elections.

I understand that the Leader of the Action Group is coming here to campaign for the Federal elections. I am informed that he is due to reach Enugu at the time when we of the NCNC are opening our own campaign.

Mr Obafemi Awolowo can be assured of a friendly welcome in the Eastern Region. By now he should realize that we are a freedom-loving people and very democratic in our way of life. That is why we have been able to adjust our differences amicably with the British and other peoples who form the various communities in this country.

We have been bred in a democratic atmosphere to believe that only by tolerating different shades of opinion, whether they are agreeable to us or not, can we free this beloved country of ours from the shackles of tribalism and oppression. I hope that Easterners of all shades of political belief will help the NCNC Government impress upon Mr Awolowo and his Action Group followers a salutary lesson on the cultivation of goodwill and fellowship in the relationship of human beings. We welcome opposition, so long as it is responsible and constitutional in its methods.

It is with regret that we learn of the wave of terrorism which is now sweeping the Western Regions, due to the forces of intolerance and bigotry which have been unleashed by irresponsible elements. This is to be deprecated. Whilst the Eastern Region will readily grant asylum to any political refugee or *emigré*, yet I must emphasize the fact that Easterners resent intolerance and bigotry, no matter from what quarter they stem, and we will not allow their importation into the Eastern Region without protest.

Speech opening the debate on the second reading of the Criminal Procedure (Adaptation) Law, 1954, in the Eastern House of Assembly on December 15, 1954.

Mr Speaker, I beg to move that a Bill entitled The Criminal Procedure (Adaptation) Law, 1954, be read a second time. With your permission, I propose that this Bill should be dealt with in the same manner as the Magistrates Court Law, 1954, and the second reading be treated formally. I would like to call the attention of honourable members to the second schedule of this Bill, with particular reference to Section 385 of the Criminal Procedure Ordinance; it will be noted that it is there proposed that that section be deleted.

The significance of this amendment will not be easily grasped, but the intention is to abolish flogging as a means of punishment in this Region. Government feels that flogging is bestial and that it is one of the relics of the mediaeval system of penology. Respecting the Biblical injunction not to spare the rod and spoil the child, we shall continue to submit juvenile offenders to this type of punishment, because it has been considered since the development of human beings as one of the best means of dealing with children. When it comes to adults all are agreed that it is bestial. I am not so sure whether this is not equally applicable to juveniles!

Secondly it is the intention of the Government in this Bill to delete part 45 of the original Ordinance. If you refer to the relevant law, you will see that the title is 'Deportation'. The political history of this country is filled with stories of deportation—from the days of King Jaja of Opobo to those of Ovonranwon and Benin and Tita Fokum of Bamenda. We feel that in our legislation we should grant freedom of movement to any person in this Region so that they can come and go in the Region, subject to due process of law.

It is the intention of Government that this obnoxious section should be deleted and should not be part of the laws of the Eastern Region.

CHAPTER 4

ZIK ON AFRICA

Excerpts from a speech which was made before his political colleagues of the Mambi Party, at the Palladium, Accra, on January 12, 1937, after his conviction for seditious libel.

I am becoming convinced day by day that the New Africa is destined to become a reality. No force under the heavens can stem it. Even my death cannot postpone its crystallization. If because I am an instrument of destiny through which imperialism in West Africa is to be challenged and liquidated, and if in this mission I am compelled to pay the supreme penalty, then there is no need for me to quake or to quiver.

Gethsemane was there to be conquered. Golgotha was there to be trodden under the feet of man. Calvary was to be overcome. And when a son of the New Africa is faced with the travails and tribulations of Gethsemane, and Golgotha and Calvary, there is no need for the spirit to weaken. At this stage of my life, I cannot be mere flesh. I cannot be part of the corruptible phase of man's organism. I am a living spirit of an idea—the idea of a New Africa. I am a living spirit of an ideal—the ideal of man's humanity to man. I am a living spirit of an ideology—the ideology of the effacement of man's inhumanity to man.

Happily for the gospel according to the New Africa, there exist today on this continent Renascent Africans : literate and illiterate, poor and wealthy, high and low; and they have expressed to me, by their words and deeds, during the last few days of the crucial moments of the existence of my flesh on this earth, that the New Africa is born to me.

Conceived in the indestructible nature of the spirit, and born of a selfless desire to utilize culture for the service of humanity, it is destined that Renascent Africans must carry the torch of this gospel of a new awakening from West to East, and from North to South, Africa.

From a birthday message delivered at 72 King George Avenue, Yaba, on November 16, 1940.

I abhor being a politician or participating actively in colonial politics for four reasons : I have no political ambitions whatsoever in life, if I am destined to spend all my life in a country with a crown colony system of government and administration. I have never believed that a colonial legislature of the crown colony type of government is a place where I could honestly serve my country and my race, without being untrue to my God and my conscience.

I know that in any form of political control of human beings, man's acquisitive instinct, man's love of power, and the vanity of human wishes must make man a target of his fellow man, especially when the spoils of politics constitute the issue which confronts them. I prefer to be a king-maker to a king, knowing full well that I could be king, if I would, and having the satisfaction of appreciating that Nature is so generous in distributing her talents to humanity that she has given to some human beings the power to make and to un-make.

My great tomorrow, if my life is spared, should be spent in an idyllic atmosphere, in an environment of pastoral grandeur, in a campus, where the shades and spirits of by-gone eras, the bubbling youths of Renascent Africa, the corps of academicians and professors of Old Renascent Africa, shall gather round a cloistered hearth with me, firing the imagination of African youth, steeling the spirits of African youth, and building the foundation and superstructure of a New Africa.

From a funeral oration delivered on May 11, 1946, at the graveside when the remains of Herbert Macaulay, First President of the NCNC and founder of the Nigerian National Democratic Party, were interred at the Ikoyi Cemetery.

Herbert Macaulay has left us a great legacy—the struggle for the attainment of social equality, economic security, religious tolerance and political freedom in our life-time. It is our duty to hold aloft this torch of democracy so that our posterity shall be free. It is an obligation for us to prevent repetition of the fatal mistake of living in servitude and in want even in the midst of plenty. Let us venerate the memory of our fallen hero because he has paid the price of leadership. Let us perpetuate his ideas of freedom because he has discharged the penalty of leadership. Let us erect a monument on this sacred spot, as a fitting climax to his glorious life, so that we close a page in our national history and open a new chapter in the story of our onward march towards the attainment of freedom for our country.

Our leader, we mourn for you. Our hero, we weep for you. To leave us at this stage of the battle is a pill that is too bitter to swallow, but man cannot stay the hand of destiny. Fare thee well, my political father, the candle of liberty which you have lit shall never be extinguished.

A birthday message delivered on November 16, 1946, at Ikare, during the Pan-Nigerian and Cameroons tour of the National Council of Nigeria and the Cameroons.

I believe in the God of Africa.

I believe in the black people of Africa.

I believe that it is not the will of the God of Africa to sentence the black people of Africa to servitude in any form for ever.

I believe that there is a destiny for the black people of Africa, and that such destiny can only be realized successfully under the aegis of free and independent African nations.

I believe that by a firm resolve on the part of the black people of Africa, undaunted by fear of imprisonment or exile or death, unaffected by ostracization or victimization or persecution, the black people of Africa will live in free and independent African States in the community of a world society of free and independent nations.

I believe that if I am obliged to pay the price of leadership, in the cause of African freedom, no matter how extreme and severe are the penalties, the prosperity of the black people of Africa shall enshrine my memory for ever in the national pantheon of Africa.

I believe that Nigeria will pass through the acid test of oppression, to which we are now subjected, and shall emerge triumphant.

I believe that the freedom of Nigeria shall come to pass and Nigeria shall become a sovereign State in our life-time, in spite of the might of the oppressor.

I believe that the God of Africa has so willed it.

From an address delivered in Friends House, Euston Road, London, under the auspices of the Pan-African Federation, on July 31, 1947, in celebration of the centenary of the Republic of Liberia.

There is one aspect of Liberian democracy which cannot be overlooked in this brief study of Liberia after a hundred years. I have in mind the role of Liberia in world politics, or shall I say, the part Liberia is destined to play in the field of international relations. Since it is obvious that among the most degraded and oppressed races in the world today are people of colour, among whom are Negroids, it devolves upon Liberia to support the cause of colonial and dependent peoples at the various forums of the United Nations. At international conferences, Liberian delegates should not content themselves with merely voting or abstaining from doing so on any issue. They should express an opinion one way or the other. If any State defends a measure which would protect human rights, Liberia should support the same by making a statement which should leave no doubt as to where she stands on such matters. It is obvious that certain States have undertaken to fight the cause of so-called backward peoples; Liberia should support such States in making a united front against all kinds of oppression.

I look forward to the day when, of her own accord and free will, Liberia will submit a resolution at any of the deliberations of the United Nations asking for the right of self-determination to be extended to millions of people in Africa, who are now suffering from their colonial rulers. Liberia and Haiti and Ethiopia have an

60

opportunity to espouse the cause of freedom for the black races. There is no doubt that India, Pakistan, Egypt, USSR, and the Arab States would support them. God grant that the Republic of Liberia shall continue to enjoy an independent national existence in the comity of nations. God grant that Liberia shall continue to strive towards the path of democracy. Whilst the republic may be proud that, in the last hundred years, she has been the 'Lone Star' in the firmament of Africa, she should not rest on her oars, but she should make it possible for other African communities to join her as free and sovereign States in the family of nations.

From an address delivered at the Plenary Session of the British Peace Congress held at the Lime Grove Baths, Goldhawk Road, Hammersmith, London, on October 23, 1949.

Take a look at the map of Africa. You will notice that its contour presents a shape which reminds one of a ham-bone. To some people this ham-bone has been designed by destiny for the carving knife of European imperialism; to others, it is a question mark which asks whether Europe will act up to its ethical professions of peace and harmony. Yet the paradox of Africa is that its wealth and resources are among the root causes of wars. Since the Berlin Conference, the continent of Africa has been partitioned and dominated by armies of occupation in the guise of political trustees and guardians, represented by the following European countries: Britain, France, Belgium, Portugal, Spain, Italy, and also the Union of South Africa.

When the Allied Powers sounded the tocsin for World War I, Africa played a leading role not only as supplier of men, materials and money, but as a theatre of war in which German colonialism in the Cameroons, in East Africa, and in South-West Africa was destroyed. Again, when the Allied Nations beat the tom-tom for World War II, the African continent was used by military strategists in order to destroy the Fascist aims of Germany, Italy and Vichy France. It is very significant that in the last two world wars, African peoples were inveigled into participating in the destruction of their fellow human beings on the ground that

61

Kaiserism and Hitlerism must be destroyed in order that the world should be made safe for democracy—a political theory which seems to be an exclusive property of the good peoples of Europe and America, whose rulers appear to find war a profitable mission and enterprise.

Now the peoples of Africa are being told that it is necessary, in the interest of peace and the preservation of Christianity, that they should be ready to fight the Soviet Union, which the war buglers allege is aiming at world domination. Since the end of World War II, Field Marshal Lord Montgomery has been visiting several countries in Africa, including my country, Nigeria, which harbours uranium-233. Military roads are being constructed under the guise of economic development. American technicians are flooding Africa, and feverish preparations are being made for World War III. Certain factors have necessitated the stand which my organization, the National Council of Nigeria and the Cameroons, has taken in respect of the next war. In Nigeria and the Cameroons we face the inescapable reality that the blood of our sons has been shed in two world wars in vain. We remember that when during World War II the speaker requested Mr Winston Churchill to confirm that the provisions of the Atlantic Charter applied to Nigeria, as was asserted by his Deputy, Mr C. R. Attlee, the War Premier's reply, couched in diplomatic language and delivered with a soothing manner, contradicted President Roosevelt's interpretation to the effect that the Atlantic Charter applied to the whole world.

Today, in Nigeria, thousands of ex-servicemen are unemployed; they are disillusioned and frustrated, while some of them have been maimed for life, because they had been bamboozled into participating in a war which was not of their making. In spite of their war efforts, the people of Nigeria and the Cameroons have been denied political freedom, economic security, and social emancipation. Our national identity has been stifled to serve the selfish purposes of alien rule. We are denied elementary human rights. We are sentenced to political servitude, and we are committed to economic serfdom. Only those who accept slavery as their destiny would continue to live under such humiliating conditions without

62

asserting their right to life and the pursuit of freedom, and joining forces with progressive movements for peace.

If I may be allowed to be frank, I must say that it is not enough for us to congregate here and adopt manifestoes for peace. We must search our hearts and be prepared to accept some home-truths. Someone has rightly said that 'Peace is indivisible.' One half of the world cannot enjoy peace while the other half lives in the throes of war. You may succeed in averting war between the two great blocs, but yours will be a hollow victory so long as any part of the world remains a colonial territory. It is clear that imperialism is a perennial source of war.

From a Presidential address delivered at the sixth Annual Convention of the National Council of Nigeria and the Cameroons which was held in the Mapo Hall, Ibadan, on May 5, 1955.

The Colombo Powers and certain Asian countries, which have recently been liberated from the yoke of colonialism, convened a conference of Asian and African States at Bandung last month. They meant well and demonstrated the essential unity of all human beings. The fact that they did not invite Nigeria has led some people with an inferiority complex to begin to doubt the will of Nigeria to play its role in the history of this continent.

I may say without fear of contradiction that any decision made at Bandung on the future of this continent that does not take into account the fact that every sixth person in Africa is a Nigerian, is bound to be like a flower that 'is born to blush unseen and to waste its sweetness in the desert air.' I appreciate that the con-veners of this conference did make it clear that it was exploratory. I realize that they were in difficulties when deciding who should be invited. But it is obvious that they blundered when they decided to invite one West African State-to-be and chose to ignore the other West African State-to-be.

When I gave audience to an official Indian emissary at Enugu, some months ago, I told him that the conveners of that conference were not up-to-date in their knowledge of events on the African continent. I emphasized the fact that both the Federal and the

63

Regional Governments of Nigeria were capable of being represented by their accredited leaders or representatives and could give worthy account of themselves like other statesmen of the world. I added that failure to grasp the opportunity of winning the goodwill of Nigeria might militate against those who chose to ignore Nigeria at this her hour of national humiliation. He promised to bring these facts to the knowledge of the Indian authorities but admitted that he was amazed at the constitutional progress made in Nigeria.

I have read almost all the remarks made by Nigerians, at home and abroad, about the failure to invite Nigeria to Bandung. As I said before, most of the observations strike me as evidence of an inferiority complex. Why should Nigerians whine simply because conveners of a particular conference invited the Gold Coast and did not invite us? Why must we be so weak as to cry and blame the new Constitution as being responsible for the failure of the conveners to treat Nigeria with the dignity that is befitting her? I feel that most of these critics are poorly informed about the implications of federalism and, in particular, about the principles governing the recognition of states according to International law.

The Asian Powers will do well to appreciate the historic mission and manifest destiny of Nigeria on the African continent. As Lord Chandos wisely pointed out when he was Secretary of State for the Colonies, the world has yet to appreciate that the least populated member of the Federation of Nigeria, which is the Western Region, has more population, outside Egypt and eight other African countries, than the rest of the fifty countries in the whole of the African continent. Naturally, we cannot be silent about the future of Africa. If we give the impression of not being interested, that is no reason to assume that we shall not join issue with those who exploit this continent when the opportunity is offered to us to play our historic role.

Therefore, I implore members of this great Party not to feel hurt because we were not invited to the Afro-Asian Conference. We have followed with keen interest the trend of the statements made by the delegates. We have watched the reaction to their deliberations in the United Kingdom, the United States and the rest of the world. We shall keep our powder dry, and when we have arrived, instead of demanding respect, we shall command it. Moreover, there is nothing to prevent us from convening a Pan-African Conference or a Pan-Afro-Asian Conference when the time comes. Nevertheless, the Asian Powers must be warned that Asians in Africa should live up to expectations in their relations with Africans, and that they should not exploit Africans; I have in mind Afro-Asian relations in East Africa and the Union of South Africa. We shall not brook the yoke of any other foreign country, once our country is ultimately liberated from the forces of British imperialism. So that it makes no difference whether we are ignored today or not. Our time will come, and when it comes, as dawn follows dusk, we shall reserve to ourselves the right to pick and choose our friends. In the meantime, we bear no malice towards any people, whether they hurt our feelings or not.

An address delivered at a reception given by Dr M. A. S. Margai (now Sir Milton), Chief Minister of Sierra Leone, in the Executive Council Hall, Freetown, Sierra Leone, on July 20, 1957.

The Honourable Chief Minister, Honourable Ministers, Honourable Members, by honouring me and my colleagues in this august assembly, you have demonstrated your 'good neighbour' policy without any shadow of doubt. Not only that, you have given us an opportunity to express the gratitude of Nigeria to Sierra Leone for benefits which have been derived in the course of the past century. Indeed, we are happy to be your guests but also we must assure you that we regard your noble gesture as an honour done to our country.

Nigeria's debt to Sierra Leone cannot be calculated in material terms alone. It is enshrined in the hearts of those who love humanity and believe in the brotherhood of man. Barely a century ago, the Right Reverend Samuel Adjai Crowther joined the noble band of martyrs who laid down their lives so that Christianity should flourish in Nigeria. Since then hundreds of Sierra Leone missionaries, teachers, traders, administrators and workers have found their way to Nigeria and have given impetus to the ferment which has now placed Nigeria at a vantage point in the struggle for freedom.

Within the last twenty years it was common in Nigeria for Sierra Leoneans to occupy leading posts in the Church and State. They were an inspiration to us and they have left us a heritage which cannot be forgotten. From the earliest beginnings of our civil service, Sierra Leoneans helped to shape the course of our history. We cannot readily forget that as early as 1866, ninety-one years ago, some parts of Nigeria were administered from Sierra Leone, which is an indication that, other things being equal, a confederation of West Africa is a possibility, if not on the political level then on the economic plane.

I would be misleading this audience if I left you under the misapprehension that the relationship of Nigeria and Sierra Leone all along had been a one-way traffic. On the contrary it is a two-way traffic. Many Sierra Leoneans are happily settled in Nigeria and have made it their home, just as many Nigerians are happily settled here and made it their home. There have been so many marriages between Nigerians and Sierra Leoneans that it is practically impossible to distinguish one from the other. Many Sierra Leone students have taken advantage of our educational facilities just as many Nigerians have studied at Fourth Bay College and other centres of learning in Sierra Leone. In other words, the two countries have encouraged an amicable relationship between themselves through the years and it has borne fruitful results. I pray to God that this spontaneous development of a spirit of one-ness and identity of purpose shall continue to flourish. God has ordained that our two countries shall be good neighbours and the reception which you have given us today is a shining example of your determination to forge this link of goodwill and fellowship into an indestructible chain of friendship. Mr Chief Minister, we reciprocate your spirit of good neighbourliness and we hope that it will not be long when you will re-visit Nigeria so as to renew acquaintances and make new ones. I thank you and your honourable colleagues for this memorable reception.

An address of welcome presented on behalf of the Government
and people of Eastern Nigeria, to Dr the Hon. Kwame Nkrumah,
Prime Minister of Ghana, on the occasion of his visit to the Eastern
House of Assembly, at Enugu, on February 3, 1959.

Mr Speaker, a rare honour is being done to this honourable House today. It is not a common thing for the Head of Government of an independent country to visit the Legislature of another territory, and to accord it the honour of addressing its House of Assembly. We sincerely appreciate this visit and we welcome to this House, with hearts overflowing with joy, Dr the Honourable Kwame Nkrumah and his galaxy of patriots.

It is a very special pleasure to us, because Dr Nkrumah is not merely the Prime Minister of Ghana, but is an outstanding pioneer in the fight for the freedom of a sister nation in West Africa. We who are battle-scarred and are now on the verge of attaining our statehood and who eagerly await the great day, 1st October, 1960, when, God willing, our dreams shall be realized, have been especially emboldened by the tenacity of purpose of Dr Nkrumah and his immortal comrades to make Ghana free. Indeed, Ghana's independence is the successful accomplishment of their lives' mission.

Mr Speaker, may I recall the pertinent milestones in this historic struggle :

On 16th December 1947, Dr Nkrumah arrived back in his own country, after 12 years of study and preparation in the United States of America and Britain.

On 12th June 1949, Dr Nkrumah founded the Convention Peoples' Party.

On 13th February 1951, Dr Nkrumah left his place of lodging as a 'special guest of His Majesty's Government' and became the Leader of Government Business and ultimately the first Prime Minister of his country.

On 18th December 1956, the British House of Commons passed the Ghana Independence Bill.

On 5th February 1957, this Bill was also passed by the House of Lords.

The Ghana Independence Act received the Royal assent on 7th February 1957.

On 22nd February 1957, the Ghana (Constitution) Order in Council 1957 was made at the Court at Buckingham Palace.

On 6th March 1957, the Sovereign and Independent State of Ghana came into being and its first Parliament was opened.

These are some of the happenings in the life-time of all of us, of which we are living witnesses. But they are not the end. Honourable Members are fully aware of the Pan-African Conference which was held in Accra last year. I have no hesitation in saying that this conference has opened a new chapter in the history of this continent. We are on the eve of great events. A future Federation of independent West African States has made a beginning. It is my earnest hope that the Federation of Nigeria, soon to be independent, will play a worthy part in that larger Federation.

The very diversity of our peoples, and customs and languages, means that we have much to contribute to each other. If we can keep the larger vision in view, if we do not spoil the opportunity that lies before us by petty and inglorious side issues, these African States may yet achieve what the independent and warring States of Europe and the volatile and sometimes undemocratic States of the Americas have never yet accomplished, that is, a unity undreamt-of; and become models of honest and democratic government, which will give hope to all Africa and offer a challenge to the rest of the world.

Mr Speaker, permit me to add a personal note in this address of welcome to my old friends. It gives me a personal pleasure that is indescribable to have Dr Nkrumah with us in our House of Assembly and to have him designated Prime Minister of Ghana. I remember so well the days, nearly twenty-five years ago, when, in spite of handicaps, many nationalists aspired and struggled together in order to win freedom for the country which used to be called the Gold Coast. I was then a new arrival at Accra and an energetic journalist in charge of the *African Morning Post*, whose motto was: 'Independent in all things and neutral in nothing affecting the destiny of Africa.'

Those were the days when party politics, even at their inchoate stage, reached a crisis at Accra, and for the first time in the history of Gold Coast politics, the Ratepayers' Association, composed mainly of the aristocrats, intellectuals and the landed gentry, was decisively defeated by the Mambii Party, the common peoples' party. That was during the 1935 municipal election to the Legislative Council. It was not long before I found myself in the warm embrace of the Sedition Ordinance : I and another nationalist, Mr I. T. A. Wallace Johnson of Sierra Leone, were the first to experience a baptism of fire at a criminal trial under this most unpopular law.

It is all history now, it is true, but I can still see the gleam of hope and the dream of greatness which flashed in the eyes of a young 'merchant of light' who left us in Accra in 1935 to study in the United States and later covered himself with academic and political honours to the glory of his country and our race. He is now a fellow alumnus and a fraternity brother. On behalf of my Government and the eight million people who inhabit Eastern Nigeria, I salute him as one who has proved himself a victor after many bitter political campaigns, and I congratulate him as the first Prime Minister of the first sovereign and independent State in West Africa to emancipate itself from colonial tutelage.

May I also acclaim the entourage of my worthy comrade in the cause of human freedom. These men have made history and it is proper that we should honour them today. There is the Hon. Minister of External Affairs, Mr Kodjo Botsio. How can I forget the gentleman who came down from Oxford University to London and volunteered to assist me and my colleagues in our secretarial work during the Pan-Nigerian delegation to London in 1947? He was one of the best partners I ever had the privilege of playing with on the tennis courts. And we were a formidable combination! Then there is the Prime Minister's Adviser on African Affairs, Mr George Padmore, whose association with me goes back to our university days in America, thirty-two years ago. He has proved himself to be a relentless fighter for the liberation of mankind.

Mr Speaker, I welcome our distinguished guests in this

honourable House with joy because their struggle and ours are identical in many respects. Indeed, history has shown that the struggle for freedom in Africa is an epic in the annals of humanity. Welcome to Nigeria, Kwame Nkrumah! Welcome to this corner of West Africa, Kodjo Botsio, Krobo Edusei, Kofi Baako! Welcome to Africa, the land of your grandsires and the land of your dreams, George Padmore!

Finally, may I say that I look forward eagerly to the day when Nigerians, as citizens of a fully independent and sovereign State, can join our honoured guests and the people of Ghana not only in enjoying political freedom, but also in participating in the titanic struggle for the freedom of all Africa from exploitation in every form and, under God, create a hate-free, a fear-free, and a greed-free continent peopled by free men and women. And I pray that Almighty God may give us the strength to accomplish this herculean task which it has pleased history to assign to us.

From an address delivered by Dr Nnamdi Azikiwe, Premier of Eastern Nigeria and National President of the National Council of Nigeria and the Cameroons, on July 31, 1959, at the Carlton Rooms, Maida Vale, London W.9 under the auspices of the London Branch of the NCNC with Dr T. O. Elias, LL.M., Ph.D., Teaching Fellow in Law at Oxford University, in the chair.

In connection with the relationship between Nigeria and the other African States, the need for economic, social and political integration has been mentioned. Since many views have been propounded on how the free African States can be linked the situation is rather confusing. Perhaps it may be pertinent for me to pursue this matter further in order not to leave any room for doubt or confusion.

Nigeria should co-operate closely with the other independent African States with the aim of establishing unity of outlook and purpose in foreign policy. The pursuing of this objective should make for better understanding among the African States and a realization of identity of interest among them. Moreover, it would advertise the importance of Africa in world affairs and help to heal the wounds that have been inflicted on this continent and which can be a basis of a revanche movement.

There are many schools of thought on how the African States should be aligned. One school favours a political union of African States now. Another school favours an association of African States on the basis of community of interests. Still another school favours an alignment of a rigid or loose character on a regional basis. Other schools develop this splendid idea further and there can be no doubt that more will be heard from other quarters.

My personal opinion is that there is great need for close co-operation between Nigeria and the other African States. The nature of such close co-operation need not delay sincere efforts to attain such a desirable goal, but we must be realistic in pursuing this matter lest we plunge the continent of Africa in a maelstrom of conflicting personal ambitions and interests.

I would suggest that Nigeria, in the first instance, should explore with its nearest neighbours the possibility of a customs union. This would lead to the abolition of tariffs between the two or more countries and would encourage 'free trade' in areas which might ultimately turn into a common market. With a free flow and interchange of goods, Nigeria and its neighbours would come closer in their economic relationship which is very fundamental in human relations.

I would also suggest a gradual abolition of boundaries which demarcate the geographical territory of Nigeria and its neighbours. The experience of Canada and the United States has been encouraging and should be explored. Once travelling is freely permitted, other things being equal, people will forget about physical frontiers and begin to concentrate on essential problems of living together.

I would suggest further that Nigeria should interest its neighbours in a joint endeavour to build international road systems which should link West African countries with East African territories, on the one hand, and North African countries with Central African territories, on the other. By encouraging the construction of *autobahn* systems across strategic areas of Africa, and by providing travelling facilities, in the shape of hotels, motels, petrol-filling stations, we should be able to knit the continent of Africa into a tapestry of free-trading, free-travelling, and free-living peoples.

I would finally suggest cultural exchanges on a wider scale than is practised at present. Students, dancers, artistes, traders and holiday-makers should be able to cross the frontiers of Nigeria and its neighbours with full freedom. They are usually the ambassadors of goodwill and they can help to produce the sense of one-ness which is so lacking in most of Africa at present. Given official support these ordinary folk would become the harbingers of a new era in Africa, because once a sense of one-ness has permeated the social fabric it facilitates the crystallization of common nationality, as the experience of Nigerian history vindicates.

I believe that economic and social integration will enable Nigeria and its neighbours to bring to pass the United States of Africa, which is the dream of African nationalists. It would be capital folly to assume that hard-bargaining politicians who passed through the ordeal of victimization and the crucible of persecution to win their political independence will easily surrender their newly-won political power in the interest of a political leviathan which is populated by people who are alien to one another in their social and economic relations. It has not been possible in Europe or America, and unless Africa can show herself different from other continents, the verdict of history on this score will remain unchallenged and unaltered.

Lest there should be any mistaken notion of my stand on the alignment of interests of African States, may I reiterate that I firmly believe in the attainment of an association or union of African States either on a regional or continental basis in the future. I would regard such a future as not within the life-time of the heroes and heroines who have spearheaded the struggle for freedom in Africa, these four decades. But I honestly believe that social and economic integration would so mix the masses of the various African territories into an amalgam of understanding that the objective might be realizable earlier than we expected.

In other words, the prerequisites of political integration in Africa are the economic and social integration of African peoples.

Otherwise, we shall be precipitating a crisis which will find African leaders jockeying among themselves for leadership of peoples who are not only alien to each other but are unprepared for such a social revolution. This would be disastrous to the ideals of Pan-Africanism which all of us, as sincere nationalists, have been propagating all these years. It means going the way of Europe, which gave top priority to political integration before social and economic integration, only to disintegrate into unimportant nation-states after the Peace of Westphalia in 1648.

The role of Nigeria in world politics can inspire respect if, in addition to creating a healthy relationship, she either spearheads or associates herself actively in the movement to revive the stature of man in Africa. This implies the downright denunciation of the spurious theory of racial inferiority which has no scientific basis. Nigeria should not hesitate to consider it as an unfriendly act for any State in Africa to proclaim or to practise this dangerous doctrine of racialism.

We can revive the stature of man in Africa by associating Nigeria actively with all progressive movements which are busily engaged not only in demolishing racial bigotry but also in spreading knowledge of the fundamental equality of the races of mankind. Nigeria should use its good offices to persuade African States which practise racial snobbery to mend their ways, and Nigeria should dissociate itself from organizations which condone the practice of race prejudice by their members.

The existence of colonies in Africa can no longer be justified in the light of science and history. It should be the manifest destiny of Nigeria to join hands with other progressive forces in the world in order to emancipate not only the people of Africa but also other peoples of African descent from the scourge of colonialism. Science has demonstrated that no race is superior to another. History has shown that no race is culturally naked. That being the case, Nigeria should be in the vanguard of the struggle to liberate Africans from the yoke of colonial rule.

May I at this stage refer to the reported plan of France to use the Sahara Desert as a site for testing its atomic bombs? I am not concerned in this lecture about the desirability or otherwise of using the atomic bomb as an instrument of war, but I am deeply concerned that a European State, which rules millions of Africans as colonial people, should calculatedly endanger the lives of millions of African people in a mad attempt to ape the Atom Powers.

The leaders and people of Nigeria are already reacting and I do not hesitate to warn France, with respect and humility, as I did in November 1958, when I first called the attention of the world to this attempt by France to perpetrate an atrocity against the peoples of Africa, that we will regard this Sahara test not only as an unfriendly act, but as a crime against humanity, in view of the dangers of radio-active fall-out and in view of the effect of the Sahara Desert on the climate of Nigeria.

CHAPTER 5

ZIK ON NATURAL RULERS

From an address delivered in the Native Court Hall at Opobo on June 25, 1946, under the chairmanship of Chief and Rev. Stephen U. Jaja, in connection with the nation-wide campaign of the NCNC against the Appointment and Deposition of Chiefs Ordinance and other national issues.

Our case is that this new law is an unnecessary interference with the tradition and custom of our people. True, the Governor can make inquiry and consult our people in case of a dispute arising out of such issues, but it is evident that he is not bound to respect or accept the advice of either the majority or minority disputants or advisers. Therefore, we raise serious objection to foreigners interfering and deciding for us who should be our rulers. This is an inalienable right. Why then should we be so humiliated as to allow a law to be enacted which virtually transforms our rulers into minions of Great Britain, since he who has the power to appoint or depose rulers must necessarily wield a great influence on them? We do not want hand-picked kings in our country.

We say that neither the descendants nor the agents of a party signatory to a treaty have the right to nominate, appoint, select, elect, reject, depose, change or demote the descendants of another party signatory to that treaty, unless the doctrine is no longer acceptable that the parties to a treaty are presumed to be equal in law.

If you agree with us that the Governor, who is a rank foreigner, should not interfere with our customs, as is envisaged under this law, as a sole judge, then we feel that we have established our case beyond a shadow of doubt, which should merit your giving us your mandate to fight this cause to its logical conclusion.

From a speech delivered in the Legislative Council at Ibadan, on March 31, 1949, on democratization of local government and enforcement of law about conspiracy against, or attempt to undermine, the lawful power of Chiefs and statutory authorities.

The third and fourth preambles refer to tribal institutions which the native peoples have evolved for themselves. According to Yoruba law and custom—and this is equally true of the customary laws of the Ijaw, Edo, Urhobo, Itsekiri, Etsakor, Ibo, Ishan and other tribal units of the Western Provinces—traditional rulers are not absolute, but constitutional, monarchs. They rule by virtue of their obedience to the will of the people. In the Yoruba State, particularly, any monarch who entertains absolutist intentions or seeks to place himself above the reach of the law, is usually asked either by the King-Makers or Ogboni to commit *hara kiri*. In Yoruba parlance, *Nwani ki lo shigba*. We should be careful not to stultify traditional institutions or to vest traditional rulers with absolutist powers which were undreamt of, before the coming of the British.

Paragraph 13 of the Motion has been amended in the light of the opportune, constructive, desirable, and justifiable press criticism, but what is left of this badly mutilated paragraph still gives an impression of an attempt, direct or indirect, to create a privileged class, outside the ambit of the law. I hope this is not the case, hence the need to clarify what is meant by 'conspire against or in any way attempt to undermine the lawful power of statutory authorities'.

Traditional rulers and Native Authorities are now Unofficial Members of the Legislative Council. They thereby exercise equal rights with other legislators, and are addressed in the same way as any other legislator. Personally, I feel that this should not have been the case, because it is a stand-down for traditional rulers, and it is thus subversive and derogatory to their status. But since

76

they have weighed up all the factors and agreed to mix with legislators on an equal basis, the propriety of this Motion must be questioned. It will be remembered that at one of the meetings of this legislature, the Honourable the Oba of Benin justified his presence in the Legislative Council because, he said, it enabled him to mix with the 'common' people and to appreciate the problems of the country.

From a speech protesting against the recommendations of the Ibadan General Conference for the Revision of the Constitution to vest Chiefs with legislative powers, delivered in the Legislative Council, in Enugu, on April 3, 1950.

The trend of general opinion, particularly in the Southern Provinces, is that Chiefs should be encouraged to perform their traditional, that is, ceremonial and religious roles; and that when they exercise political power it should not be based on privilege but should be democratically exercised. . . .

Naturally, the Northern Region, which is heavily weighted with what Sir Donald has described as 'feudal autocracies',[1] favoured, by an overwhelming majority, the continued existence of the House of Chiefs. In this connection, it is refreshing to recount Sir Donald's observation on the tendency to make the North a refuge for reactionary and obsolete institutions under the pretext of religious tradition. 'The policy accepted for some considerable time,' he asserted, 'that the Moslem administrations should be sheltered as far as possible from contact with the world was due no doubt to a feeling, however unformulated, that an unreformed feudal autocracy could not be expected to stand up against the natural forces of a western civilization that was gradually but quite perceptibly creeping further and further north in Nigeria; a curtain being drawn between the Native Administrations of the North and the outer world, so far as it was possible to maintain the integrity of that curtain. But we have advanced now to the stage that the curtain is being gradually withdrawn

[1] *Principles of Native Administration,* paragraphs 21–23.

and, I hope, will be fully withdrawn within a comparatively brief period.' [1]

Although the North has always been isolated as a sort of museum specimen, and in spite of the efforts of certain high officials to lull its rulers and inhabitants into a false sense of security, a gradual desire for change is slowly becoming manifest. Although the Sokoto delegates to the Northern Regional Conference suggested that the Sultan should preside over the House of Chiefs instead of the Chief Commissioner, the Ilorin Provincial delegates have the distinction of being the only Northern group to join the Western Provinces in demanding that the function of the House of Chiefs should be advisory and not legislative. Zaria and Bauchi Provinces suggested modifications along the lines of the relationship between the House of Commons and House of Lords. Bornu and Bauchi advocated ultimate election of an African President. Plateau Province, which is a 'Pagan' area, decided that the House of Chiefs should not exist. The North is not unanimous in the effort to vest the House of Chiefs with legislative powers concurrent with the regional legislature.

From a speech delivered in connection with the suspension and deportation of the Alafin of Oyo, at a rally which was held at Isalegangan Square, Lagos, on June 17, 1955.

The Government of the Western Region is legally right in suspending the Alafin of Oyo, under the Western Region Local

---

[1] *Ibid,* paragraph 21. When informed that it had become necessary to change the Richards Constitution, the Emir of Zaria, Ja'afaru, C.B.E., said: 'If the Governor asks what changes are required in the Constitution let us tell him that so far as we are concerned it is quite satisfactory now. If, however, any other Region desires a change, then let it say what it is that it wants. For ourselves we do not want any change yet.' See *Northern Regional Council of Chiefs Debates,* Third Session, 1949, p. 20. Contrast Sir Donald's opinion with the panegyrics of Mr H. M. Foot, Chief Secretary, on 'the religion of Islam which stands today, as it has always stood, for discipline, dignity, generosity and chivalry,' and his appreciation of the Western Region with its 'example of a sense of public responsibility provided by a progressive aristocracy.' (*Nigeria Legislative Council Debates,* Second Session, 1948, Vol. II), p. 622.)

Government Law, 'On being satisfied that the suspension . . . is necessary in the interests of peace, order and good government'; but it is morally wrong to have done so (a) without making public the reasons which led that Government to become satisfied of this, especially in view of the fact that the Lloyd Commission, an impartial body, had exonerated the Alafin and absolved him from six out of the seven charges alleged against him, and (b) without making public any official arrangement made for payment of stipend to the Alafin during the period of suspension.

The Government of the Western Region is legally justified in deporting the Alafin, under its laws, 'in the interests of peace, order and good Government'; but that Government is not normally justified in doing so, since this is tantamount to the imposition of an extreme form of penalty upon an individual who has been declared innocent of blame, and who was not given any opportunity by the Government to show cause why he should not be banished.

The Government of the Western Region is legally justified, under its laws, in using deportation as a form of punishment, but the Government is not morally justified in doing so if the members of the Executive Council of the Western Region, apart from their Governor, still regard themselves as Nigerian Nationalists, whose forebears were victims of this vicious weapon of British imperialism.

The Government of the Western Region is legally justified in deporting the Alafin of Oyo, but it is not morally justified in doing so without making public any arrangement it has made for paying the Alafin some sort of subsistence allowance during the period of banishment, as was the case with Nigerian deportees when the British were in full control of our Government.

The Government of the Western Region showed lack of moral courage when it resorted to the exercise of a statutory power to deport a prominent Yoruba Chieftain, knowing full well that the exercise of such power could not be contested in any court either in the whole country or in the Privy Council, since it is an executive act which is beyond the competence of the judiciary.

From a speech delivered in the Eastern House of Assembly on March 28, 1956, when moving the second reading of a Bill entitled Recognition of Chief Law, 1956.

It is my intention to belabour honourable members with a critical inquiry into the existence of Chiefs with social or political power in this Region. Eminent ethnographers like Thomas, Talbot, Basden, Meek, Jeffreys, Jones and others have given this subject critical study and have produced works of literary merit and first-class academic worth. As I am speaking to you today, a scholar of anthropology, who is a former colonial administrator of many years' experience in Nigeria, has been officially constituted into a one-man commission of inquiry to investigate the issues of chieftaincy in this Region.

This Bill does not conflict with the terms of reference of the Jones Commission of Inquiry. It merely seeks to accord official recognition and to withdraw same at the pleasure of the Government. It is devised to minimize chieftaincy disputes and to preclude the hearing and determination of such causes in any court of the Region. It defines Chief to mean 'Any member of a tribe or clan or local community whose authority and control in that behalf is recognized by such tribe or clan or local community.' After due enquiry and consulting with certain persons, the Governor-in-Council may recognize a person to be a Chief, and such recognition is final, until it is officially withdrawn.

At the instance of the Royal Institute of Public Administration, a conference was held at Queens' College, Cambridge, last September, and discussions on Development in Local Government in the Colonies brought out the following suggestions on traditional authorities :

The position of the Chief is undergoing a change due to the growing complexity of modern local government, the assumption by the Chief and Council of collective responsibility, and the realization that the responsibility of the traditional council is to the public rather than the Chief.

The position of chiefs and other authorities holding office based on custom depends largely on the historical background of the country, on religious factors, and on the feelings of the local population. Where such a Chief has traditionally played an important part in local affairs, he should occupy a prominent position on the appropriate local authority, so long as public opinion approves.

Pending the report of the Jones Commission, the Government intends to exercise the power conferred by this law in order to demonstrate to the people of this Region that this Government is not necessarily opposed to chieftaincies, as some trouble-brewers have deceived the Chiefs and their followers into believing. After studying the findings and recommendations of the Jones Commission, the Government will make a statement of policy which will be a pointer to its stand at the next constitutional conference, in connection with the establishment of a House of Chiefs in the Eastern Region.

The Bill is an assurance to the Chiefs of this Region and other parts of the country that this Government is not antagonistic to the institution of chieftaincy, where it is the established tradition and custom of the people. Where the role of chiefs is practised by elders or whatever name they are called, the Government will give due consideration to the findings of the inquiry which is now being conducted into the status of Chiefs in this Region. I, therefore, commend this Bill to the House, and Mr Speaker, I beg to move.

CHAPTER 6

ZIK ON DEMOCRACY

From a speech delivered to the graduates of Storer College, in the Anthony Memorial Hall, Harpers Ferry, West Virginia, U.S.A., on June 2, 1947, on the occasion when the honorary degree of Doctor of Literature was conferred on him.

According to the leaders of the Allied Nations, we fought the last war in order to 'revive the stature of man' and to make the Four Freedoms a living reality. I interpret those war and peace aims to mean the enjoyment of political freedom, social equality, economic security, and religious freedom, everywhere in the world. Political freedom is understood to mean the right of self-determination, freedom of speech and press, and the right of the citizen to participate in the government of his country. Social equality implies the right of a human being to associate with his fellow human being, regardless of such extraneous factors as race, colour, creed, or station in life. Economic security means the right of a human being to have sufficient food, convenient shelter, comfortable clothing and some of the luxuries which go to make life tolerable. Religious freedom implies freedom to worship according to conscience.

After we had won the war, can we say conscientiously that we have won the peace? Are the fruits of victory, namely, political freedom, social equality, economic security, and religious freedom, enjoyed today by all the peoples who gave their moral and material support to the cause of the Allied nations? The answer is definitely 'NO' because I come from the part of the world where, in spite of our sacrifices in man-power, money and materials so as to destroy Nazism, we are still living under a political system of benevolent despotism. And when we demand to exercise elementary human rights not only are we silenced by our self-appointed ruler, but the outside world seems to close its eyes, stuff its ears, and seal its mouth on the subject of what is to us a righteous cause.

In my humble opinion, democracy is the hope of a confused world. Having been globally engaged in totalitarian warfare in order to preserve this political philosophy as a way of life, we are not being consistent if we either restrict the development of democratic institutions or limit the enjoyment of the fruit of democracy to a few, regionally. In the interest of world peace, democracy is indivisible; one-half of the world cannot be democratic and the other half undemocratic, otherwise we are sowing the seeds of future war for, as Tacitus said, 'A desire to resist oppression is implanted in the nature of man.'

From a Presidential address delivered at the Fourth Annual Convention of the National Council of Nigeria and the Cameroons held in the Lagos City College Auditorium on August 17, 1952.

I have demonstrated that the Macpherson Constitution is bad, because it destroys our national solidarity, it denies us basic human rights, it makes a mockery of democracy in Nigeria and the Cameroons, it perpetuates the era of benevolent despotism in our country, and it postpones political emancipation in the Cameroons; I have urged that revolutionary means must be used in order to effect its change and that constitutional methods must be adopted for these changes; I have suggested that if it becomes necessary for us to seek for moral support outside the confines of our country, then our only criterion should be this one test; whether in our time of political bondage and national humiliation, such quarters were complacent or energetic in hastening our political manumission?

Our stand should be definite and we must prepare for the zero hour, dedicating ourselves to the complete destruction of the Macpherson Constitution, after which we shall, through political organization, gain power and

(1) Make universal adult suffrage a right of all our people;
(2) Organize a plebiscite for convening a Constituent Assembly for framing a Constitution which will be acceptable to our people;
(3) Declare the independence of our country from colonial status;
(4) Obtain recognition from the family of nations and establish diplomatic relations with them;
(5) Apply for admission into the United Nations as a free and sovereign state.

If we adhere to the above principles, then we must also be ready for the consequences that are bound to follow our actions; but we must not be goaded into any rash action which would either distort our motives or give the enemy an opportunity to misrepresent us or even to seek or be in position to destroy us. Come what may, comrades, we must keep our powder dry, and we need not worry for, as Bernard Shaw has said : 'The most anxious man in a prison is not the prisoner, but the warden.'

Are we satisfied with the seemingly lethargic and complacent condition of our country's politics or are we making preparations in order to launch an all-out assault for the freedom of our country from foreign bondage? True, we are the Government of the Eastern Provinces and the Opposition in the Western Provinces, but what hopes shall we hold out to millions of our supporters? Should we be satisfied with the crumbs or should we now marshal our forces in order to come into our own? If we must be satisfied with the status quo, then some of us must revise our concept of politics. I have read with satisfaction the statement made by Dr Y. M. Dadoo, President of the South African Indian Congress, before he was sentenced to six months' imprisonment for his civil disobedience activities. He told the magistrate that he and his associates were law-abiding citizens and were prepared to obey all laws made for peace, order, and good government, but they would fight bad and unjust laws in every legitimate way. He concluded by saying that he had entered the political field to fight for a fully democratic country. One European trade union leader and an African member of the executive of African National Congress were also implicated and gaoled.

To my mind, that is the correct approach to politics. I regard politics as synonymous with public service buttressed by a sincere desire to make life in this country worthwhile for all who live within its borders. In the attainment of such an objective, compromises on fundamental principles must be rigorously discouraged and renounced, and no sacrifice should be too great to be made. Under such a definition, I cannot parley with those who regard politics as a synonym of ambition animated by an unbridled quest for leadership and power. If I did so, then I would be giving support to opportunists and thereby deceiving the masses upon whose support we have relied, and must continue to rely, as a political organization.

From a Presidential address presented at the meeting of the National Executive Committee of the NCNC held in Owerri Hall at Port Harcourt on October 3, 1952.

Thanks to the growth of political consciousness in this country our people are becoming acquainted with the practice of parliamentary democracy. This has been used as a criterion to determine the political maturity of any people under the rule of others and we can be no exception. As a matter of fact, it is a declared policy of Britain that no colony can be considered ready for self-government until it has made parliamentary democracy a political reality. In plain words, Britain is unwilling to confer the honour of self-government on any of its colonial territories until there is a full-fledged two-party system in operation. Our meeting today can be rightly regarded as a test of the efficacy of parliamentary democracy in Nigeria, because the items on the agenda indicate that we are due for serious heart-searching so far as the workings of the party system are concerned.

I must remind you that the party system of government is based on the control of public opinion. It is a systematic attempt by an interested group to control the political attitude of people through the use of suggestions and consequently to control their actions. Naturally, this arises from interested motives which have the primary purpose of obtaining public support for a particular idea or course of action. This makes it quite clear that the party system is a political medium to control the behaviour of the public through diverse means of propaganda. The machinery of such institution works smoothly on the basis of majority rule. In the words of John Locke: 'A State is established through the agreement of a number of persons who unite themselves to live together in peace and to protect themselves in common against others, and who, for this purpose, subject themselves to the will of the majority. That was—and only that could have been—the beginning of every legally constituted government'.

You will remember that on the eve of the Macpherson Constitution, we decided to constitute ourselves into a political party in order to persuade the majority of voters that our policy is the best suited for the political advancement of this country. We carried out propaganda and gained a considerable following which has enabled us to crystallize into an autonomous government in the Eastern Region, and an opposition party in the Western Region. We have now to take stock of our stewardship and chart our bearings on the boisterous sea of Nigerian politics. In doing so, we should attempt to detect the flaws in our party machinery, repair them, rebuild the machinery and give it a new lease of life; but we must not destroy it.

Unless we are not conscious of our obligations to our various electorates, it is patent that none can denounce the system of party government in our country today without betraying the public trust. That being the case, I propose to make a résumé of the rationale of party politics in our country. As you are aware, a political party is an organization of voters freely and voluntarily formed, for the attainment of common ends. There is, however, an irresistible tendency actually to control the reins of government, and in so doing, there is a concentration of power in the hands of the few people who are willing and have the time and ability to practise those arts by means of which executive control is obtained and exercised. Since there must be conflict of views and clash of opinions among human beings, on a range of issues, it is but rational that those who hold substantially similar views upon any subject should draw together into co-operative effort in order to attain these ends, hence Edmund Burke defined a political party as 'a body of men united for promoting by their joint endeavours the national interest, upon some particular principle in which they all are agreed'.

It is universally accepted that the party system is the only effective *modus operandi* of parliamentary democracy. It is the result of the experience of sovereign nations through the ages and no better substitute has been devised. The nature of its functions is variegated but these run a gamut in almost all the ramifications of political activities, to wit :

(1) disseminating political propaganda and doctrines of the party;
(2) formulating positive policies which find expression in party platforms or manifestoes and other official pronouncement of party leaders;
(3) nominating candidates for public offices and pledging the vote of the party to its candidates;
(4) conducting election campaigns involving the use of every conceivable device for convincing and persuading the electorate that the policies which its candidates represent are preferable to those of their rivals;
(5) controlling, after elections, the policy-forming organs of government so as to materialize the principles embodied in the party platform.

Thus it can be broadly stated that, 'Political parties function in order to make representative democracy workable, especially over large areas, through elections, referenda, and crystallization of public opinion. They facilitate decisions on vital issues by becoming an avenue through which the electorate may subordinate lesser differences of opinion for the good of the country. They also serve as a unifying force by controlling the various organs of government and thereby secure harmonious and consistent policy and administration.' There can be no doubt that party control is essential to an effective practicalization of democracy. As a former President of the United States said : 'This is a government by parties, and there should be a party responsibility. When a policy has been pledged, the party should carry it out, and the leader who leads his party to performance is to be commended'.

Since our party has been entrusted with the sacred responsibility of directly and indirectly guiding the destiny of two regions of the country, we have an obligation to make the party system of government a constructive force in our national life. We can do this by becoming consistent in our policy. Any party member who deviates from the norm of party policy must be seriously censured since his behaviour will stultify the ideal of party system of government. Therefore, we cannot accept party politics on the one hand and then reject it on the other. We are either party-conscious or we are not. If we belong to the former category, then we must be loyal to the party without qualification. By this I do not intend to imply the cultivation of servility or clannishness which generate friction of an acrimonious nature, but within the bounds of reason one can be a party man without necessarily being regarded as chauvinistic or unpatriotic. To think otherwise is either advertising ignorance of the party system of government or indicating distrust of it.

An inaugural speech delivered at his installation as Premier of Eastern Nigeria, in the Eastern House of Assembly, on October 1, 1954.

Mr Speaker, I rise to thank those who have been very gracious in their reference to my elevation to the premiership of Eastern Nigeria. Their kind sentiments were full of inspiration. Their message of congratulation was couched in beautiful language; it was expressed in words that stimulated my thoughts and challenged my emotions. It is with humility that I reciprocate the good wishes extended to me today.

When I returned to Nigeria, almost twenty years ago, little did I expect to be a living witness to what is happening before our very eyes today. I had no ambition for public life, in spite of the fact that I was trained in the art and science of Government. Then, I was convinced that the time would come when the Lion and the Palm Tree would appreciate the need for co-existence in their mutual interest, but I never reckoned that I would be an actor in such a drama. I only assumed that if my life was spared, I would merely be one of the spectators whose role would be evanescent.

Seventeen years ago, I returned from the Gold Coast, as a fully fledged nationalist. There, I had received my baptism as a militant journalist. I did not hesitate to join hands with my Nigerian counterparts and we proceeded to proclaim aloud the gospel of freedom. We converted many who believed in this gospel to nationalism, whilst many were confused as to the correct path to a fuller, richer and more abundant life. This process of social evolution continues apace.

The transformation which has taken place in Nigerian society, in the last quarter of a century, has been phenomenal. Political freedom has become a reality. Social freedom is no longer a dream. Economic freedom has been accepted as a matter of course. Religious freedom is a fact. As we enjoy the fruits of the labours of our predecessors, let us not forget those who, among others, made the foundations of liberty in Nigeria secure—William Pepple, Ovonramwon, Jaja of Opobo, Herbert Macaulay, Horatio Jackson—names for ever enshrined in our national pantheon.

Today marks another milestone in our march towards political emancipation. Aware of the foibles of humanity, we must not allow the mistakes and disappointments of the past to act as a stumbling-block to the hopes and achievements of the future. There must not be any scope for disintegrating forces to decoy us into a situation where we shall point an accusing finger at our fellow man, whilst we cannot claim to be without blemish. Nor should we encourage the exploitation of the ignorance and poverty of our people in order to satisfy the mercenary natures of the more privileged ones.

I count it a great honour to be alive at this stage of Nigerian history. I regard it as an immortal privilege to be an instrument of social change for the rehabilitation of my people. But I realize how puny I am at the hands of fate and I know how insignificant I am for this historic role. Therefore, I must be humble, I must be God-fearing, I must be self-effacing, if I am to prove equal to this rare opportunity!

Mr Speaker, this is a chance of a life-time to serve those who have been placed in unfavourable circumstances by the social forces of history. I pray to God to give me the faith and the courage so that I will live up to expectation. I entreat all of you assembled here on this august occasion to give me your moral support, lest I fail and bring contumely to my race and country from quarters below the equator which continue to doubt our capacity for self-government.

> So let it be, Creator mine,
> Whose skilful hands and thought divine
> Did mould my frame without a blame.
> And gave to me this fleeting flame :
>
> That in this span of strife and hate,
> Buttressed by irony and fate,
> Grant that I live to love mankind
> And thoughtless prejudice rescind;
>
> And may I live to help the weak,
> And learn to serve the poor and meek,
> That when Death wins, I should not miss
> That Path-way to eternal bliss.

Now that we have been offered freedom on a platter of gold, let us welcome this unique opportunity by consecrating our lives anew to the service of African humanity, and, in this re-dedication, let us renew our pledges to the land of our birth, in the form of sixteen canons of rectitude in public life : that we shall not seek to reap where we have not sown; that we shall not covet our neighbour's yam patch or his pay-packet or his material wealth; that we shall not deliberately exploit the ignorance of our under-privileged folk; that we shall not design or manipulate the downfall of the upright; that we shall not conceal or adulterate the truth; that we shall not pervert the course of justice; that we shall not allow ourselves to be corrupted; that we shall not worship filthy lucre; that we shall not be a conscious vehicle for the immolation of the guiltless; that we shall not mislead the innocent; that we shall expose and excoriate evil in any shape or form; that we shall be constructive in all we say or do; that we shall resist injustice with all our might; that we shall commend and not discredit merited achievement; that we shall serve without the hope of gain; that we shall willingly surrender the reins of office in the usual democratic manner.

The Premier is a senior servant of the people. No servant is ever greater than his master. From today, I am a senior, but your humble servant. If I fail to discharge my duties efficiently, it is your obligation to call me to order. It is your responsibility to discipline me. By the grace of God, I promise to do my best, but if that is not good enough, then I am in honour bound to submit myself humbly to your pleasure. Thereafter, I will not complain. One main thing I beg of you : give me a fair chance to serve my country, and if my services are inadequate, then dispense with me in the usual constitutional manner.

From a statement made in the Eastern House of Assembly on March 18, 1955, in connection with the honest difference of opinion between the Governor and the Executive Council of the Eastern Region on the questions of expatriation allowance, abolition of vacant posts, and down-grading of certain posts in the public service.

Lest there be any misgiving about the determination of the Executive Council to eschew absolutism and sustain parliamentary democracy based on constitutional Government in this Region, it is imperative that emphasis be placed on the idea that 'good government is not an acceptable substitute for self-government, and that the only form of self-government worthy of the name is government through Ministers responsible to an elected legislature.' That was the idea which pervaded the atmosphere in which the Joint Select Committee on Indian Constitutional Reform worked in 1934, and it harmonizes with the British conception that 'good government cannot endure unless it is self-government'.

From a speech delivered in the Eastern House of Assembly on March 20, 1956, seconding the motion for the second reading of the Abolition of the Osu System Bill.

Mr Speaker, this Bill is a milestone in the long history of the struggle of African humanity for social equality on the continent of Africa. I would equate it with the Magna Carta of 1215, the Petition of Right of 1628, the Abolition of Slavery Act of 1806, the Emancipation Proclamation of 1863, and the Untouchability Act of 1954. The Magna Carta laid the foundation of civil liberty in England. The Petition of Right secured political liberty in the United Kingdom. The Slavery Act abolished slavery from the British Empire for ever. The Emancipation Proclamation manumitted all slaves in the United States of America and gave them citizenship rights. The Untouchability Act guaranteed social equality to all the Indian untouchables and secured for them full liberty under the law. Today, we are treading the path which was trodden by the reformers of history and I pray to God to give us the vision and the strength of conviction to stand firm in the cause of righteousness.

This Bill seeks to do three things: to abolish the Osu system and its allied practices including the Oru or Ohu System, to prescribe punishment for their continued practice, and to remove certain social disabilities caused by the enforcement of the Osu and its allied systems. The objects and reasons for the Bill are humanitarian and altruistic. They are a positive attempt on the part of your Government to implement one of the recommendations of the Balonwu Bride Price Committee, which found as a fact that certain persons suffered social disabilities and were stigmatized from the point of view of marriage simply because they were labelled as Osu or descendants of Osu, or Oru, or descendants of Oru.

What is the Osu system and why must it be abolished? If any honourable member of this House should ask such a question, it is a perfectly fair one. . . . After all, we must define our terms clearly so as to appreciate the issues at stake. According to this Bill, the Osu system includes any social way of living which implies that any person who is deemed to be an Osu or Oru or Ohu is subject to certain prescribed social disability and social stigma. An Osu may be a person who has been dedicated to a shrine or a deity and that person and his descendants are therefore regarded as social pariahs with no social rights which non-Oru are bound to respect. An Osu may be a person who is descended or can be

92

proved to be descended from a slave and that person and his descendants are for ever proscribed as social pariahs. . . .

Mr Speaker, I call upon all nationalists on both sides of this House to dissassociate themselves from a satanic practice which sentences our kith and kin to social degradation. Mr Speaker, I appeal to all patriots of this country to join this Government in its noble crusade against a vicious social system. Let us recognize a person for what he is and not who he is. Mr Speaker, I demand the emancipation of our people from a social stigma which has instilled in them an inferiority complex. Some of them have scaled the ladder of progress in many spheres of human endeavour and have proved their ability as human beings. What right have we to destroy their personality on the altar of tradition? What kind of tradition shall we revere? A tradition which enslaves the human soul and destroys human virtues? A tradition which sacrifices man's humanity to the passion of man's inhumanity? Why must we question the need for a law of this kind, when it is obvious that it is the right thing to do so as to justify our faith in our ability to rule ourselves justly and righteously? I will not be a party to any social proscription of my fellow man. I will not support any stigmatization of human beings simply because they are said to be descended from a certain family—after all, our descent is something over which none of us has any power. I will not join in the encouragement of a system of society where one stratum can superciliously claim to be descended from the best strain and would therefore consign the others to a scrap heap of their own invention and ostracize them socially. They tell me that somebody is descended from a slave, and they tell me that he must be treated as a social pariah, that what they believe is not a cock-and-bull story based on legends and fairy tales that were told long, long ago.

Mr Speaker, this Bill offers a challenge to the morality of the Easterners. I submit that it is not morally consistent to condone the Osu or Oru or Ohu system. I submit that it is devilish and most uncharitable to brand any human being with a label of inferiority, due to the accidents of history. I submit that human beings are entitled to the right of social equality. Because of my personal convictions, I am seconding this motion. It is my prayer that God may guide us to do the right. Mr Speaker, I beg to second.

From an electioneering address broadcast over the Nigerian Broadcasting Service on May 20, 1956, in connection with the Elections to the Western House of Assembly.

Another legacy of British rule to which I would like to draw your attention is the canon that good government must win public confidence by being truthful, modest, courteous and peaceful. Truth ensures full faith and credit in the pronouncements of those who govern. It means that those who are placed in authority must not trifle with the destiny of those whom they are called upon to govern by telling half-truths or untruths or by suppressing the truth. Modesty implies a tendency not to be proud or arrogant in making claims or stating facts or clarifying official policy. It means that those who govern must be humble in their words or in their deeds because they have been privileged to control the destiny of their fellow man through the will of the people collectively expressed in a democratic manner. Courtesy is an indication of good breeding. It means proper upbringing in a home that is stable, religious and ethical, in order that the foundations of society may exert a good influence on public opinion and morals. Peace ensures harmony. It means that the maintenance of law and order is the basis of good government and is the foundation of a stable society.

From a speech delivered in the Eastern House of Assembly on June 27, 1956, during a debate of confidence in the Government of the Eastern Region.

Mr Speaker, I am grateful to the honourable mover for his moral courage in tabling this motion. In recent months, there has been a spate of challengeable utterance questioning the right of this Government to continue in office. These have emanated from various sources. Some have come from Opposition quarters, whose insatiable desire to replace the present Government can be understood. Some have come from certain chronic grumblers whose fault-finding obsession has become a pathological feature of Nigerian politics. The motion is, therefore, timely, because it will provide the Opposition, the grumblers and diverse critics of Government policy with a platform on which to ventilate their views. If this motion has achieved nothing else, the fact that it forces the Government and its critics to a showdown is commendable, hence my appreciation of the spunk of the honourable gentleman who proposed it.

I am speaking to this motion for five reasons: to reaffirm my faith in the parliamentary system of government, to assess the confidence of the legislature in the present Government, to test the validity of the claim that this Government has outlived its usefulness, to expose the chicanery of those who are demanding the dissolution of this House, and in order to justify the mandate of this Government to speak on behalf of the Eastern Region at the forthcoming London Constitutional Conference.

I believe that in a parliamentary system of Government, the duly accredited representatives of the electorate must decide the composition of the Government of the day. I believe that by organizing themselves into political parties they facilitate the expression of the collective will of the electorate. I believe that the party which succeeds in gaining a majority of seats in any legislature is entitled to form the Government by approving or rejecting the composition of the Executive Council. I believe that such an Executive Council owes its life to the legislature. As a matter of fact, I participated in the constitutional crisis which confronted this House in 1953, for no other reason than my firm conviction that the Executive Council must submit absolutely to the will of the legislature.

I hereby reaffirm that faith in the supremacy of the legislature over the executive and, in doing so, may I humbly assert that, if this House negatives this motion, I shall not regret it, but I will understand that it is an expression of the collective will of the duly accredited representatives of the electorate. Not to over-emphasize this point, may I refer the House to the assurance I gave honourable members, when I was appointed Premier of this Region. On that occasion, I recited sixteen canons of rectitude in public life and ended as follows:

The Premier is a senior servant of the people. No servant is ever greater than his master. From today, I am a senior, but your humble servant. If I fail to discharge my duties efficiently, it is your obligation to call me to order. It is your responsibility to discipline me. By the grace of God, I promise to do my best, but if that is not good enough, then I am in honour bound to submit myself to your pleasure. Thereafter, I will not complain. One main thing I beg of you: give me a fair chance to serve my country, and if my services are inadequate, then dispense with me in the usual constitutional manner.

Mr Speaker, this motion offers the House an opportunity to determine if my services as a senior servant of the people are inadequate. Because of my firm belief in the parliamentary system of Government, I will accept with equanimity whatever the House, as my master, decides.

My next point is to assess the confidence of the legislature in the present Government. The cabinet system of government is based on the principle of collective responsibility. This means that all the members of the Executive Council are collectively responsible for the acts of the Government. No individual Minister can be singled out and exonerated from any blame for which the Government is responsible. Whilst any individual Minister has not only full liberty but a clear duty to speak in Executive Council meetings for or against any proposal put before it, yet it is incumbent upon such a Minister to support the decision of the Executive Council once it has been arrived at and collectively expressed.

It is enjoined upon Ministers, by a conventional code of behaviour which is practised in modern democracies, that so long as a man remains a Minister, he may not speak either in public or in private against a decision of the Executive Council, although he may do so with his fellow Ministers. The same code of ministerial conduct rigidly demands that no Minister should commit the Government save as a result of a decision of the Executive Council. Since the principle of collective responsibility must be the yardstick to judge the conduct of Ministers, it is imperative that

96

Ministers should exercise that responsibility within the limits of general policy as decided in the Executive Council.

Mr Speaker, I believe in the cabinet institution as an adjunct of the parliamentary system of Government. If the acts of this Government must be submitted to scrutiny by this House, then each and every Minister is jointly and severally responsible to the legislature. Singling out any particular Minister for criticism is usually accepted, but when it comes to a question of confidence in the Government, all the Ministers are collectively responsible. The only exception to the rule is that where the House objects to any particular Minister or Ministers, but has confidence in others, it should be brought to the notice of the Premier, who should re-shuffle his cabinet at once or face a motion of censure which, if successful, must be the end of his Government. I submit that this Government should stand or fall by this universally practised principle of cabinet responsibility. Until notice has been brought to the Premier concerning any particular Minister or Ministers, and provided there is still confidence in the Premier, I can only assume that in fairness to this Government, a motion of the type we are now debating is an opportunity to assess the confidence of the legislature in the present Government.

From an address delivered by Dr Nnamdi Azikiwe, Premier of Eastern Nigeria and National President of the National Council of Nigeria and the Cameroons, on July 31, 1959, at the Carlton Rooms, Maida Vale, London, W.9, under the auspices of the London Branch of the NCNC, with Dr T. O. Elias, LL.M., Ph.D., Teaching Fellow in Law at Oxford University, in the chair.

The domestic policy of Nigeria will be framed on the assumption that Nigeria shall continue to be a parliamentary democracy. The Government of Nigeria shall exercise power so long as it retains the confidence of the legislature. It will express its belief in parliamentary democracy as government by discussion, based on the consent of the governed, whose will is collectively expressed by the majority of the duly accredited representatives of an electorate that is based on a universal adult suffrage and that votes by secret ballot at periodic elections.

The expression of such belief in parliamentary democracy should take the following forms:

First, the Government should recognize the existence of an Opposition as an essential ingredient of democracy, and vote a salary in its budget for payment to the Leader of the Opposition; this salary should not be diminished during the tenure of office of such Government.

Secondly, the Government should express publicly its adherence to the rule of law and respect for human dignity and should scrupulously act accordingly.

Thirdly, the Government should at all times be prepared to support and not hesitate to enforce the fundamental human rights in order to ensure particularly freedom of speech, freedom of the press, freedom of peaceful assembly, freedom of association and freedom of movement.

Fourthly, the Government should protect the property of the citizen by ensuring and enforcing the right of the individual to enjoy his private property and to be justly and adequately compensated if he is compulsorily deprived of the same.

Lastly, the Government should act energetically and proclaim its belief in the right of the people of Nigeria to live in a society which respects free enterprise and which provides social security for its inhabitants.

Unless an Opposition, as a 'Shadow Cabinet' which is capable of replacing the Government, exists, democracy becomes a sham. We should not hesitate to put our stewardship as a Government through the crucible of organized public opinion. We should be tolerant and allow our official actions to be thoroughly scrutinized no matter how it hurts. Failure to tolerate the existence of an Opposition party would be disastrous to the existence of democracy. It is the easiest invitation to dictatorship and we should eschew autocracy in any form. We should not give the impression that we have extinguished British Colonial rule only to enthrone in its stead its Nigerian counterpart.

By adhering to the rule of law, we shall protect Nigerians from the forms of arbitrariness which are a speciality of power-drunk politicians. We shall ensure the independence of the judiciary and insulate the civil service, the Police and the armed forces from being subverted for political ends. All Nigerians should be equal before the law and justice should be done without fear or favour. Discrimination should not be practised on account of race or tribe or creed or station in life. A Nigerian should be free to enjoy citizenship rights and privileges anywhere in Nigeria without molestation.

CHAPTER 7

ZIK ON NIGERIAN CONSTITUTIONAL DEVELOPMENT

From a speech delivered in the African School at Calabar on July 13, 1946, at a mass meeting convened on the occasion of the visit of the NCNC delegation.

The Richards Constitution divides the country into three zones which are bound to departmentalize the political thinking of this country by means of the bloc vote. Whether Richards intends it or not, it is obvious that regions will now tend more towards Pakistanization than ever before, and our future generations will inherit this legacy that is born out of official sophistry. If, therefore, there spring forth schools of thought tomorrow, making requests of a parochial nature which would ordinarily rend this country into a multiplicity of principalities, mark it down, men and women of Calabar, as one of the crops to be harvested from this curious constitution of a curious political regime which has just introduced a general strike into the economic annals of this great country.

The Public Relations Department of this country and that of the Colonial Office in London are busy spreading propaganda to the effect that the Richards Constitution has created an African unofficial majority. Writers, travellers, students, statesmen and administrators of the world have swallowed this political bunk— hook, line and sinker. But is it a fact that we are to have in the Legislative Council of Nigeria an African unofficial majority, without qualification? Of course not. This claim is misleading, because the official propagandists fail to tell their innocent victims the whole truth. Having fed them with half-truths, which is the technique of the expert propagandist, they congratulate themselves on having accomplished their devilish plans according to the gospel of Goebbels.

The true fact is that Chiefs and Native Authorities constitute the majority of the unofficial membership of the Houses of Chiefs and Assembly in the regions, which form electoral colleges for the Legislative Council. This is how it works. In the Northern Provinces House of Assembly fourteen members are selected by the Native Authorities, and six are nominated by the Governor to represent certain special interests;[1] whilst the official members number nineteen. In the House of Chiefs, thirteen first-class and ten second-class Chiefs are nominated. In the Western Provinces three Chiefs are nominated by the Governor, seven members are selected by Native Authorities, five members are nominated by the Governor 'from prominent citizens representing important aspects of life not otherwise represented among the unofficial members', and there are fourteen official members. In the Eastern Provinces, nine members are selected by the Native Authorities, five are nominated by the Governor à la Western Provinces, and there are thirteen official members. It is from these 56 Chief-cum-Native-Authority-dominated regional legislative set-ups, including 16 nominees of the Governor, that we have the basis of the unofficial 'majority' of the Legislative Council, after an electoral selection.[2]

This is how this political legerdemain works. The Legislative Council, not having direct elections (apart from the three elected members for Lagos and one for Calabar) will have six Chiefs, 18 Native Authorities and nominees of the Governor (three of whom will represent commerce and industries, shipping and mining) and 17 official members. That is to say that in a legislature of 45 members, 25 are Africans! Here you have the myth of the African 'majority'!

[1] 'The Pagan community, smaller Native Authorities, the Sabon Gari community, industry and commerce or any other important aspects of life not otherwise represented among the unofficial members.' Cmd. 6559 of 1945, p. 8.

[2] In other words, electoral colleges will select from 26 Chiefs, 30 Native Authorities, and 16 nominees of the Governor, the 24 Unofficial Members of the Legislative Council, excluding the four Elected Members and 16 Official Members.

From the opening speech to a Motion standing to his name appealing for national unity, delivered in the Legislative Council at Kaduna, on March 4, 1958.

This country, Nigeria, can no longer be regarded as a mere geographical expression. It is also an historical expression. The various communities or nationalities inhabiting this country have great traditions and a rich heritage of culture which, if pooled together, can make Nigeria great and enable her to take her rightful place among the family of nations. I have great respect for the Hausa-speaking peoples. Studying their historical background, which goes back through centuries of medieval and ancient history, one is proud of the achievements of the Ghana, Melle, Mellestine and Songhay empires. The same is applicable to the Nupe, the Tiv, the Kanuri, not to speak of the Yoruba, Ibo, Edo, Ibibio, Ijaw and other tribes and nationalities forming the various communities in Nigeria.

It is essential that ill-will be not created in order to encourage a Pakistan in this country. The North and the South are one, whether we wish it or not. The forces of history have made it so. We have a common destiny; so, too, have the East and the West. Any attempt from any source to create dissension and make the North feel that it is different from the South and the West from the East, or to make any particular nationality or tribe in Nigeria feel it is different from the others, should be deprecated.

It is from these points of view that I feel that this House should place on record their condemnation of such a practice, and I have in mind the New Year's message of Your Excellency when you appealed to the various communities of Nigeria to appreciate the need to live in harmony so as to make Nigeria a worthy place for all to live in.

From a speech introducing a motion in the Legislative Council held at Kaduna on March 5, 1948, which sought to pay Nigerian legislators £600 per annum for their law-making services.

My honourable friend, the First Member from the Western Provinces, raised the point that it would ultimately ruin this country to spend £16,800. I do not understand what he means by 'ultimately ruin' the country. I suppose he used the expression relatively, but I want to assure him that to spend £16,800, rather than ruining the country, would make conditions much better for members of the Legislative Council for the following reasons. Members of the Legislative Council are expected to be incorruptible, they are expected to have a clear conscience and, like Caesar's wife, they must be beyond reproach. I am not insinuating that the contrary is the case when I assert that it is quite clear that an empty sack cannot stand upright. It is however evident that a person who is not economically secure cannot be free to express his opinion without fear or favour in a legislature of this nature. If we have employees as members of this House, as undoubtedly is the case, it is difficult for them not to think first of their jobs before thinking of the public interest. By being compensated, a member of the Legislative Council will become independent to some extent and he will be free from manacles which otherwise would make it impossible for him to stand by his convictions. In fact, it will tend to strengthen his character and enable him to form sound judgments. Therefore, I feel that the argument of my friend that it will ultimately ruin this country is faulty.

My honourable friend, the Fifth Member for the Northern Provinces, was afraid that if salaries were paid to members of this House, there would be a struggle for jobs. I agree with him. Competition is the soul of business. Other things being equal, such a situation will tend to weed out mediocre personalities and give better types of legislators an opportunity to serve their country. I am sure my honourable friend will not claim that the present unofficial members are the best the country can produce.

I agree with my honourable friend, the First Member for the Western Provinces, that it is a privilege to be elected to serve the country, and I also agree with my honourable friend, the Fourth Member for the Eastern Provinces, that it is an honour to serve this country in a legislative capacity, but I would remind them that Churchill, Nehru, de Valera and others, who regard service to their country as a privilege and an honour, have to be granted some sort of compensation, perquisite or allowance for doing so.

From a speech delivered in the course of the Debate on the Appropriation Bill in the Legislative Council at Kaduna, on March 9, 1948.

In rising to address this Honourable Assembly, I wish to say that I am not doing so as a prodigal, because I and my two honourable colleagues representing Lagos, after having been elected by our constituency, decided, as a matter of principle, not to attend this Legislative Assembly, not out of spite or defiance, but because we felt, firstly, that the framers of the New Constitution ignored the taxpayers of this country by failing at its inception to bring it to their notice and also to respect the will and wishes of the people of Nigeria and the Cameroons; secondly, the New Constitution overlooked the fact that Nigerians and the people of the Cameroons have a right to political freedom and to exercise political responsibility; thirdly, we felt that the New Constitution, like the old Constitution, had enthroned our civil servants not only to exercise political privilege, but also to guide, direct and administer our finances. Consequently, we decided that the New Constitution offered us no hope and that this Legislative Council was merely a debating society where we might be heard, whereas the management of our affairs was to be left in the hands of those who felt that they knew what was best for us.

However, on behalf of my two honourable colleagues, I wish to say that, for reasons which are well known to all the Honourable Members here, the electors of Lagos have reconsidered their decision of last year and they have asked us to accept the advice of the Secretary of State for the Colonies and co-operate in order to hasten the day when this country shall have attained to a state when her people shall exercise political responsibility. We are, therefore, pleased to be here and to associate ourselves with our friends from the North, from the West and from the East, in trying to find a common solution to the problems confronting this country of ours, in spite of the fact that we are still of the opinion that this Constitution is undemocratic and is not consistent with the high hopes which were held out to those sons of Nigeria and the Cameroons who laid down their lives in the mountains of East Africa, in the deserts of North Africa, and in the jungles of Burma. These heroes died in order to make the world safe for democracy and in order to enable us, their people, to enjoy democracy.

From a speech on the Second Reading of the Appropriation Bill delivered at the Budget Session of the Legislative Council at Kaduna on March 9, 1948.

I feel and I sincerely believe that it cannot be the intention of the Government to impose direct and indirect taxation on over twenty-five million people and then expect them to be quiet so far as adequate representation on the Executive and Legislative Council for purposes of financial control is concerned. Our indirect taxation swells our Treasury, yet whilst the vested interests are represented on those august bodies, the people, the bulk of whom constitute tax-payers, occupy an extraneous position in respect of ultimate financial control. I suggest, therefore, that, in preparing our programme of reconstruction, we should realize that the tax-payers of Nigeria are entitled to have a say—I will suggest a final say—in respect of how our revenue should be disbursed. To maintain a bureaucracy and then allow it to show us how the money is to be spent is all right, because we cannot all be experts in the realm of public finance; but to allow such a bureaucracy to spend our money for us is to justify the view that we are politically immature and are also ignorant in the art of government and administration. All we ask for now, is a fair chance to prove our mettle. In the circumstances, I suggest that the following fiscal reforms be made :

(1) that payment of direct taxation should carry with it a right of control of how the taxation should be expended, by tax-payers;
(2) that maintenance of a bureaucracy should imply its control by tax-payers, through their representatives;

(3) that when public funds are disbursed for public benefit, the interest of the public should be paramount, and the welfare of the public should be given priority in all respects;

(4) that the control foreshadowed in (1) above implies the right of tax-payers of Nigeria to be represented on the Executive Council and the Legislative Council of Nigeria, on a majority basis, with other interests, official or unofficial.

A speech delivered in the Legislative Council at Lagos on August 21, 1948, supporting a motion for increased political responsibility for Nigeria.

Your Excellency, in rising to support this motion I do not know how far it is consistent with the statement made on Tuesday about the proposed changes in the Constitution, but I feel that I should support it for four reasons. It involves a fundamental change in the Constitution of this country so far as the exercise of executive power is concerned. It seeks to introduce a system of ministerial responsibility. It accords with the submissions which were made to the Secretary of State last year by a political mission of which I was a member. It represents an advance towards self-government.

This is a progressive motion when we compare it with the present Constitution, but there are certain points with which I am in disagreement. Although it is necessary for us to have Ministries of Land, Agriculture, Education, Transport, Health and Social Services, there is no reason why we should not also have Ministries of Labour, Works, Communications, Finance and other ministries which are well known to those who have studied the ministerial system of government. The granting of political responsibility should not be done on a piecemeal basis.

The people of Ceylon, after giving the Donoughmore Constitution a trial for many years, decided, after the Soulsbury Commission, to abandon this system and introduce real self-government. If our Constitution is to be changed so that we should have ministerial responsibility, rather than go through the stages of Crown Colony Government, Representative Government, and Responsible Government, why not go straight to Self-Government? If the people of this country should discuss and manage their own affairs, why should they not assume full ministerial responsibility? The question of the time element is also vital. Your Excellency indicated that in 1950 there would be a change in the Constitution, but, according to this motion, the changes envisaged are not intended to be made now. Personally I feel that they should be made now.

So far as the motion is concerned, I am supporting it; the only disagreement is that more ministries should be added, ministerial responsibility should not be done on a piecemeal basis, and the time factor should be definite.

A speech delivered at a caucus of the National Emergency Committee (formed of the National Youth Movement and the NCNC) on February 12, 1950, in Dr Randle's Resort, Victoria Beach, Lagos.

We have been invited to attend your conference in order to discuss with you 'How to achieve Political Freedom for Nigeria and the Cameroons most rapidly.' We appreciate your patriotic gesture: history has made possible for us a *rapprochement* in order to strike boldly for the freedom of our country.

This is no time to mince words. We should act now in unison. All parties should mobilize their forces and unify them under one common command towards the attainment of one common objective.

A Cabinet for a Provisional Government of Nigeria and the Cameroons should be established forthwith.

The Cabinet should consist of the following twelve Ministers of State: Prime Minister, Deputy Prime Minister, Ministers of Communications, Defence, External Affairs, Finance, Industries, Internal Affairs, Labour, Trade, Transport and Welfare.

The forces under your leadership should be privileged to select the following Ministers of State: Prime Minister, Ministers of Communications, Finance, Internal Affairs, Transport and Welfare.

The forces under our leadership should be privileged to select

107

the following Ministers of State : Deputy Prime Minister, Ministers of Defence, External Affairs, Industries, Labour and Trade.

Having formed a Provisional Government, the coalition Cabinet should summon a Constituent Assembly of the Nation (a) to prepare a Federal Constitution, (b) to declare our independence, (c) to seek for recognition, according to international law, (d) to establish diplomatic relations with the sovereign States of the world.

Mr Chairman, this is a meeting of the National Emergency Committee. We are gathered here because we mean business. Our plan is a practical way of satisfying the yearnings and aspirations of our people. We are now in a position to unify the various elements of our country and give meaning to the common task of nation-building. There is no need for me to warn you that our plan for national liberation is fraught with dangers. That is one of the penalties of leadership from which none of us dare shrink.

From a speech advocating the regionalization of Nigeria on ethnic and linguistic grounds, contrary to the recommendations of the Ibadan General Conference for the Revision of the Constitution, delivered in the Legislative Council at Enugu on April 3, 1950.

I am opposed to the division of a great country like Nigeria with an area of 372,674 square miles and a population of about 25 million into three regions, because it is an artificial system and must inevitably tend towards Balkanization and the existence of chronic minority problems. I suggest instead the division of the country along the main ethnic and/or linguistic groups in order to enable each group to exercise local and cultural autonomy within its territorial jurisdiction.

At a conference of Nigerian students held in Edinburgh between July 4 and 8, 1949, at which were delegates from England, Wales and Scotland, the following statement was enunciated: 'This conference is of opinion that one of the chief weaknesses of the 1943 [1] Constitution was the arbitrary regionalization of the country, based on the equally unsatisfactory provincial groupings

[1] Evidently 1945 is meant.

initiated at the beginning of British rule. We therefore suggest that as a necessary condition of achieving that unity in diversity [1] which was the expressed aim of the Richards Constitution, and is the desire of our people, the basis of regionalization must be re-examined.' [2]

In their opinion, 'The Constitution of Nigeria should be based on some form of federation which would permit all the nationalities of Nigeria to develop to full political and national cultural maturity, while at the same time ensuring that Nigeria as a whole progresses "towards a more closely integrated economic, social and political unity, without sacrificing the principles and ideals inherent in their divergent ways of life." ' They suggested that 'the units in this federation should be the major national (ethnic) groups in the country'; that where small and isolated groups were incapable of forming an administrative unit, they should be encouraged to form a federated unit.

These suggestions are in line with the Freedom Charter of the National Council of Nigeria and the Cameroons which recommended, in April, 1948, the organization of the country into 'States on national and linguistic bases' enjoying legal equality within the framework of a federal commonwealth.

From a speech opposing the principle of nomination of members by the Governor to represent certain vested interests in the legislature, delivered during a debate on the Report of the Select Committee on the Revision of the Richards Constitution, in the Legislative Council, held at Enugu on April 3, 1950.

I am opposed to the appointment by the Governor of three members 'to represent special interests which in his opinion are not otherwise adequately represented' in the central legislature because it is a recrudescence of the system of nomination and of

[1] Lord Milverton no doubt must have borrowed this expression from the well-known concept of 'diversity in unity and unity in diversity' of Heracleitus, a Greek philosopher.

[2] See *The Future of Nigeria*, p. 14. Also Nigeria Handbook, XIth edition, p. 22, and Obafemi Awolowo, *Path to Nigerian Freedom*, where he discusses the ten main national or ethnic groups in Nigeria.

the creation of a privileged class. The principle of nomination is a denial of the elements of democratic procedure which has been repudiated by enlightened sections of Nigerian opinion in the last thirty years. It is a system by means of which the will of a single individual is imposed on millions of people; this is unprogressive and inconsistent with the essentially democratic nature of indigenous Nigerian political institutions.[1]

The National Council of Nigeria and the Cameroons in making its commentary on the Richards Constitution observed that 'the system of nomination has not encouraged the cultivation of a sense of responsibility to any constituency by a Nominated Member, and it has tended to create a feeling of frustration on the part of the people who are now forced to conclude that since a Nominated Member is not usually a popular choice and cannot be guaranteed to serve his constituency loyally and faithfully, his presence in the Legislative Council is extraneous, so far as the interests of the people of Nigeria are concerned. The system of nomination is, therefore, an anomaly and should be replaced by popular representation based on adult suffrage.[2] . . .

In the circumstances, one cannot endorse the 'appointment' of three members 'by the Governor to represent interests which in his opinion are not otherwise adequately represented', for the following reasons:

(1) This country should not allow those who are energetically concerned in the exploitation of its agricultural, forest, and mineral resources to exercise legislative power as a matter of privilege.
(2) This country should not allow those who have established monopoly in its commercial, banking, shipping and mining activities to exercise political power as a special privilege.
(3) This country should not condone the stultification of its indigenous political philosophy by giving special representation to a particular stratum of any section of its community.

[1] *Memorandum of the West African Students Union* on the Richards Constitution (1945), p. 3. See also the Petition of the National Congress of British West Africa to His Majesty the King, 1920.

[2] *Memorandum on the New Constitution for Nigeria* (Lagos: 1945), p. 17. See also Joan Wheare, *The Nigerian Legislative Council* (London: 1950), pp. 72–81, 102, 115.

(4) This country should not allow the interests of immigrant races to be paramount over those of the indigenous races, in the light of the exposition of the idea of British trusteeship in Africa, by the Duke of Devonshire, Secretary of State for the Colonies, in 1923.

If those who represent these 'special interests' desire to participate in the politics of the country, they should exercise their rights, provided they satisfy the requirements of our electoral laws, just like any other inhabitants of the country.

From a speech disagreeing with the recommendation of the Ibadan General Conference for the Revision of the Constitution delivered in the Legislative Council, at Enugu, on April 3, 1950.

The recommendations of the General Conference in respect of the system of election would appear to ignore the strong feeling throughout the South for direct election to the regional and central legislatures, and the near-unanimous wish of the North for indirect election at the Divisional level. Ever since the deputation of the National Congress of British West Africa in London, in 1920, demands for the emancipation of the people of this country from the thraldom of indirect election have been made, because of its undemocratic nature. In the halcyon days of the Nigerian Youth Movement, the need for universal adult suffrage was felt and harped upon.[1]

In view of the divergent views on this issue, one would have thought that instead of the encouragement of 'indirect election' throughout the country by means of 'electoral colleges', the aim should be direct election. The statement of the Drafting Committee in this respect is most disappointing. I suggest direct election based on universal adult suffrage to all those Provinces which are in favour of this political instrument for the determination of the popular will, including Kabba Province, since having accepted direct election to the Divisional level, they have necessarily condoned that in principle. As for the North, I suggest that, at this

[1] See also *Political Blueprint of Nigeria* (Lagos: 1943), p. 27: 'Voting should be based on universal adult suffrage; this applies equally to elections to Parliament, Legislative Council, Municipal Council, Rural Council.'

stage, direct election be limited to the Divisional level in order to give opportunity to tax-payers of this Region to be better acquainted with this new political experiment. Surely, if a tax-payer is intelligent and responsible enough to exercise the franchise sensibly at the Divisional level, there is no satisfactory justification for limiting this right.

The electoral college is a device to stultify the will of the voter. It is incompatible with our indigenous custom and is alien to our political ideas of democracy. Throughout the progressive sections of the modern world its practice does not enjoy patronage. Not being a universal institution, it is inconsistent with democracy and contradictory to the spirit of progress which is said to animate the revision of our Constitution. It is very significant indeed that this curious political device may be said to deny the tax-payers of this country a basic human right, because Article XXI of the Universal Declaration of Human Rights guarantees to the people of this country the right to participate directly in the government of our country.[1] Therefore, I associate myself with the views expressed in a minority report attached to the recommendations of the General Conference on this issue.

Excerpts from a Presidential address to the Third Ibo State Assembly at Enugu on December 15, 1950.

The Macpherson Constitution is most undemocratic because it is based on indirect elections; at best, it is a compromise with reaction and feudal autocracy. It grants limited franchise at the village or township level and hypocritically gives to the Regions autonomy to decide the mode of elections in their territories. Beyond the primary stage, it substitutes selection for election. It denies universal adult suffrage and makes it virtually impossible for the real choices of the people to be elected as representatives without a shadow of doubt. It creates electoral colleges at the

---

[1] '1. Everyone has the right to take part in the government of his country, directly or through freely chosen representatives. . . .

'3. The will of the people shall be the basis of authority of Government; this will shall be expressed in periodic and genuine elections which shall be by universal and equal suffrage and shall be held by secret vote or by equivalent free voting procedures.'

Divisional, Provincial and Regional levels obviously in order to weed out nationalists, especially in the Northern Provinces.

It grants vested interests special representation and makes a minority bloc of twelve official and unofficial Europeans to hold the balance of power in a legislature where the North, the East and the West are disproportionately represented in the ratio of 68 : 34 : 34. In other words, if the Richards Constitution was the same old poison in a different bottle, the Macpherson Constitution is the same old bottle with a different label. Realizing the reactionary nature of the Macpherson Constitution, I warn you against displaying complacency with respect to its operation. In the Western Region, the Egbe Omo Oduduwa has been very active in seeing to it that only nationalists and patriots who are pro-nationalist should enter the Western House of Assembly. In the North, the feudal autocrats and their minions have spared no time in making it easier for non-English speaking ciphers and illiterate dummies to flood the Northern House of Assembly. With due deference, may I say that these marionettes are entitled to about fifty per cent of the seats in the central legislature.

In the Eastern Provinces, it will be your supreme task, as the most numerous people there, to make it impossible for genuflecting Uncle Toms, shameless stooges, servile stool-pigeons, mercenary traitors, unemployed spivs, and professional sycophants from approaching the entrance of the Divisional Council or Provincial Council or the Eastern House of Assembly. Throughout the Divisions of Benin, Calabar, Ogoja, Onitsha, Owerri, Rivers, and Warri Provinces, which Ibo-speaking peoples inhabit in large numbers, I exhort you, fellow Ibo compatriots, not to support the candidature of those spineless parrots whose stock-in-trade is to denounce nationalists without provocation and without cause.

Excerpts from a speech delivered at the Legislative Council on March 7, 1951.

The new Constitution is now in the offing. Without attempting to prejudice its effect on this country, I must say that it is my sincere belief that like all makeshifts it will flounder and call for

113

early revision. No Constitution which fails to measure up to the highest standards of democratic living can have lasting benefits for the people. It is patent that the life of such a Constitution will be as chequered a one as that of the Richards Constitution which is now on the verge of burial.

Based as it is mainly on the principle of indirect election, it will yet be shown by history to be a panacea and not a cure for our political malady. As my honourable friend, the Second Member for the Northern Provinces, said on October 1, 1948, during the debate on local government, at the African Conference held in London:

The system of election is a democratic instrument. . . . The system of indirect election to the central legislature is recognized as an immediate compromise in view of the high proportion of illiteracy now prevailing in the African colonial territories. It is not acceptable, Sir, as a final method of choice, and we hope that the ultimate policy must aim at the polls and the ballot box as the final method of choice for selection of members of the central legislature.

That, Your Excellency, is a correct diagnosis of the disease which is bound to hasten the new Constitution to an untimely grave.

A statement made at a caucus of the NCNC Working Committee which was held in the Managing Director's Office of the 'West African Pilot', 34 Commercial Avenue, Yaba, on May 12, 1953.

I have invited you to attend this caucus because I would like you to make clear our stand on the issue of secession. As a party, we would have preferred Nigeria to remain intact, but lest there be doubt as to our willingness to concede to any shade of political opinion the right to determine its policy, I am obliged to issue a solemn warning to those who are goading the North towards secession. If you agree with my views, then I hope that in course of our deliberations tonight, you will endorse them, to enable me to publicize them in the Press.

In my opinion, the Northerners are perfectly entitled to consider whether or not they should secede from the indissoluble union which nature has formed between it and the South, but it would be calamitous to the corporate existence of the North should the clamour for secession prevail. I, therefore, counsel Northern leaders to weigh the advantages and disadvantages of secession before embarking upon this dangerous course.

As one who was born in the North, I have a deep spiritual attachment to that part of the country, but it would be a capital political blunder if the North should break away from the South. The latter is in a better position to make rapid constitutional advance, so that if the North should become truncated from the South, it would benefit both Southerners and Northerners who are domiciled in the South more than their kith and kin who are domiciled in the North.

There are seven reasons for my holding to this view. Secession by the North may lead to internal political convulsion there when it is realized that militant nationalists and their organizations, like the NEPU, the Askianist Movement, and the Middle Zone League, have aspirations for self-government in 1956 identical with those of their Southern compatriots. It may lead to justifiable demands for the right of self-determination by non-Muslims, who form the majority of the population in the so-called 'Pagan' provinces, like Benue, Ilorin, Kabba, Niger and Plateau, not to mention the claims of non-Muslims who are domiciled in Adamawa and Bauchi Provinces.

It may lead to economic nationalism in the Eastern Region, which can pursue a policy of blockade of the North, by refusing it access to the sea, over and under the River Niger, except upon payment of tolls. It may lead to economic warfare between the North on the one hand, and the Eastern or Western regions on the other, should they decide to fix protective tariffs which will make the use of the ports of the East and West uneconomic for the North.

The North may be rich in mineral resources and certain cash crops, but that is no guarantee that it would be capable of growing sufficient food crops to enable it to feed its teeming millions, unlike the East and the West. Secession may create hardship for Easterners and Westerners who are domiciled in the North, since the price of food crops to be imported into the North from the

South is bound to be very high and to cause an increase in the cost of living. Lastly, it will endanger the relations with their neighbours of millions of Northerners who are domiciled in the East and West and Easterners and Westerners who reside in the North.

You may ask me whether there would be a prospect of civil war, if the North decided to secede? My answer would be that it is a hypothetical question which only time can answer. In any case, the plausible cause of a civil war might be a dispute as to the right of passage on the River Niger, or the right of flight over the territory of the Eastern or Western Region; but such disputes can be settled diplomatically, instead of by force.

Nevertheless, if civil war should become inevitable at this stage of our progress as a nation, then security considerations must be borne in mind by those who are charged with the responsibility of government of the North and the South. Military forces and installations are fairly distributed in all the three regions; if that is not the case, any of the regions can obtain military aid from certain interested Powers. It means that we cannot preclude the possibility of alliance with certain countries.

You may ask me to agree that if the British left Nigeria to its fate, the Northerners would continue their uninterrupted march to the sea, as was prophesied six years ago? My reply is that such an empty threat is devoid of historical substance and that so far as I know, the Eastern Region has never been subjugated by any indigenous African invader. At the price of being accused of over-confidence, I will risk a prophecy and say that, other things being equal, the Easterners will defend themselves gallantly, if and when they are invaded.

Let me take this opportunity to warn those who are making a mountain out of the molehill of the constitutional crisis to be more restrained and constructive. The dissemination of lies abroad; the publishing of flamboyant headlines about secessionist plans, and the goading of empty-headed careerists with gaseous ideas about their own importance in the scheme of things in the North is being overdone in certain quarters. I feel that these quarters must be held responsible for any breach between the North and South, which nature had indissolubly united in a political, social and economic marriage of convenience. In my personal opinion, there is no sense in the North breaking away or the East or the West breaking away; it would be better if all the regions would address themselves to the task of crystallizing common nationality, irrespective of the extraneous influences at work. What history has joined together let no man put asunder. But history is a strange mistress which can cause strange things to happen!

An address delivered on the return of the NCNC delegation to the United Kingdom conference for the revision of the Macpherson Constitution, at a public meeting held in the Glover Memorial Hall, Lagos, on August 29, 1953, under the auspices of the NCNC Caretaker Committee.

As your humble servants in the service of our country, we went to London seeking unity and freedom. We are proud to say that we have returned with the unity of Nigeria intact and her freedom guaranteed. Before we flew to the United Kingdom, you requested us to place the interest of the country before party politics, and we pledged ourselves to be patriotic, no matter what sacrifice it entailed. On the eve of our departure, I made a statement to the nation on the aims and objectives of the NCNC at the London Conference. This was done at the instance of our Working Committee and on that occasion I said:

We are leaving Nigeria and the Cameroons with the determination of achieving national unity through a workable Constitution based on common nationality and respect for human dignity. In pursuing this objective we shall tackle our common problems with an open mind and a warm heart for the rights of our compatriots, no matter from what region they may emanate.

We shall learn from them as well as teach them; we shall give as well as take; we shall accommodate to the same extent that we are accommodated; and we shall not depart from the fundamental philosophy that has guided great nations to build a heritage of freedom.

As for Great Britain, we must say at once that we shall discuss our problems with her officials with a sense of decorum and responsibility. We shall be tolerant and understanding, but we shall not swerve from our goal, and we shall not be servile.

At the opening session of the London Conference, it was my privilege to state the stand of the NCNC. I informed the audience that this was an opportunity to render service to the cause of unity and freedom in Nigeria and the Cameroons. Realizing the complexity of the problems confronting the Conference, I assured my listeners that the NCNC delegation believed that wise statesmanship could resolve whatever differences might exist among the various delegations.

It is a great sacrifice for a party whose members, since its inception, have suffered privations in order to keep alive the agitation for unity and the spirit of freedom, to express willingness to forgive and forget; indeed, it is a testimony of political sincerity. From the speaker to many patriots in this historic hall, how many of us have not suffered persecution, prosecution, or imprisonment for our convictions? How many of us have not paid heavy fines perennially for alleged sedition so that the country might be free? Yet there are some foolhardy day-dreamers who will not hesitate to jump to immature conclusions and pass unfair judgment on their fellow man. It kills the spirit when those we try to salvage from ignominy resort to the use of the vile tongue and the crooked pen. This is base ingratitude and it is sufficient to chill the ardour of the most red-blooded patriot. Joshua whom the Greeks called Jesus must have felt this way when he admonished :

'O generation of vipers, how can ye, being evil, speak good things? For out of the abundance of the heart the mouth speaketh. . . . For by thy words thou shalt be justified, and by thy words thou shalt be condemned.'

We approached the London Conference animated by a desire to co-operate with the North, the West, the East and the Cameroons. We knew that 'Constitution-making is not an art in essay writing', because it is said that 'in politics we are unlikely to achieve the best' and 'we should remain satisfied if we get the second best'.[1] We knew that in seeking to withdraw our Constitution, we admitted the need for change, both in outlook and in

---

[1] 'The New Federation in Pakistan' in S. D. Bailey, *Parliamentary Government in the Commonwealth* (The Hansard Society, London, 1951), p. 155.

attitude. Benjamin Disraeli said that 'Change is inevitable in a progressive country. Change is constant.' In this vein, my friend, the Hon. Aliyu Makaman Bida, Minister for Education and Social Service, Northern Region, did say at the Ibadan General Conference : 'Nobody likes changes more than we do but ... changes are the law of nature, we want natural changes and not radical ones which will result in nothing else but failure.'

It was, therefore, our considered opinion that events had moved so swiftly in our national life that sweeping changes must be made in our way of thinking and living so that any constitutional arrangements, no matter how radical, might redound to our benefit as a nation in the building. As a party, we made five major proposals which should be borne in mind in redrafting the Macpherson Constitution. They were :

(1) Its objective should be self-government in 1956 or as soon as necessary constitutional administrative arrangements for transfer of power had been made before 1956.
(2) Its form should be federal and based on common nationality.
(3) It should guarantee the practice of parliamentary democracy in our exercise of internal sovereignty.
(4) It should preserve the basic human rights.
(5) It should respect our right to external sovereignty.

As experienced statesmen, we knew that to achieve these desirable objectives, there must be unity in the country based on goodwill and fellowship among our different communities. We, therefore, refused to subscribe to the curious thesis that we were not a nation, or that we could not become a nation, because of our ethnic and linguistic differences. We opposed the idea that because we differed in language, culture, tradition, and outlook, therefore we could not achieve national unity, even at the constitutional level. We remembered the opinion expressed by a group of British parliamentarians, whose views we value highly : 'Experience shows that, given plenty of time and favourable circumstances, differences of race, language, religion and culture need not prevent the growth of a feeling of national unity.'

This point of view is correct because history is replete with such experiences. For example, in spite of these differences the desire for constitutional unity grew in Switzerland among the French, German, Italian and Romansch-speaking communities of that country; today, the Swiss Confederation is one of the world's models of democratic federal government. The English and French-speaking communities of Canada were impelled to form a federation in spite of these differences. In short, we told the London Conference that we believe deep down in our hearts that we could achieve constitutional unity in our country without uniformity. To put it in classic phraseology, we can achieve what the Greek philosopher, Heracleitus, described as 'unity in diversity and diversity in unity'.

In the balance sheet of our activities at the London Conference, there are twenty-four assets and four liabilities. The role of the NCNC as a political party has been creditable and commendable. Our first major proposal was that the objective of the re-drafted Constitution should be self-government in or before 1956. The Conference accepted this proposal and on August 19, 1953, the Right Honourable Oliver Lyttleton, Secretary of State for the Colonies, made a historic declaration of policy 'that in 1956 her Majesty's Government would grant to those Regions which desired it full self-government in respect of all matters within the competence of the Regional Government', provided that the existence of the federation was not endangered by any region and subject to the usual constitutional safeguards. If I may say so, this is a signal victory for the NCNC, which at the Kano Convention of 1951 fixed the year of our Lord 1956 as the target date for self-government. The constitutional significance of this declaration of policy is yet to be fully appreciated. It is the first time in British colonial history that Britain has offered self-government to a colonial territory on a platter of gold. I make this statement in all seriousness because not only will this new Constitution give us semi-responsible government but the offer of self-government in 1956 was made by Britain of her own volition, without warfare, without bloodshed, without conflict, and without rancour. Be it remembered that Ceylon achieved semi-responsible government of this nature in 1946 and by 1948 Ceylon had become a Dominion.

Our second major proposal was that the form of government in

Nigeria should be federal with the residuary powers in the Regions. We based our argument on the ground that such form of government would preserve our unity and guarantee common nationality, in view of the large area of the country and its heterogeneous population factors which make federalism imperative. The Conference accepted this proposal and Nigeria will become a federation of equal states, with the jurisdiction of the Federal Government prescribed, leaving the residuary powers to the co-ordinates of the federation, as is the practice in Switzerland, the United States of America, and Australia.

In other words, each Region will become autonomous and will be headed by a Governor. In the event of a clash between a federal law and a regional law on concurrent matters, the federal law will prevail.

Our third major proposal was that parliamentary democracy should be practised in Nigeria in our exercise of internal sovereignty. The Conference accepted this and endorsed the following decisions:

(1) There shall be direct elections in all Regions to the House of Representatives, which shall be dissolved forthwith. No person shall be a member of the Central and regional houses at the same time.

(2) Any Region is at liberty to introduce universal adult suffrage. The North will revise its electoral register and change its system of representation from a provincial to a divisional basis. The Eastern and Western Regions will guarantee that each division is represented in the regional and central houses.

(3) The House of Representatives will have a membership of 184 (North 92, East 42, West 43, Cameroons 6, Lagos 2). This represents an increase of 36 seats.

(4) The Eastern House of Assembly will have a membership of 84. This represents an increase of 17 seats in view of the greatly increased population of the Eastern Region and the proposal to give the Cameroons a separate legislature.

(5) The three Lieutenant-Governors and Special Members will no longer be members of the House of Representatives.

(6) All official members (Civil Secretary, Legal Secretary, Financial Secretary and Development Secretary) will no longer be members of the Eastern House of Assembly and the Western

House of Assembly. The North prefers them to remain in the Northern House of Assembly.

(7) Special Members representing commercial, banking, shipping, mining and other interests not otherwise represented will no longer be members of the Eastern House of Assembly. The Western Region and the Northern Region prefers them to remain. In the case of the West, it is reported that women will be nominated as Special Members.

(8) The three Lieutenant-Governors will no longer be members of the Council of Ministers.

(9) The official members (Civil Secretary, Legal Secretary, Financial Secretary and Development Secretary) shall no longer be members of the Executive Council of the Eastern and Western Regions. The North prefers them to remain in the Northern Executive Council.

(10) There shall be a Premier in each of the three Regions. This does not preclude a Prime Minister's being appointed in the Council of Ministers subsequently, as was the case in the Gold Coast.

(11) All Ministers (excepting the Chief Secretary) shall be African and they shall have full responsibility and power over all departments, which shall become Ministries.

(12) Ministers shall be appointed and dismissed by the Governors of the Regions on the recommendation of the Premier.

(13) Excepting the usual reserved discretionary powers, the Governors shall always act in accordance with the wishes of the regional Ministers.

(14) The Governor-General shall appoint the leader of the majority party to form a government in the centre; failing which he shall appoint leaders of the majority parties of the regions to do so, and he shall always act in accordance with the wishes of the central Ministers.

Our fourth major proposal was that the redrawn Constitution should preserve the basic human rights with particular reference to freedom of speech, press, peaceful assembly, association, processions, demonstrations, and movement. Whilst the Conference did not accept the incorporation of these fundamental rights in the Constitution, yet it recommended the establishment of Federal and State courts, which we had proposed, for the protection of the rights of the subject, who will have a right of appeal from the lowest to the highest court of the land. In view of this new arrangement, it is unlikely that the West African Court of Appeal will continue to function in Nigeria, where we shall have a State High Court and a Federal Supreme Court, whence one can appeal directly to Her Majesty's Privy Council.

Our last major proposal was that our right to exercise external sovereignty should be respected and we should reserve the right to delegate same until Dominion status had been achieved. This proposal was accepted. Other proposals of the NCNC which were accepted are as follows:

(1) There shall be Federal and State civil services and separate Public Service Commissions shall be appointed to ensure that the civil service is administered strictly on merit. The Governor-General and the Governors shall consult the African Ministers before appointing members of the Public Service Commissions.

(2) There shall be Federal and State Police forces. The Federal Police shall be armed and will be under the direct control of the Governor-General and Governors. The State Police shall be local police for constabulary duties and will be under the control of African Ministers.

(3) If the people of Southern Cameroons desire it, and if they are financially able to bear the burden of budgetary autonomy, then the Southern Cameroons shall become a separate region with its own legislature and executive.

(4) The municipal area of Lagos shall become the federal capital and no longer part of the Western Region. Its government and administration shall be under a central Minister.

(5) The redrafted Constitution shall be reviewed not later than August 31, 1956, when the people of Nigeria shall have an opportunity to express their views on the nature of changes they envisage for the attainment of self-government in that year.

So far for the assets on the balance sheet of the London Conference. If I may be allowed to inject a personal note, it is with humility that I make public today that I have derived a measure of personal satisfaction in the decisions which favoured the NCNC proposals, because they formed the basis of the minority report which I, as Second Member for Lagos, submitted to the Legislative Council at Enugu in March 1950, following the adoption in that House of the Report of the Ibadan General Conference by an overwhelming majority of votes. It will be recalled that I was the only person to dissent from the recommendations of that conference when it was debated in the Legislative Council. It was during that meeting of the legislature that I and Sir Hugh Foot, now Governor of Jamaica, had occasion to cross parliamentary swords.

Coming to the liability side of the balance sheet, I propose to direct your attention to four issues which we raised, three of which were not acceptable to the Conference. We proposed that in a true federation the following four ingredients were essential :

(1) Elections must be direct and based on universal adult suffrage.
(2) Electoral laws must be uniform.
(3) Electoral Commissions must be constituted for the purpose of supervising elections and guaranteeing free and fair elections.
(4) The boundaries of the regions must be so delimited that no one region can be in a position to dominate the others, individually or combinatively.

Certain delegations were not prepared to accept the above proposals. In fairness to the North, they accepted in principle the first three proposals, but submitted that, in view of the fact that they were still behind the South in the race for self-government, they needed time to reconsider the whole issue. Since these four points threatened to engulf the Conference in a stalemate, and the North had accepted the principle of direct election, and it was made clear that any Region was at liberty to introduce universal adult suffrage at any time, the NCNC delegation decided not to press these matters, but to compromise on them whilst emphasizing positively that they would be made an election issue in 1956 when the Constitution was reviewed and self-government was attained.

In the light of the above facts, how can any fair-minded person say that the London Conference was a waste of time and money? How can any reasonable Nigerian expect us to place national interest before party politics, and then turn round and blame us for not pressing our points home—which would have made us extremely partisan? How can any responsible Nigerian, who loves

Nigeria and believes in Nigerian unity and freedom, accuse us of compromising principles and working without plan simply because we preferred to co-operate with the North and the West, and then expect us or the outside world to take him seriously?

If we had placed party interest before national interest and insisted on having our way, there is no doubt that we have the leaders with the academic background, the professional qualifications and the political experience to shake the Colonial Office to its very foundation; but the Conference would have floundered on the rocks of erudition, logic, mistrust and selfishness, and the very lips which shout glibly that the NCNC are plan-less followers of a party which they imagine had pocketed our leaders, would have accused us of inexcusable parochialism.

In conclusion, let me say that it was a rare privilege to work with my fifteen colleagues in London. They were patriotic, loyal and co-operative; but they were people with conviction and were neither servile nor hypocritical. I am proud to have been a member of a delegation where, unlike my experience of six years ago, team spirit was the rule and the issue was not who was right but what was right for Nigeria. Here you see them, leaders in their own right, unrelenting fighters in the cause of Nigerian unity and freedom; yea a collection of sincere nationalists who had been tried and tested in the crucible of time. We are happy warriors because we have fought a fight that will go down in the history of our country as a clean and noble one. We have no cause to regret our visit to London, and we are not apologetic when we admit that we were impressed by the impartiality of the Secretary of State, Mr. Oliver Lyttelton. He showed vision and imagination in the handling of Nigerian affairs. Our posterity will remember him.

All that remains for us all to do now is to roll up our sleeves, buckle down to hard work and sweat profusely so as to maintain unity and freedom in Nigeria. In our daily lives we can further it. The way we speak of other Nigerians and the way we behave towards other Nigerians will decide whether there can be unity in Nigeria or not. In spite of handicaps, let us forge ahead, facing the stark realities of life, admitting our shortcomings and changing our preconceived notions about our fellow human beings. That is the way to win the confidence of our people, be they Northerners, Easterners, Westerners or Cameroonians. That is the only basis to justify our march in unity to freedom.

From a statement made as leader of the NCNC Delegation during the resumed Conference for the Revision of the Nigerian Constitution, which was held in the chamber of the House of Representatives on January 28, 1954.

Whether a member of a federation can secede or not has been given careful study by eminent scholars and jurists, in the light of practical experience of the leading federal countries of the world. In a decision of the United States Supreme Court, in 1869, Chief Justice Salmon Portland Chase enunciated the principle that the union of the states was never a purely artificial and arbitrary relation. He expounded that 'it began among the colonies and grew out of common origin, mutual sympathies, kindred principles, similar interests, and geographical relations.' In his learned opinion, the union was not only indissoluble but was perpetual: 'The Constitution, in all its provisions, looks to an indestructible union, composed of indestructible states. . . .' In this connection, we may also refer to the petition of Western Australia, which, in 1934, sought to contract out of the Australian Federation. The decision of a joint committee of the Houses of Lords and Commons emphasized the fact in the words of Professor Wheare that, 'in practice as well as in law, no right of secession rested with any state acting alone.'

It is true to say that the Western Australia case cited above does not preclude the possibility of secession but merely indicates that it can only take place with the consent of the federating units. I believe this may be a trump card of the memorandum under examination; but I must remind the Conference that Professor Wheare did warn that the right to secede unilaterally even with the consent of the federating units is not consistent with good federal government because it weakens the props of federation, especially where a discontented region uses threat of secession to create embarrassment to the federation.

126

In view of the above considerations, the NCNC delegation is opposed to the request made in the memorandum and appeals to this Conference to reject the incorporation of the right of secession in our Constitution, on the following grounds:

(1) Secession from a federation is incompatible with federalism.
(2) Secession from a federation is an illegal act.
(3) Secession from a federation is an invitation to anarchy.
(4) Secession from the Nigerian Federation between now and 1956 is suicidal.

Our first objection is the incompatibility of secession with the theory and practice of federalism. We have seen that a federation retains the sovereignty of the whole nation, as distinct from the division of powers which are exercised by the central and regional governments. If the latter, individually, reserve the right to contract out of a federation, then it is bound to affect the whole federation adversely, since sovereignty is located therein. Thus a fiction of political philosophy has become a reality in course of the centuries—that federations are compacts which are perpetual and indestructible unless destroyed by external forces. By its structure and organization, no federation can survive if any of its units secedes. Perpetuity is, therefore, an ingredient of federalism, and any attempt to secede will make perpetuity impossible.

An address delivered at a joint meeting of the NCNC Federal Parliamentary Party and National Executive Committee, held in the Assembly Hall of Lagos City College, Yaba, on January 8, 1955.

Honourable Members, Madam and Fellow Committee Men, I welcome you to the first meeting of the National Executive Committee this year and, in doing so, may I wish you all a prosperous New Year. I pray to God that this year will find the people of Nigeria working harder towards the building of goodwill and the creation of mutual understanding among themselves.

As the hierarchy of our great Party, the National Executive Committee meets today to tackle some of the burning political problems which confront our country. The composition of the

Federal House of Representatives has been determined. The personnel of the Council of Ministers is yet to be decided. You have a rare privilege in deciding who should be Ministers of State to represent the Eastern and Western Regions of the Federation of Nigeria. I hope that you will discharge this sacred duty patriotically and realistically.

The results of the federal elections have placed the political parties roughly as follows: Northern Peoples Congress 84, NCNC 63, Action Group 20, KNC 6, UNIP 5, Idoma State Union 2, Middle Belt Peoples Party 2, Igbirra Tribal Union 1, Nigerian Commoners Liberal Party 1. This means that no one political party has established a clear majority over all the other parties. According to the Royal Instructions to His Excellency the Governor-General, if such a situation arises then he shall consult with the leaders of the majority political parties in each Region in order to appoint the ten Ministers, of whom the NCNC will be entitled to six.

It is true that this constitutional pattern will present a situation in which the NCNC will have a majority in the executive and the Northern Peoples Congress will dominate the legislature. The question arises: Can the NCNC and the Northern Peoples Congress operate a government in which either party is in a constitutional position to paralyse action? If so, can such a government be stable enough to win the confidence of the people of Nigeria and the outside world? Otherwise, must Nigeria be subjected to another spate of conferences for the revision of its constitution?

I believe that the NCNC and the Northern Peoples Congress can work a government by agreement in which the former dominates the executive and the latter controls the legislature, provided that both parties genuinely and sincerely intend to give the new Constitution a fair trial. I have two reasons for subscribing to this view. In the first place, the leaders of both parties have already expressed publicly the desire to give the new Constitution a proper chance of survival. The present hiatus is an opportunity for both parties to demonstrate good faith and a sense of responsibility. In the second place, the present constitutional situation is not unique in the political history of mankind. I want you to realize that in the United States of America today, the Republican Party controls the Cabinet and the Democratic Party dominates the Houses of Congress.

The question of whether such a hybrid government can be stable has been answered in the United States, whose Constitution, by the way, is partially our model, and where the Republican and Democratic Parties have bridged the gulf of their differences by establishing an accord based on bi-partisanship. That, ladies and gentleman, is a lamp to guide our feet towards the building of goodwill and understanding in Nigeria, in spite of our political differences.

I will admit that there is an ideological chasm between the NCNC and the Northern Peoples Congress but I submit that, in the realm of practical politics, such a chasm can be bridged by a span of mutual respect for each other based on a bi-partisan policy of government by mutual accord. Therefore, the fact that the NCNC is in a position to dominate the Council of Ministers and the Northern Peoples Congress is poised to control the House of Representatives does not preclude the possibility of a bi-partisan policy which should enable each of the co-operating political parties to co-exist and to exert salutary influence on policy, be it at the executive or legislative level.

Having dispelled the mist from the atmosphere, we can now see clearly enough to enable us to determine who will be our standard-bearers in the Council of Ministers appointed from the Eastern Region and from the Western Region. As soon as this has been done, we should charge our Ministers with the responsibility of maintaining cordial relations with their colleagues in the Council of Ministers. They should be warned that, whilst they will not be expected to compromise on fundamental issues on which the party feels strongly, they should not hesitate to consult the party hierarchy for guidance and direction so as to avoid unnecessary embarrassment. The same goes for those of you who are members of the House of Representatives.

The NCNC believes that there is room in this country for different shades of political opinion. Unlike a certain other political party, we shall not seek to destroy our identity; rather, we will gladly co-operate with any political party which is honest in its intentions, sincere in its outlook, and genuine in its programme. But the NCNC will not encourage any form of Nazism in this country, no matter whether it rears its ugly head in the form of intolerance or of bigotry or of terrorism.

From a welcome address in the Chamber of the Eastern House of Assembly, at the opening session of the Eastern Region 'Summit' Conference which was held on July 9, 1956.

Compatriots, on behalf of the Government of the Eastern Region, I welcome you to this conference. It was decided that since the determination of the future status of the country is of universal concern, especially to those who are leaders of various political organizations, it would be fitting and proper to invite you to a public meeting of this nature in order to have a frank exchange of views. It will be observed that certain individuals with an independent turn of mind on some of the burning issues affecting the country have been invited also. We feel that the presence of those who are concerned in moulding public opinion is very essential, if we are to have an idea of what various shades of political opinion are thinking about the future of Nigeria.

Before the 1953 London Constitutional Conference adjourned, it was agreed 'that a conference consisting of delegations from each Region of the Federation, chosen by their respective Governments in such a manner as to ensure adequate representation of all shades of political opinion in the Federation, should be convened in Nigeria not more than three years from the 31st August, 1953, for the purpose of reviewing the Constitution, and examining the question of self-government.'

The resumed conference in Lagos was very conscious of the declared intention to hold another constitutional conference in 1956, but did not make any specific mention of it in its report, although it did record in the final paragraph that there was no wish on the part of any delegation, or of Her Majesty's Government, either to restrict the scope of this conference or to prejudice its decisions on any issue. At the resumed conference, Lord Chandos, then Secretary of State for the Colonies, indicated that it was the intention of Her Majesty's Government to participate in the constitutional conference proposed for 1956.

At a meeting held in Government House, Lagos, on January 5 and 6, 1956, to discuss preliminary arrangements for the 1956 Constitutional Conference, which was attended by representatives of the Governments of the Federation, the Northern Region, the Eastern Region, the Western Region, and the Southern Cameroons, including the Governor-General and the Governors of the Regions, it was unanimously agreed that in spite of the fact that arguments to the contrary had been carefully considered, the 1956 Constitutional Conference should take place in the United Kingdom. In view of the representations made to Her Majesty's Government, the meeting decided that it would be necessary that there should be not only delegations from each Region, but also representatives of the federal territory of Lagos and of the Southern Cameroons. It was also agreed that such delegations should include persons with direct experience of the working of the Federal Government during the operation of the present Constitution, hence it was decided that the Federation of Nigeria should be represented by the Governor-General, the Regional Governors, the Commissioner of the Cameroons and such advisers as they might wish to take with them.

It was agreed that each Region should be represented by ten delegates, the Southern Cameroons by five, and the federal territory of Lagos by two persons who would be appointed by the Federal Government, on the recommendation of the two main parties in Lagos, namely the NCNC and the Action Group. It was further agreed that each Regional delegation should be permitted to have advisers or alternates not exceeding five in all, and three in the case of the Southern Cameroons.

Before the meeting adjourned, it was agreed that the agenda for the London Conference should be settled by a steering committee which would be formed when the conference met. With reference to the question of the allocation of revenue, the Secretary of State asked the meeting whether in accordance with the recommendation made by Sir Louis Chick, who conducted the 1953 fiscal commission, his proposals should be revived as a matter incidental to the Constitutional Conference; the meeting agreed that no review should take place before the conference and that the latter should determine whether or not there should be a review and, if so, it should draft the terms of reference and determine the composition of the fiscal commission which would undertake this task.

We have summoned this All-Party Conference because we appreciate the heavy responsibility which rests upon each of the Governments in the Federation to ensure that 'all shades of political opinion' are adequately represented in the delegations from each Region. Naturally, the problem is fraught with difficulties, some of which cannot be anticipated. Moreover, the agitation all over the country for separate states has intensified our difficulty in ensuring adequate representation for 'all shades of political opinion'. It has been suggested that representation at a constitutional conference of this nature should be limited to the major political parties, in view of the fact that parliamentary government is now a reality throughout the Federation of Nigeria. But the issue of separate states has become an electoral one in isolated local, regional and federal elections. Another suggestion has been made that some persons or bodies of persons should be entitled to be heard on this specific subject, even though they may not be entitled to attend the conference as delegates.

The task of your Government is to unravel this tangled skein, and we hope that in course of our deliberations a workable solution will be found. Perhaps it might be more practical to invite representatives of the major political parties as accredited delegates to the conference, and to invite also those who agitate for separate states as advisers with the status of alternate delegates, giving them the liberty to express their views as delegates when the conference begins to discuss the subject of separate states.

Two main problems will confront the forthcoming London Conference which will influence all the deliberations of the delegates and their advisers. They are the problem of self-government for the Federation and the problem of self-government for the Regions. It will be recalled that Her Majesty's Government made a declaration in respect of self-government in these words:

This question had been placed on the agenda at the request of the three principal political leaders attending the Conference and the Conference devoted two plenary sessions to a lengthy discussion of this matter. The Secretary of State for the Colonies informed the Conference that Her Majesty's Government were not prepared to fix a definite date for self-government for Nigeria as a whole, the more so as the Northern delegation, representing over half the population of Nigeria, was unable to depart from its policy of self-government as soon as practicable.

The Conference eventually accepted a declaration of policy that in 1956 Her Majesty's Government would grant those Regions which desired it full self-government in respect of all matters within the competence of the Regional Governments, with the proviso that there should be safeguards to ensure that the Regional Governments did not act so as to impede or prejudice the exercise by the Federal Government of the functions assigned to it now, or as amended by agreement in the future, or in any way make the continuance of federation impossible.

This declaration was welcomed as an opportunity to put our houses in order before 1956. It was thought that the 1953 Conference demonstrated the need for a compromise in order to avert the liquidation of Nigeria as a political entity. Since the North promulgated its Eight Points for a loose federation, which would be tantamount to a customs union, the South, through a short-lived alliance between the two major political parties, decided to compromise on a number of fundamental issues with the understanding that in 1956 all delegations would be free to press their points home as they see fit. The North ultimately abandoned its Eight Points and the present Constitution emerged but not without a lot of unfortunate incidents, including walk-outs staged by two delegations, the issuing of press statements attacking the political integrity of certain delegates, the declaration of Her Majesty's Government regarding self-government, and the decision to review the Constitution and the question of self-government not later than the 31st of August 1956.

An address delivered in the Eastern House of Assembly on December 14, 1956, on the occasion of Sir Robert de Stapledon's assumption of office as Governor of the Eastern Region.

Your Excellency, as Premier I have the privilege of extending a warm and hearty welcome to you and Lady Stapledon from the people of the Eastern Region. In doing so, we are particularly glad to recall that you do not come to us as a stranger, since you had served as an Administrative Officer in Nigeria for nine years between 1931 and 1940.

You will no doubt notice many changes since you were last here. The rate of development in both the social and economic fields has been very rapid, and we are proud of our achievements. A great deal, however, still remains to be done, but we look forward with confidence to the future.

Today, a new page is being turned in the history of this Region and a new chapter will begin. With all that lies ahead of us, it will undoubtedly be a most important chapter, but with mutual confidence and trust, we are convinced that, together, we shall succeed in overcoming the many problems which must be resolved in achieving the goal of self-government based on democratic principles.

I make this observation since the Eastern Region is unique because of the keen sense of justice and the deep abiding faith in democracy which permeate the social institutions of its peoples. An appreciation of this fundamental principle is a useful point of reference for understanding the behaviour patterns of the inhabitants of this part of Nigeria.

Your Excellency, this is not an occasion for a long speech, but on behalf of the Government of the Eastern Region I assure you of our whole-hearted co-operation with you and of our loyalty to Her Majesty the Queen.

From a statement made in London on July 11, 1957, on the occasion of his departure from the United Kingdom to Nigeria, after leading the NCNC delegation to the Constitutional Conference.

In my humble opinion, the Constitutional Conference was a painful disappointment, although one must admit that it was not a total failure. It is true that among the achievements are a large measure of internal autonomy for the Federation and a somewhat circumscribed form of self-government for the Eastern and Western Regions. Nevertheless, the Colonial Secretary studiously ignored the feelings of Nigerians who, through their duly accredited representatives, had demanded independence for 1959. This failure to respect our natural aspiration is bound ultimately to disturb Anglo-Nigerian relations.

Two factors have been responsible for the partial failure of the Conference: the immaturity of the Nigerian delegations, and the clever diplomacy of the Colonial Secretary. The argument that there were difficult problems to be solved, which could have stalemated the activities of the Conference, but for the fact that they were referred to certain commissions of inquiry for future resolution, is irrelevant because these problems are not necessarily basic; rather, they are incidental and are neither unique nor peculiar to Nigeria.

The Nigerian delegations demonstrated their immaturity by committing two lethal but avoidable errors. At the instance of the Colonial Secretary, they decided to place the subject of independence for 1959 as the second item on the agenda, contrary to a gentlemen's agreement made between themselves that it should be the first item. Again, they accepted the suggestion that since much preparatory work must precede independence and interim arrangements between now and its attainment would take a long time to mature, the date-line for independence should be shifted from 1959 to 1960, contrary to the mandate which their people gave to them.

Naturally, the commission of such errors exposed vividly the inexperience, if not the ignorance, of certain Nigerian leaders in the art of diplomacy. Had the Conference discussed primarily the subject of independence and stuck to the 1959 deadline, the Nigerian delegations would have brought home to the Colonial Secretary their unanimous demand that Britain's powers of control over Nigeria must terminate in 1959. Instead, they have allowed themselves to be manoeuvred into a position where they have left a wrong impression that their immediate goal is to diminish British rule gradually in Nigeria.

The decisions of the Conference in respect of the circumscribed forms of internal self-government for the Federal and Regional Governments confirm my argument. Surely, no territory can be said to be self-governing in the true sense of the word when its civil service, which is the machinery for implementing its policy, is under the control of a superior political power to whom civil servants must primarily owe their loyalty.

The second factor which spelled the doom of the Conference, in spite of its obvious achievements, was the diplomacy of the Colonial Secretary. He and his galaxy of experts spared no effort to play on the vanity of the Nigerian delegations, whose gullibility in swallowing the soothing opium of flattery administered by experts in this branch of 'White Magic' beats the imagination. Having allowed the subject of Regional self-government to take precedence over independence for 1959, they put the Colonial Secretary into the position of an arbiter and thereby enhanced the popular belief that Britain is the cement which holds Nigeria together.

The spate of claims and counter-claims for separate states, the volley of allegations of oppression fired at a certain Regional Government, the exaggerated fears expressed by representatives of minorities against certain majority groups, and an apparent general feeling of insecurity, should the British depart from Nigeria, placed the Colonial Secretary at a vantage point. As a clever politician, he wasted no time in making capital out of these imponderables; hence he made it clear that he was not prepared to give a blank cheque for Nigerian independence.

From a message relayed over the Nigeria Broadcasting Corporation system on the occasion of the attainment of self-government by the Eastern Region, on August 8, 1957.

It is appropriate that I should speak to the people of the Eastern Region today, which marks another major advance in the constitutional and political progress of the Region and of Nigeria towards full independence. Today an Order by Her Majesty the Queen in Council was promulgated and it implements in part the undertaking given by the Government of the United Kingdom in 1953 to grant self-government to the Eastern and Western Regions. I will explain just what this Order-in-Council means and will describe the further steps that will follow in the immediate future.

First, in accordance with an agreement of the recent Constitutional Conference in London, His Excellency the Governor will no longer preside at the Executive Council of the Region. The Premier will do so instead, but His Excellency will be kept currently informed of the business of the Executive Council.

Secondly, the Governor's general reserved powers not to consult with the Executive Council, or to act otherwise than in accordance with the advice of Council, will no longer be exercised. He will, as far as possible in advance of the making of the main Constitutional Instruments, act on the advice of his Ministers. In short, the Governor becomes the constitutional representative of Her Majesty in this Region.

A third major change that must follow, in accordance with the decisions of the Conference, is the future of the Civil Service. Hitherto, the Public Service has been under the ultimate control of the Secretary of State for the Colonies; but it will now come under the aegis of an executive Public Service Commission. From now on, the Governor will act on the advice of the Public Service Commission in respect of appointments, promotions, transfers, dismissals and other matters of discipline. This implies a very great change in the conditions of service of civil servants who were appointed originally by the Secretary of State and it affects a large number of the expatriate officers working in this Region.

So great is the change that it has been agreed that such officers may have three options; either to retire with due compensation, or to remain in the Public Service of the Region, or to join Her Majesty's Overseas Civil Service. Here I should like to repeat the assurance which I gave publicly on my return from the Constitutional Conference that, we want our expatriate friends to give us the benefit of their expert knowledge, to help to formulate and implement our policies, and we want them to work *with* us and not for us. It is my hope that a great number of expatriate officials will stay with us, especially during the difficult transitional period that lies ahead.

We agreed also at the Conference that the independence of the judiciary should be ensured. To this end, a Judicial Service Commission will be established to deal with the appointment and disciplinary control of judicial officers, in the same way as the Public Service Commission will deal with other civil servants.

A fifth change to be made is that the Attorney-General, who is the Chief Law Officer of the Government, will no longer be a civil servant; this office will be a political appointment and the qualifications for the post will be those of a High Court Judge: i.e. ten years of post-call experience at the Bar. There will, in addition, be a Director of Public Prosecutions, who will be a civil servant whose office will be protected by the new Constitution, and who will be charged with the sole responsibility for the conduct of prosecutions.

I would like to take this opportunity to place on record my Government's appreciation of the work done by pioneer civil servants who laid a sure and enduring foundation for the public service we know today. Their successors have joined them in moulding it to accord with the best traditions of the highly respected British Civil Service, of which we are proud. I must confess that at every stage in the evolution of our public service in Nigeria, both expatriate and indigenous civil servants have acted with a missionary zeal and a remarkable sense of duty for which this Government must be eternally grateful. I would be failing to do justice to my conscience if I did not pay this tribute publicly, especially to that early band of gallant heroes who defied the tropical climate in order to generate the social mechanism which has enabled us to bridge the gap between the days of the porters and the hammock bearers on the one hand, and this modern era of mechanical progress and atomic bombs on the other.

Another matter on which the Conference agreed, and which I know is arousing great interest, is the creation of a second legislative chamber, the Eastern House of Chiefs. I am aware that speculation is rife and that there are many rumours current about this. It may help if I say that the report written by Mr G. I. Jones of Cambridge is now being considered by the Government and arrangements have been made for its publication in the immediate future. The problem of determining how the Chiefs and Natural Rulers shall be represented in both the second chamber and in the Local Government Councils is not an easy one; but it is my aim to create the House of Chiefs early next year.

A statement made on the occasion of the celebration of the fifty-fourth anniversary of his birth, on November 16, 1958, at sea, on board the M.V. 'Aureol'.

This is a glorious day. It is an occasion for personal rejoicing because it reminds me that now is the beginning of the end of our political servitude. The announcement that Her Majesty's Government will recognize October 1, 1960, as the date of our national independence is a message of hope. It is also the fulfilment of my life's mission and the realization of the dream of Nigerian patriots.

In 1937, when I returned from Ghana, I joined forces with my compatriots in order to fight for the freedom of Nigeria. We fought for political autonomy, economic security, social equality and religious toleration. Those were the days of the colonial regime, with its trappings of economic inequality, social discrimination and religious intolerance. It is gratifying to realize that today these spectres of the past are being swept away by the forces of nationalism. Indeed, we have not fought in vain.

Our struggle for freedom has been protracted and painful. We have had to overcome many obstacles put up not only by our own people but also by those who have a vested interest in our continued political bondage. Our Quislings betrayed us and they were commended by our oppressors for doing so. Our exploiters entrenched themselves unshakeably in all the strategic positions of our national life and applied various pressures to us. We did not retreat and we did not surrender. We fought relentlessly and we have now forced them to concede to us our birthright. The vista is now clearing. The dawn of freedom is no longer a dream. It is reality.

How many times have we not been persecuted because of our honest conviction in the ultimate freedom of our country? As individuals, have we not suffered humiliation and privation of different sorts? Have we not lost our jobs? Have we not experienced losses in our business undertakings? Have we not gone through hell on earth because of our political beliefs? How many of us are poor today, who should have been rich but because of our faith in Nigerian freedom? How many times have we not been victimized because we had dared to assert our rights as human beings? We have one consolation: history has vindicated our stand.

On this fifty-fourth anniversary of my birth, I appeal to all nationalists to forget the injustices and the provocations of the past. Only God can avenge man's inhumanity to man. Only time can heal our wounds. Although truth was crushed to earth and fair play was trampled into the dust, I never doubted that it was a temporary triumph for the forces of evil. Today, we know the truth and it has made us free.

When Marcus Garvey preached of African freedom, what was his reward? They called him a visionary. They prosecuted him. They silenced him. And he died broken-hearted. When the National Congress of British West Africa advocated freedom for us, their leaders were ostracized and made objects of scorn. Most of them died unsung. When Herbert Macaulay organized the National Council of Nigeria and the Cameroons in order to liberate Nigeria from colonial status, he was snubbed in an unholy attempt to crush his spirit of freedom. But we gave him a burial befitting a hero. And when the Zikist Movement became militant in the cause of Nigerian freedom, they imprisoned its youthful leaders and banned it so as to stultify our just and natural aspirations.

In spite of the fury of the oppressor, we are still standing firm. In spite of the canards of the traitor, we are still as constant as the Northern Star. In spite of the treachery of the inordinately ambitious, we are still upholding the banner of Nigerian freedom. In spite of the provocations of the literary hirelings, we are still firm in the belief that Nigeria is destined to take its place as a free, sovereign state in the comity of nations. No amount of inspired vituperations can cause us to swerve from this goal, and no amount of aspersions on our character can provoke us to forget our mission. The insults and misrepresentations of yesterday have been replaced by a polite admission of our sincerity of purpose.

For our part, we shall not be bitter and we shall not recriminate over the past and we shall not retaliate in kind because it is the price patriots must pay for their country's freedom. But henceforth, we shall take dictation from none. Henceforth, we shall be satellite to none. Henceforth, we shall assert our national identity without apologies. Henceforth, we shall plan our national destiny as God gives us the vision and wisdom to determine.

But when I ruminate over the events of the last twenty-one years, I have every reason to be thankful to God for sparing my life to survive this historic struggle. Like Simeon of the New Testament, I am happy because I am a living witness of our imminent salvation. I can now see the Nigerian not appearing like a drooping spineless slave, but a freeman who stands erect and commands respect. And I am satisfied.

The valediction which Zik delivered at Premier's Lodge, Enugu, on 17th December 1959, at a caucus of Ministers and Parliamentary Secretaries of the Government of the Eastern Region, after relinquishing office as Premier of Eastern Nigeria.

His Excellency has just appointed Dr the Hon. M. I. Okpara to succeed me as Premier of the Eastern Region, and I am taking this opportunity to bid farewell through you to the people of the Eastern Region.

During my tenure of office it was a pleasure for me to serve the Government and people of the Eastern Region and I very much appreciate the privilege of having come into contact with many people in all walks of life.

I am proud to testify that my Cabinet colleagues were loyal to me and dedicated themselves to the service of the Region. Our relationship was happy because it was based on team spirit and mutual respect for each other.

I commend the new Premier to you, my parliamentary associates, and trust that you will give him your unalloyed loyalty both in the Legislature and in the Cabinet. I know that the policy of our great Party has been progressive and it has enabled the Government of this Region to be among the foremost so far as administrative competence and the provision of essential social services are concerned. Therefore, I urge the people of this Region to give their fullest co-operation to Dr Okpara and his Government.

My five years of legislative activities in this Region have been very instructive to me and I count them among the best years of my life. I am sorry that I am obliged to leave the Eastern Region but I will be carrying away with me pleasant memories of my happy association with the people of this part of Nigeria.

May I also express my gratitude to all the officials of the Public Service of the Region for their devotion to duty and loyalty to the Government of the day. Without their sober advice, it is possible that the Government machinery might have floundered; but our firm belief in insulating the civil service from politics has helped considerably to cement the mutual respect and cordial relationship which existed between my Government and members of our Public Service.

Finally, my wife and family join me in thanking the very many friends who in their own way helped to lessen the burden of public office and make our stay in the Eastern Region pleasant and memorable.

Honourable Senators :

It is with humility that I express my gratitude to you for electing me to be President of the Senate. I deeply appreciate the kind sentiments expressed by the Honourable Mover and his seconder and I promise to do all that lies in my power to discharge conscientiously and efficiently the responsibility of this high office.

Upper Houses of the legislature usually attract to their deliberations a certain aura of dignity that is based on tradition and immemorial custom. From these has evolved the idea that members of the Upper House constitute 'elder statesmen' of the nation whose knowledge of the world and grasp of practical human problems entitle them to be respected not necessarily as paragons of perfection but as repositories of the accumulated wealth of wisdom about the manners and mores of mankind.

Bi-cameral legislatures are popular not only in the dominions of the Commonwealth but also among many sovereign nations which practise democracy as a way of life. Upper Houses were devised to enable after-thoughts to be given to bills which may not have been given careful consideration at their initial stages. Hence the introduction of the delaying technique of a stated period after which the legislation becomes operative.

In keeping with the cherished traditions of parliamentary government, Honourable Senators are expected to study objectively any Bill that is tabled before this Honourable House. If there is any cogent or substantial reason for delaying such a bill, then our will should be collectively expressed in the usual parliamentary manner. We are expected to use the delaying technique constructively. Our duty is to delay, if we deem it necessary to do so; but it is not our duty to obstruct the passage of legislation. We have not been constituted into an 'opposition' House so as to oppose any bill passed by the Lower House. Our main function is to allow time, the healer of all wounds, to steady but not to arrest the robust hands of the accredited representatives of the electorate.

Let us, therefore, face our sacred duty with a sense of devoted service to our people.

This Honourable House is charged with a joint responsibility with the House of Representatives for making laws for the people of the Federation of Nigeria. This concurrent power can be exercised untrammelled, save that the Senate has no power to initiate or delay money bills and it can only delay other bills for a period not exceeding six months.

In exercising our legislative power, I appeal to Honourable Senators to bear constantly in mind that the welfare of the people is the supreme law. This great political principle is universally acknowledged to be the bedrock of the theory and practice of democracy, to which all the shades of political opinion represented in this Honourable House are committed.

As many Honourable Senators are aware, the deliberations of the House will be conducted in accordance with the rules of dialectics, which are expressly described in our Parliaments as the Standing Orders. Since we are the Upper House of the nation, we will be expected, both in our utterances and in our demeanour, to set the example that would be worthy of emulation. You will assist in making my task easier by conforming strictly to the Standing Orders.

As I solemnly promised earlier on, I will do my best to discharge my duties as the President of the Senate as is compatible with the highest traditions of parliamentary democracy; I shall not only have to rely on the decorum of the Honourable Senators, but I shall have to draw from the rich experience acquired over the years by the respected officials of this Honourable House who, I hope, will readily co-operate in order to ensure the smooth operation of the Upper House.

Finally, may I express my thanks, once more, to you, Honourable Senators, for electing me to be your President. I pray to God to give us the wisdom to serve our people conscientiously, and may He guide and bless our deliberations, to the end that we may prove ourselves to be worthy of being respected as elder statesmen of our nation.

A speech delivered by Zik in the Senate after the debate on an adjournment motion on 4th May 1960, when he clarified the issues in connection with the outline of a proposed Defence Agreement between the United Kingdom and Nigeria.

. . . Honourable Senators have had the opportunity to hear various comments on the draft Defence Agreement. As one of those who initialled the draft heads of agreements in 1958 I am in a position to make relevant contributions to this debate. It is called 'Outline of Proposed Defence Agreement' and what was initialled in 1958 was entitled 'Draft Heads of Agreements'. Honourable Senators appreciate that a draft is not a final copy and a proposed Agreement is not a concluded Agreement.

The outline of the proposed Defence Agreement merely gave an idea of what was at the back of the mind of the British Government when it invited the heads of Nigerian Governments to study the draft Heads of Agreement they proposed to negotiate with the Federal Government on the attainment of independence. The effect of the initialling by the heads of the Nigerian Governments of the outline of the proposed Defence Agreement was, to my mind, to place on record the agreement of its signatories on the need to further explore the issue by negotiation between the interested parties *in futuro*.

The proposed Defence Agreement is merely a proposal which has no binding effect either legally or morally on the Federal Government, whose representatives are free to negotiate its details with the British Government in the national interest of Nigeria. In my view the concluding of a Defence Agreement between Her Majesty's Government and the Government of the Federation is not a condition of the granting of independence to Nigeria and has never been so stipulated by Britain, either secretly or publicly, because it would be inconsistent with the cherished ideals of the Commonwealth if the sovereignty of a prospective member were to be restricted in any manner before its attainment of political independence.

The Prime Minister of the Federation has declared in the House of Representatives and recently in the United Kingdom that the

Federal Government will not enter into any agreement of this nature with Her Majesty's Government without the previous approval of Parliament. The effect of this announcement is therefore that the Federal Government is free to negotiate the basis of a defence agreement with the United Kingdom Government, bearing in mind the proposals initialled in the form of draft Heads of Agreement in 1958, before the attainment of independence.

In the circumstances, it would be most unreasonable and ungenerous to prejudice the issues involved by assuming that an 'Outline of proposed Defence Agreement' is a Defence Agreement which will be signed at the forthcoming Constitutional talks, in spite of the fact that Nigeria is still an object and not a subject of international law and is therefore not capable of negotiating a legally binding treaty.

Personally, I feel that the Federal Government has a great responsibility to the people of Nigeria, and I have made up my mind that, when attending the constitutional talks, I will support the Federal delegation in negotiating actively at all stages of the proposed Defence Agreement, bearing in mind the forthright assurance given to the Members of the House of Representatives on the 12th of April, 1960, by the Prime Minister that he would not support the signing of a Defence Agreement without the prior approval of the Nigerian Parliament.

The matter of enlarging the powers of the Governor-General is extraneous to the constitutional talks because all the Premiers of the Federation had already agreed with the Secretary of State that the prevalent practice in Commonwealth countries serves as a creditable precedent from which we cannot depart.

I hope, therefore, that this honourable House will set its mind at rest, knowing full well that under no circumstances will the Federal delegation commit this country to the signing of a military pact without the prior approval of parliament, and I hope that Honourable Senators will constantly distinguish between 'draft Heads of Agreement' and 'Heads of Agreement' on the one hand, and 'outline of proposed Defence Agreement and 'Defence Agreement' on the other.

CHAPTER 8

ZIK ON THE COLOUR BAR

From a speech delivered at a mass meeting which was held in the Glover Memorial Hall, on March 5, 1947, under the chairmanship of the Honourable Sir Adeyemo Alakija, Barrister-at-Law and Member of the Executive Council of Nigeria.

The problem which is agitating our minds today is the colour bar. We are resolved to exterminate it, in all its forms, in this country. But before we engage in a death struggle with it, we should be objective in our approach. The colour bar is the practice of racial distinction based on a social attitude of prejudice. Racial prejudice is not instinctive in man. No human being was born prejudiced; it is an acquired trait which develops and reacts on the emotionality of man so that he behaves unreasonably and unfairly. In the words of Professor H. A. Miller: 'Prejudice is the bias of judgement that comes from either caprice or training. Caprice is individual and sporadic, and may sometimes be explained by psycho-analysis, and sometimes is too subtle to be accounted for. Trained prejudice is social and persistent'.

As far as we are concerned, Mr Ivor Cummings, an African, was a victim of racial prejudice at the Bristol Hotel. Why was this African so victimized? I will say that it was due to the education of non-Africans with regard to the place of the African in world society. Through the various media of education—the film, the radio, the press, the school, etc., the world has been mis-educated to regard people of African descent as backward, primitive, uncouth, boisterous, and ignorant. Consequently, the language of science has been prostituted to rationalize the myth of the racial inferiority of the African. The natural consequence was the creation of stereotypes of African personality and character. In our country, the servile and cringing types, better known as Uncle Toms, were canonized by the master-race as paragons of faithfulness and loyalty. In the films, the 'scared-stiff' type was portrayed as a racial character. In literature, either the menial type was glorified to demonstrate the docility and complaisance of the African, or the primitive type was shown to be bound by superstition and ignorance. Those Africans who did not conform to such stereotypes were branded as 'the irresponsible intelligentsia', 'agitators', 'know-all niggers', etc. The resultant effect is seen in the diverse ways in which the member of the master-race proceeds to justify his racial attitude in order to guarantee social control. This takes two shapes : segregation and discrimination.

From a speech delivered in the Legislative Council at Kaduna, on March 5, 1948, supporting a motion for the introduction of an ordinance to prohibit discrimination against any person on account of his race or colour in any public place in Nigeria.

No attempt is being made to suggest that any person of the white or the black race consciously goes out of his way to segregate or discriminate, but what we say is that, through faulty information, particularly of a scientific nature, it was thought in the past that the mixing of African with non-Africans made certain people susceptible to malaria and other tropical diseases; therefore, it became necessary that races should be segregated. I think, Sir, that this theory has been exploded, and it has been shown that with the advance of modern science and the various researches made on this subject, it cannot be said now that such an idea is warranted or justified.

Because of this, we feel that in our country—an African country —it would be most demoralizing for our children to grow up in an atmosphere where they are made to feel that they are inferior, when all the voices of science proclaim the contrary to be the case. In the interest of racial and international goodwill, it is essential, therefore, that Nigeria should make this innovation, although, in fairness, I must remark that immediately after the interview with the Governor, the Attorney-General introduced legislation in respect of licensed premises, and it is a part of our laws today. Many of us feel proud that Nigeria has made history because, so far as I know, and I am open to correction, this is one of the very few places in the world where racial discrimination has been made an offence in this particular respect. If we introduce this legislation, we shall have gone one step further, because Nigeria will be among the first (if not the first) to have it clearly written in black and white in a statute book that any person who lives in this country is allowed to do so in peace and on a basis of racial and social equality so that man shall learn to respect his fellow man.

From a speech delivered in course of the debate on the Appropriation Bill in the Legislative Council at Kaduna on March 10, 1948.

I regard the Royal West African Force as a nucleus of a Nigerian Army. But unfortunately, throughout its long and brilliant history it has fostered and encouraged racial segregation and discrimination in many ways. The uniforms of African soldiers are not designed on the same basis as the uniforms worn by their non-African opposite numbers. The word uniform implies similarity or oneness of some kind, but it is strange that an African corporal wears a different uniform from a non-African corporal, whilst both serve in the same army. Besides, I have yet to learn of any Nigerian combatant or any person of Nigerian or Cameroons descent who has been commissioned since the founding of the Nigeria Regiment. I feel that this state of affairs needs impartial scrutiny. Sometime last year, during an interview with the late Governor of this country, assurance was given to a deputation to Government House led by Sir Adeyemo Alakija that the whole question of the commissioning of Nigerian and Cameroonian soldiers was receiving the active consideration of the Government. Personally I have not heard anything further on this score. Perhaps the Government will be disposed to make a statement.

Such conditions are very challenging because they make it clear to us that no matter how intellectually or physically qualified a Nigerian or Cameroonian may be, he will find to his chagrin that he is not required in the army of his country. The testimonies given by the military leaders of the world, after the first world war and the second world war, about the martial ability of our soldiers are very good indeed. Their valour and gallantry in action have been praised, so I cannot see and I cannot appreciate what is the reason at the back of such a reactionary policy.

Usually, it is said that our soldiers lack initiative and lack leadership qualities. I remember that some years ago, during the war, Lord Swinton visited this country and gentlemen of the Press had an interview with him. This issue was raised by me and the noble lord explained that if we had men with leadership ability and initiative they would be commissioned. Up till today, no one appears to know the criteria of initiative and leadership. I say this because the evidence of science at our disposal shows that martial quality is not innate and it is not inborn in man. It has to be acquired and it has to be developed. Throughout history there can be no doubt that persons of African descent have distinguished themselves as leaders of men in war, and I need not bother this House by a recital of the famous generals of African descent who have played an important role in the history of the world in ancient, medieval and modern times.

I hope that this Government will be more circumspect on this subject and see that this disparity is removed so as to enable our youth to seek a career in the army of their country. I have yet to be convinced that the people of Nigeria and the Cameroons would not seek a career in the army. If that impression exists it is because of the discouraging conditions; once these are removed, many of them will flock in, as they did in the early days of the war when we had a Local Defence Force Ordinance and our youths believed that with a secondary education and military training they would be eligible for commissioning in the army. Unfortunately, that Ordinance was repealed for reasons best known to the Government. It is very challenging to notice that in our military establishment Africans, no matter how educated or accomplished, can only attain to the rank of Sergeant-Major; and even an African Sergeant-Major is regarded as inferior to his non-African opposite number.

During the last war efforts were made to bring it home to the African soldier that he was inferior to Europeans. I regret having to raise this point, but as I said yesterday, if such facts are not exposed, it is impossible for Government to appreciate why some of us feel very discouraged and bitter when we think of the future of our country. In a directive issued to European soldiers instructing them not to fraternize with African soldiers, it was said *inter alia*: 'Fraternization or excessive familiarity between the African and European population of conquered territories must be discouraged.' This was a directive entitled 'Instructions on the treatment of Black People in the Central Mediterranean Forces.' This curious document continues:

At the present stage of his development the African will derive no benefit from fraternization. On the contrary he may suffer much harm because he is bound to make a comparison between the social equality which the type of Italian he meets is ever ready to afford him and the inequality which he has to contend with in his own country. Furthermore, dealings with the degraded type of European he meets can result in the lowering of his estimation of the white man, which would be detrimental to the policy adopted by the Government of the Protectorates and might have unfortunate repercussions in the neighbouring European States, where a great per cent of these young men find employment.

Your Excellency, I disagree *in toto* with this directive because it is scientifically faulty and I do not believe that any type of European is necessarily inferior. The Italians belonging to the Mediterranean sub-race of the Caucasoids cannot be said to be inferior to the other sub-races, that is Nordic or Alpine, from the point of view of anthropological science, but here this false assumption has been used to prevent fraternization on the part of the African soldiers who are fighting for democracy. What we need is equality of opportunity in our army and respect for human personality, irrespective of race, colour, creed or sex or station in life.

From a speech made at the introduction of a motion concerning films which are humiliating to the Negro race in the Legislative Council held at Ibadan, on March 30, 1949.

Not only is there a tendency to portray certain races and nationalities in a stereotyped fashion, but it appears to be the vogue to lower the moral standards of film fans by the sympathy of the audience being thrown on to the side of crime, wrong-doing and evil.

In connection with the first tendency, it is becoming habitual for Hollywood, particularly, to ignore the rights, history and feelings of certain races and nationalities by not giving careful consideration and respectful treatment to those concerned. This may be due to the environment of Hollywood as an American community influenced by social factors of race prejudice and discrimination. The portrayal of Negroes on the screen perennially as menials, bellhops, red caps, janitors, stable boys, clowns, eccentric dancers, lazy and happy-go-lucky people may be justified in certain respects, but not as a yardstick to describe the Negro race to the whole world.

The strange thing about this deliberate distortion of the social behaviour of a long-suffering race is the anomaly of seeing prominent American Negroes, especially some very talented members of the entertainment world, willing to proselytize what cannot be justified scientifically—all for the love of money! It is, therefore, not uncommon to hear such objectionable epithets used to identify Negroes on the screen as these: Nigger, Sambo, Smoky Joe, Snow-ball, Gawge, Zigaboo, Jig, Coon, etc. Among more articulate and influential groups pressure has been applied in order to compel Hollywood to respect the feelings and susceptibilities of certain races and nationalities, for example:

(1) Griffith's famous film *The Birth of a Nation* was vigorously denounced by the National Association for the Advancement of Coloured Peoples in the United States, on the ground that it portrayed American Negroes in an unfavourable light as a servile people who prefer slavery to freedom. Public reaction

of this nature is bound to have effect on the motion picture industry.

(2) When *Devil's Island* was screened in America, the Government of France threatened to place a ban on all the distributing companies' products if the picture was shown anywhere in the world. This had a salutary effect.

(3) The Government of Italy has successfully protested against the portrayal of Italians as villains and comic characters.

(4) British censors have been punctilious in banning any film showing cruelty to animals.

(5) *Spain in Flames* was banned in Pennsylvania by the State Board of Censors because words like 'Fascist', 'Nazi', 'Italian', 'German' were used in uncomplimentary fashion. That was before World War II.

(6) The epithet 'as thick as flies in a Greek restaurant' brought a chorus of successful protests from the American Society of Greek Restaurateurs.

(7) *School and Society,* a journal devoted to the teaching profession, protested on August 11, 1945, against the tendency of Hollywood to portray school teachers as 'neither animal, nor vegetable, nor mineral' since they are always shown as anaemic and emaciated old maids who are victims of protein deficiency.

(8) The American Bar Association has also protested against the practice of Hollywood in portraying lawyers as crooks, shysters and flim-flammers.

This motion is designed to curb in any feasible way open to us in this country, through our Board of Censors, films which portray the Negro race in a derogatory and humiliating manner, because they tend to create a spirit of resentment and bitterness on the part of Africans, thus embarrassing race relations in this part of the world.

CHAPTER 9

ZIK ON COLONIALISM

Excerpts from an address delivered in the Hotel Pennsylvania, New York, on June 27, 1947, whilst responding to the toast in his honour.

The present colonial policy of the British Government can be a reliable index of the prospects for the future. I mean no harm when I say without equivocation that such policy has been formulated in accordance with the logic of imperialism, buttressed by a false belief about the incapacity of the colonial peoples to develop initiative. To an extent, this policy was justified in the past, for historical reasons, but it can hardly stand the test of impartial analysis and criticism today.

Politically, British colonial policy has been to grant dependent peoples constitutions which are essentially autocratic. In spite of treaty obligations, Britain has ruled British protectorates and mandates as if they were British Crown colonies. The idea and implications of trusteeship have been misapplied or flouted so that the terminology is meaningless to the colonial peoples. Denial of elementary human rights such as freedom of speech and of the Press and freedom of association and assembly is rife.

Socially, the ogre of racial segregation and discrimination makes it extremely difficult for the colonial to develop his personality to the full. Education is obtainable but limited to the privileged. Hospitals are not available to the great number of the people but only to a negligible minority. Public services are lacking in many respects; there are not sufficient water supplies, surfaced roads, postal services and communications systems in most communities of Nigeria. The prisons are medieval, the penal code is oppressive, and religious freedom is a pearl of great price.

Economically, the colonial peoples have been made to appreciate that colonial possessions constitute 'undeveloped estates' specially reserved as a legacy for exploitation by the Colonial Power in control, either through a closed-door policy or a system of preferential tariff, or as a dumping ground for the unemployed of the 'Protecting State'. This policy has affected the colonial peoples adversely. There exists in colonial territories a regime of monopoly which has a stranglehold on the country's economy. The system of taxation is arbitrary and inequitable. The civil service is not as efficient as it should be, owing mainly to favouritism, nepotism and racism. The agricultural programme is often antediluvian, as no energetic effort is made to introduce and popularize labour-saving machinery and modern farming techniques. The mining policy is definitely despotic, for whilst State control may be desirable in a democratic State, yet the Governor of a colonial territory 'may in his absolute discretion' grant, cancel, modify or renew any prospecting or mining right. Labour is exploited and victimized galore. And in spite of the catalogue of disabilities indicated above, the colonial policy of the British Government seems to be dedicated to the gospel according to 'the man on the spot' whose word is law and whose maladministration often entitles him to be kicked upstairs with a G.C.M.G. or a peerage as his reward.

I am convinced that as a Colonial Power Britain's stock is high, in spite of the fact that her moral influence is not as salutary as could be desired because of her adherence to the antiquated ideas of imperialism and the *herrenvolk*. However, it is obligatory for Britain to examine herself more critically and be willing to adjust herself to the changing conditions of contemporary colonial thought and international society. It is highly desirable for Britain to cultivate the goodwill and loyalty of the colonial peoples, and thereby earn the approbation of the outside world.

From a speech delivered at Oxford University on Friday, August 15, 1947, spotlighting some of the problems raised in the relationship between Nigeria and Britain, before a select audience of British teachers, at the ending of their summer course under the auspices of the Oxford Delegacy for Extra-mural Studies.

The NCNC is convinced that the criterion of ability of any state to govern dependent territory is the degree of social and material welfare and development made possible and available, by the protecting state, to the people of the protected state. In Nigeria and the Cameroons, education is limited to a privileged class at the expense of the majority of peasants. Hospitals are inadequate and not available to the greatest number of people but to a negligible minority. Social services are lacking in many respects; in spite of the fact that we pay heavy taxation, there are few water supplies available, there is a limited mileage of surfaced roads, there is an inefficient transportation system, there are insufficient bridges, there are little or no lighting services, there is no fire-fighting organization outside of Lagos and Port Harcourt, there are inadequate hospital and postal and telecommunications services, and there is no police protection for the masses of the population. And the Governor expects us to be satisfied!

We cannot be satisfied with the 'discussion' of our own affairs, as envisaged in the Richards Constitution. We are unwilling to continue the reactionary policy of making our legislative chamber a debating society for the amusement of British colonial administrators. We resent the idea of our paid civil servants being an untrammelled bureaucracy, able to make, interpret, and administer our laws, without our knowledge and consent, and without our being effectively represented in such a chamber by councillors or legislators of our own choice.

We demand the right to assume responsibility for the government of our country. We demand the right to be free to make mistakes and profit from our experiences.

A speech delivered in the course of the debate on the Appropriation Bill in the Legislative Council at Kaduna on 10 March 1948.

By virtue of a series of about 400 treaties negotiated between Her Majesty Queen Victoria and the Kings of several territories which are now known as Nigeria, Britain assumed a Protectorate in all our country except Lagos township. The existence of these treaties is a recognition that the Protectorate thus established is not British territory, and its inhabitants are not British subjects. This is consistent with English Constitutional law. After almost 100 years of British connection, certain factors have necessitated re-examination of our relations in order that the bond of fellowship between the two countries be either strengthened or disintegrated. We belong to the school of thought which prefers the former course, and we feel that the future of Anglo-Nigerian relations need not be a subject of conflict. Rather it should be a question of adjustment of the political and administrative organization. . . .

At present, we who are regarded as the articulate element in our country have the sense to make a friendly gesture towards strengthening the bond of fellowship with Great Britain. Self-government is our aim within our life-time. The only way for the British in Nigeria to prove their sincerity is to implement their professions by actual deeds. I will admit that an effort is being made, but I submit that this can be increased. Some of us are be-gining to think like Count Tolstoy that there is too much talk of working towards self-government and not enough working to-wards it. He said : 'I sit on a man's back, choking him and making him carry me, and yet assure myself and others that I am very sorry for him and wish to ease his lot by all possible means—except by getting off his back.'

I have never suggested, and I do not suggest, the wholesale evacuation of the British from Nigeria, but I hold that since Anglo-Nigerian relations are based on treaty obligations founded on friendship and commerce, there is no reason why Anglo-Nigerian condominium should not be the nucleus of a great Federation of States in the immediate future, to enable us to take our rightful place in the British Commonwealth. If the British mean well, then they must trust us and allow us to participate actively in the management of our affairs. It was Emerson who said : 'Trust men and they will be true to you, trust them greatly and they will show themselves to be great.'

Your Excellency, Nigeria offers a serious challenge to Britain, not in the sense of a test of strength, but in the realm of moral values. I love Nigeria, just as any other patriot loves his country, and I have expressed my views in the only way I know, that is, candidly and with sincerity. I cannot always be right but that does not mean that I am always wrong. After all, I am human like any other human being. My country groans under a system which makes it impossible for us to develop our personality to the fullest. That is why some of us appear impatient. I hate nobody on account of his race or colour, or sex, but I detest any system of Government which destroys the best that is in man and makes man rebel against man's inhumanity to man.

From an address of welcome delivered at the annual convention of the NCNC held in Tom Jones Memorial Hall, Lagos, on April 4, 1949.

I conceive the cult of imperialism, anywhere it exists, as a crime against humanity, because it enables any section of the human race which is armed with the techniques of modern scientific knowledge without justification to dominate less fortunate sections of humanity, simply because the latter are unequal to the task of resisting the force which buttresses such domination. As I see the problem of imperialism in the world today, it is the only yard-stick by which I can judge the good intentions of any nation or race. Continuance of such a philosophy cannot but be regarded by me as a chronic disease which must invite drastic remedy. . . .

I had hoped against hope, and reposed confidence in those whose good motives I had not sufficient reason to doubt. But age is creeping upon me, and I am beginning to realize that there is no conclusive evidence for me to believe that those who have will be disposed voluntarily to surrender their swag; and experience has taught me that I have misplaced my confidence. You will remember the very timely sentiments expressed by Charles-Maurice Talleyrand in January, 1796: 'Ils n'ont rien appris, ni rien oublié.' ('They have learnt nothing, and forgotten nothing.') How can I trust people with such a memory? What guarantee have I that they will not forget any promise when it suits their purpose?

From an address delivered at the Second Annual Conference of the Congress of Peoples Against Imperialism on 'Colonies and War' held at the Civic Theatre, Poplar, London, on October 9, 1949.

Every sixth man on the Continent of Africa is a Nigerian. Every other person in the British Colonial Empire is a Nigerian. Add the British Isles to Belgium, Holland, Portugal and the Irish Free State, and then you have an idea of the area of Nigeria. There is gold in Nigeria. Coal, lignite, tin, columbite, tantalite, lead, diatomite, thorium (uranium-233), and tungsten abound in Nigeria. There is palm oil galore. Rubber, cocoa, groundnuts, benniseeds, cotton, palm oil and palm kernels are there in very large quantity. Timber of different kinds is found in many areas of this African fairyland. Yet in spite of these natural resources which indicate potential wealth, the great majority of Nigerians live in want.

. . . It is our considered opinion that factors of capitalism and imperialism have stultified the normal growth of Nigeria in the community of nations. We are confident that only by the crystallization of democracy in all aspects of our national life and thought—political, economic and social—can we develop *pari passu* with the other progressive nations of the peace-loving world. We are determined that Nigeria should now evolve into a fully democratic and Socialist Commonwealth in order to enable our various nationalities and communities to own and control the essential means of production and distribution and thereby more effectively promote political freedom, economic security, social equality, religious toleration and communal welfare.

For these reasons, we define imperialism as the enforced rule of one nation by another nation. This we hold to be an antithesis of democracy, for the realization of which our sons have shed their blood in two world wars. Therefore, we are compelled to denounce imperialism as a crime against humanity, because it destroys human dignity and is a constant cause of wars. And in doing so, we make the following declarations :

159

1. That we shall no longer be scared by false alarms sounded by imperialists and their venal press in respect of any ideology which is basically Socialist in its concept.

2. That we shall no longer be prepared to pull the chestnut out of the fire for blundering war-mongers.

3. That we shall no longer be dragooned to act as cannon-fodder in the military juggernaut of hypocrites who dangle before our people misleading slogans in order to involve humanity in carnage and destruction.

4. That we regard imperialism as our primary mortal enemy against which should range all the various nationalities and communities of our country.

5. That we assert that we are entitled to be consulted and our consent obtained before we are stampeded into another world war.

6. That in the event of another world war, we reserve the right to adopt an independent attitude and a line of action which would accelerate our national liberation, by casting in our lot with any people whose attitude towards our national struggle for freedom warrants such an alliance.

7. That in the next world war, we shall pitch our tent in any camp which by word and deed satisfies our immediate national aspirations.

An address of welcome presented on behalf of the people of Enugu to the Secretary of State for the Colonies, the Right Honourable Alan T. Lennox-Boyd, P.C., M.P., on his first visit to Enugu, capital of the Eastern Region, in the Federation of Nigeria, on January 18, 1955.

We the people of Enugu, on behalf of Her Majesty's subjects and protected persons in the Eastern Region, heartily welcome you here today. Your visit is evidence of an established tradition of the Colonial Office to acquaint Ministers responsible for colonial affairs with the people of the colonies, by personal contact. It is, therefore, a pleasure for us to know you and to welcome you to the capital of the Eastern Region.

Following the decisions of the London and Lagos constitutional conferences, this Region became an autonomous unit in the Federation of Nigeria. We are happy to say that the government of this Region has been entrusted by our people to the responsible hands of a right-minded political party, whose tact and statesmanship have acted as a cement to blend in friendship and comrade-ship the seven and a half million peoples of Eastern Nigeria with the United Kingdom.

It is needless to remark that the Government Party discharges its duties conscientiously thanks to the vigilance of an alert, re-spected and officially recognized Opposition Party. In spite of differences of opinion on a number of issues, the Government and the Opposition Parties have many things in common. They believe in the unity of Nigeria and aim at evolving one nation out of the different tribes of this country. They work for harmony and co-operation among the component parts of Nigeria, irrespective of language or religion. Their political objective is responsible govern-ment within the framework of the British Commonwealth of Nations. It is, indeed, very unusual for the Government Party and the Opposition to be so similar in their fundamental beliefs.

The Government of this Region is determined to transform Eastern Nigeria into a model of parliamentary democracy in the continent of Africa. It has taken initiative in this respect and, for the first time in Nigerian political history, every male and female adult in this Region can freely exercise the right of franchise. This is a clear vindication of willingness to submit official actions to public scrutiny and judgement in accordance with the best tradi-tions of the British system of parliamentary government.

Nigeria is passing through a critical phase in its political evolu-tion. Occasions like this would certainly permit us to assure Her Majesty's Government, through you, that there is a reservoir of goodwill for the people of the United Kingdom in this Region. We appreciate the opportunity to work together with the British and to exchange ideas with them. In our opinion, such contacts should be a two-way traffic because, in the realm of human rela-tionships, there is much that we can learn from the British and there is much that the British can learn from us.

We are resolved that the spirit of goodwill and mutual forbear-ance shall continue to pervade the atmosphere of Anglo-Nigerian relations. The type of personal contact which was initiated by your noble and gallant predecessor has created a most favourable impression in this country, and we are gratified that you have followed this worthy example of friendship and comradeship in common loyalty and allegiance.

We are a friendly and loyal people with a highly developed sense of justice and equity. We react to others the way they behave towards us. Consequently, a friendly Britain will find us friendly towards her, and a sympathetic Britain will find us equally sympathetic. We proved this to his lordship the Right Honourable Lord Chandos in London, in 1953, and in Lagos early last year. Our sentiments today are intended to assure Her Majesty's Government that we deeply appreciate the gesture of enlightened statesmanship whereby Britain has not only respected our natural aspirations but also recognized our inalienable right to self-determination, and has encouraged our growth towards an independent national existence, and we hereby testify that it has sustained our faith in Britain and strengthened the cord that binds us together, and it has made our friendly relations with the British people stronger than it has ever been in the history of the two countries.

We hope that you will enjoy your short stay at Enugu, and that our climate, which is more salubrious than that of any other town in Nigeria, will be kindly disposed towards you. We are a very hospitable people and we feel proud to have had the honour of welcoming you publicly as an ambassador of goodwill from that historic land which gave the world Queen Victoria—that gracious sovereign of blessed memory who negotiated numerous treaties of amity and friendship with our illustrious ancestors.

CHAPTER 10

ZIK ON THE NCNC

From a Presidential address to the Annual Convention of the NCNC which was held at the Rex Cinema, Kaduna, on April 5, 1948.

The NCNC was founded in order to unify the various elements of our communities, to crystallize the natural aspirations of our people, to express in concrete form the trend of public opinion, and to emancipate our nation from the manacles of political bondage. How far these noble aims have been realized is public property, suffice it to observe that, at this critical period of our national humiliation, the road to victory is barricaded by enemies without and within.

How far have we succeeded in unifying the various elements of our communities? By the federation of several political parties, trade unions, professional and business associations, farmers' organizations, tribal unions, youth, student and other cultural associations scattered over Nigeria and the Cameroons, active steps have been taken to create a spirit of oneness among our heterogeneous peoples. Have we crystallized the natural aspirations of our people? I would answer in the affirmative. Yesterday, our people had a variegated idea of the object of our relations with Great Britain. Today, galvanized by the existence and activities of the NCNC, even the humble village peasant appreciates that he is being exploited and yearns for a politically-autonomous Nigeria and the Cameroons.

Since our existence, have we expressed in concrete form the trend of public opinion? I would say yes. The New Constitution, the four obnoxious ordinances, the practice of the colour bar, the exploitation of our wage-earners, the restraint of trade prevalent due to the existence of a regime of monopoly in our country, these, among others, have given the NCNC opportunity not only to ascertain, but to mould, direct and crystallize the trend of public opinion and give it expression in diverse forms. What active efforts have been made, since our inception, to emancipate our nation from the manacles of political bondage? We sent a delegation to all the Provinces of our country and to the British Isles. We protested against the defiant attitude of the Colonial Office and accused the Secretary of State for the Colonies of having 'treated our national Delegates and the national cause we sent them to present in a most summary, unpleasant, unfavourable and disappointing manner which we regard as a great insult to our entire nation'. Then we pledged 'ourselves anew to continue the struggle for freedom and democracy in our country with all the forces and resources in our power and to see to it that the struggle continues to the bitter end, even if we have to pay the supreme sacrifice for it'.

As a matter of fact, the four main objectives of the NCNC are being realized, maybe on a less pretentious scale, as witnessed by the resolution made by the people of Lagos on August 15, 1947, part of which has been cited above, and part of which reads thus:

We hereby enjoin our delegates to carry on the fight abroad for a little while yet and make the world know our plight, and we assure them that the attitude of the British Colonial Office cannot and will not kill the living spirit of nationalism and our determination to secure freedom, democracy and a better and fuller life for our suffering people and a noble legacy for posterity; on the contrary, it has merely spurred us to greater and yet more determined action and with unprecedented unity, co-operation and loyalty to our noble delegates, we shall carry on with the fight vigorously and side by side with them until victory is won. We are tired of political and economic slavery; we are tired of continued subjection, oppression, suppression and frustration. We are united and desperate.

A careful analysis of the above shows that the various elements of our communities have been unified, their natural aspirations have been crystallized, the trend of public opinion has been expressed in concrete form, and the nation is set for redemption from the forces of oppression. True, in realizing the above, we have been beset by difficulties of our own creation as a people, and those engineered by the oppressor and his agents. Nevertheless, we are progressing step by step towards a Federal Commonwealth of Nigeria and the Cameroons, and in spite of handicaps and barriers which might appear insurmountable, we shall hurdle over them and let our nation take her place in the family of free nations.

. . . One distinguishing element between the NCNC and other organizations is our readiness to graduate from the 'talking stage' to that of 'positive action'. It should be understood by adherents to our cause that the future is pregnant with possibilities for the realization of our political dreams. In years gone by, I believed staunchly in Great Britain and in her ability to set us free, without fuss. Even when I was in the United Kingdom with the NCNC delegation, I had to debate with myself whether I should continue to have faith that Great Britain would make self-government possible within the 15 years, as I have been advocating since 1943.

In reading through certain excerpts from one of Barere's speeches during the French Revolution, I ran across the following: 'The tree of liberty grows only when watered by the blood of tyrants.' In view of what has happened in the history of many countries, it saddens my heart to think of gaining the independence of our country in this inhuman way. In truth, my faith in Great Britain has waned and I am compelled to admit openly my belief that freedom for Nigeria and the Cameroons can no longer be expected to come to us easily without tremendous sacrifice. I shudder at this thought but history has yet to convince me otherwise. If we mean to liberate our country, we must reckon with these realities and cease living in a fool's paradise. I have doubted the wisdom of these thoughts in the past. I have waited vainly for one positive act on the part of those who govern to prove me wrong and now I am free, for I am no longer wishful in my thinking. As I become free from the manacles of my blind faith and belief in the good sense of those who govern, there is no longer any reason why I should not suspect the intentions of those who have succeeded in making a simpleton of me all these years.

Now that you know where I stand, I charge you to realize the gravity of the task ahead. In the struggle for national liberation, we must not count on publicity hunters, for after obtaining publicity, they will reverse their loyalties. We should shun office-seekers, for after being elected to office they will desert us. We should not hanker after those who regard their vested interest as more important than the cause of the country, for they will ignore us at the first test. Let us grapple to us with hoops of steel those comrades of ours who have stood by the NCNC throughout the storm and stress of our short existence. Let us draw them closer and inspire them to share with us the bitter experience which must lie in wait for us. We must depend in the main upon our youths, our wage-earners, our world-war veterans, our patriots, and our peasantry, if we expect to make our bid for national freedom successful.

And by the God of Africa, I pledge anew my faith in the common people of this blessed country. All of us spring from them. The masses hold the key to the future of our country. They can make and unmake those who dare to be in the vanguard of our national cause. If we break faith with the common people, then we are done. We must not betray the masses. They are our backbone. God bless them. Blessed are the masses. Blessed are the common people. God loves them, that is why he made millions of them.

From an address of welcome delivered at the annual convention of the NCNC held in Tom Jones Memorial Hall, Lagos, on April 4, 1949.

The existence of the NCNC has been of great value to our country, in that it has presented our people with a rostrum on which individuals can play an honourable or an ignominious role in the political history of the nation. Those who are convinced that the crusade for human rights in Nigeria and the Cameroons is worth the sacrifice required, are expected to appreciate that they have joined the holy crusade not out of deference to, or worship of, any individual crusader, but because they are deeply convinced that the cause is worth fighting for and worth dying for, if need be. There should be no haven for charlatans, black-guards, turn-coats, Uncle Toms, and other undesirable elements in our organization. Wherever they rear their horrid head, or raise their treacherous voice, or show their traitorous face, they should be isolated and destroyed. The air of Nigeria and the Cameroons must be made unsafe for these political leeches and their kind.

In conclusion, I must assure you that, in spite of the efforts of the oppressor and reactionaries to embarrass me, in many devious ways, I am undisturbed; rather, I have chosen to exist as a dormant volcano, and to erupt at the appropriate time. I pledge faithful and loyal service to the land of our birth. I renew my vow as a crusader against man's inhumanity to man. And I give assurance that whenever the crusaders for human freedom are on the march, well-disciplined, responsible, and loyal to the general command, you will find me at my post, obedient to your will, as constant as the Northern Star, and as steadfast as the Rock of Gibraltar.

> He either fears his fate too much,
>   Or his deserts are small,
> Who dares not put it to the touch—
>   To gain or lose it all.

From a speech rescinding his decision to retire from active politics for five years, delivered at a rally of the Nigerian National Democratic Party, in the Glover Memorial Hall, Lagos, on January 25, 1951.

If we are to realize self-government for Nigeria now, then nationalist forces must forget their petty selves and work together for the greater glory of Nigeria. It is not whether one nationalist group is right or not: the supreme test is, What is good for Nigeria? We cannot forever be pointing an accusing finger at each other, whilst individually and collectively we are not without blemish. But by cultivating in our lives absolute standards of morality we can integrate, rather than disintegrate, our forces. Thus can we establish a positive ideology and proceed to realize our dreams. There is, therefore, a need for change of heart on the nationalist front. Former political enemies should rid themselves of their suspicions and distrust, resolve their differences and be reconciled.

At a great risk to my political reputation, and to your knowledge, I relinquished leadership to another patriot, about a year ago, in order to demonstrate my good faith. In doing so, I was sincere, and I had in mind the thought of Stephen Grellet: 'I shall pass through this world but once. Any good things, therefore, that I can do or any kindness that I can show any human being, let me do it now. But let me not neglect it; for I shall not pass this way again.' But the war drums of local politics have sounded once more and all sincere efforts towards establishing mutual understanding between conflicting nationalist forces seem to have gone with the wind.

It was Abraham Lincoln who in time of stress opined: 'If we could first know where we are, and whither we are tending, we could better judge what to do and how to do it.' So I decided that to talk of self-government for Nigeria now, when a crumb of discord can cause deep-seated friction within the camp of the nationalist forces, is an indication of political immaturity. I thought that if my being a leader of some sort has been an offence to any of my compatriots, then my withdrawal might ease the situation. But the tocsin of misunderstanding continues to beat at a faster tempo; yet we are telling the world that we want self-government now! Is it not true that 'In times of crisis we must avoid both ignorant change and ignorant opposition to change?'

Yesterday I had the honour of receiving in my office fourteen members of my political party, comprising men and women of repute and experience. They impressed upon me that in their opinion my decision to retire from active politics for five years had placed our country in a dilemma and they asked me to rescind it. I must confess that it was farthest from my imagination to commit any act which would deter the progress of this country or embarrass my party.

Please concede to me that I acted in good faith, thinking that it would relieve a perplexing situation; but if it is the consensus that I misdirected myself in the way I thought and acted, then I ask your forgiveness, not because I love Nnamdi Azikiwe less, but

168

because I love Nigeria more. I gladly rescind the decision, but on the understanding that efforts will be made immediately to strengthen our nationalist front by working hard to reconcile apparently irreconcilable elements and by efficient organization and strict discipline in striving towards the goal of our national ambition. Fellow country-men and -women, as usual, I am at your service, ready to obey your will.

From a speech made on April 12, 1951, in the Glover Memorial Hall, on the occasion of the call to positive action of the National Council of Nigeria and the Cameroons by the Committee on National Rebirth which dissolved itself thenceforth.

Now that the Committee on National Rebirth has entrusted the realization of a positive programme to the National Council of Nigeria and the Cameroons, I hereby call upon patriots of this great country, who believe in our cause, to join hands with us in carrying out this sacred task of emancipating our country from foreign rule. No crumbs, however tempting, should distract us from our legitimate aspiration, which is the attainment of independence for Nigeria within five years. No impediments, however formidable, should deter us from our goal. No person, however powerful, should so dampen our ardour as to demoralize and frustrate us in the pursuance of our national ambition. Fellow Nigerians, I have been authorized by the NCNC cabinet to say publicly that, in view of the fact that the recommendations of the Committee on National Rebirth are consonant with our beliefs and aspirations, we accept them with an iron will which knows no defeat.

Join our colours, fellow crusaders of Nigerian Freedom! On to the battle with us, fellow bondsmen of alien rule! Forget the disappointments of the past, overlook the misunderstandings of yesterday, discount the recriminations which might well up in your bosom. Come forward, compatriots, let us smash the ramparts of imperialism and establish an independent State of Nigeria, so as to redeem this continent from the obloquy of its slanderers and the rapacity of its exploiters. Let us organize ourselves in the

West, in the East and in the North. There is no reason why we should not contest the next elections and expose in all its nakedness the deception hidden under the cloven hoof of the Macpherson Constitution. We must give battle to the forces of reaction and conservation, and by the God of Africa, there is no force on earth to stop us in this grim struggle to emancipate our race from oppression.

From a Presidential address to the Third Annual Convention of the NCNC at Kano on August 30, 1951.

We meet today in Kano, a historic city which placed Nigeria on the map during the middle ages. When the Ghana Kingdom reigned supreme, Kano was famous as an emporium of commerce in the Sudan. And when the Songhay Empire shone brilliantly in all its splendour and glory, Mohamed Askia the Great realized the importance of Kano, not only as a military outpost, but as a bastion of the Holy Koran. And now in the twentieth century, and on this day when His Highness the Emir of Kano is visiting Mecca, we have assembled here for the welfare and benefit of our country.

On behalf of the cabinet, I bid welcome to each and every one of the delegates from all corners of Nigeria and the Cameroons to Kano, which is making history today, owing to the great awakening which has shaken Northern Nigeria to its foundations, through the patriotic efforts of the Northern Elements Progressive Union, to which organization I hereby doff my hat in appreciation of the sacrifices of its members for human freedom.

After two years during which our national armour has been pierced through by the forces of imperialism, buttressed by a clique of reactionaries, we have congregated today in order to assess our gains and losses in our common struggle for the freedom of our country, and to plan for the future. Since the Second Annual Convention, we have been crippled into inertia by many factors. In the first place, some of our member-unions have been confronted with internal factions and strife for leadership. Secondly, the strong arm of the law has taken its toll on the nationalist front. Thirdly, we have been faced with the problem of putting our house in order, because of disintegrating elements within the framework of the building. Lastly, our common enemy has intensified his grip on our country to the sorrow of those of us who still believe that our people must be free from alien rule.

Because our people are just emerging from the darkness of ignorance into the light of knowledge, it has not been possible to inculcate discipline in the rank and file of our organization. Consequently, a lack of sense of proportion has been evident in their activities and has given rise to unnecessary squabbles and a scramble for leadership, irrespective of the fitness or otherwise of the ambitious ones. The result has been a dissipation of energy into channels which led to separatist tendencies and egomania. Some of our labour movements and political parties have been afflicted by the scourge and this has affected us adversely.

The seething cauldron caused by man's dominion over man with its demoralizing effect has created a militant spirit which was generated by a sincere desire to give battle to the authors of our unenviable fate. But the troops were an aggregation of ebullient humanity whose patriotism could never be in doubt, even though they lacked the experience of war strategy. Throwing all caution to the wind, this band of noble warriors charged the Maginot Line of colonialism, unmindful of the consequences. Like their counterpart in history, theirs was not to reason why, theirs was the charge of the Light Brigade at the Balaclava of our time. Yet their gallantry and heroism will forever be enshrined in our national pantheon.

The home front was not without its pains. Some soldiers of fortune within the ranks played the role of Quisling for filthy lucre. Some stalwarts became disillusioned and resorted to fault-finding and lack of faith in the leadership. Some valiants who, hitherto, had distinguished themselves in various theatres of the war of liberation, lost faith and became discordant. In spite of these obvious misfortunes, the faithful few carried on the struggle without surrender, and this example of steadfastness in the common cause became an inspiration to a leadership which almost wavered and was becoming discouraged. When now the clarion for rebirth sounded, ranks were shuffled, files were closed, and the army resumed the march to freedom.

The concentrated offensive against the Richards Constitution has caused the enemy to capitulate. A truce has been made and an armistice concluded. Unfortunately, this was a ruse, as the common foe used it as a respite to consolidate his gains, reconstruct his lines, and begin a counter-offensive in the form of a totalitarian war with all its craftiness and ferocity. And now a new Constitution has been prepared and imposed upon us like a Carthaginian treaty. As soldiers of honour, we have unsheathed our swords and we are now battering the enemy forces wherever they are vulnerable.

The kaleidoscope of the last two years is an effort to remind you of the grim struggle that lies ahead and to steel your hearts for the uncertain future. The outcome of the struggle cannot be in doubt. I have supreme confidence that, sooner or later, Nigeria and the Cameroons shall be free. I have implicit faith in the capacity of our people to rise to the occasion by resisting injustice and oppression. And I know that if we do not surrender our inalienable rights, no matter the temptation to concede the apparent invincibility of the enemy, a glorious victory awaits us in the end.

From a speech delivered during the electioneering campaign for the Western House of Assembly on November 17, 1951, at Obalande Square, Lagos.

Now that the 'Battle for Lagos' is drawing to a close, will you allow me to discuss with you the main differences between the NCNC and its political opponents. There is really one major opponent—the Action Group. As for the other party, we can afford to be less serious with them at this stage, not because they are of no consequence, but because their programme is not basically different from ours, in spite of their obvious political opportunism.

We have drawn the battle-line with the Action Group on three fundamental issues: (1) *Self Government:* Despite their profession to the contrary, they do not believe in self-government in

Nigeria now or within five years; (2) *Democracy:* Although they parade the slogans, 'Freedom for All', and 'Life more Abundant', the Action Group do not believe in democracy but prefer Fascism for Nigeria; (3) *One Nigeria:* In spite of lip service towards Nigerian unity, the Action Group do not believe in one Nigeria but prefer in its stead a tri-sected Pakistanized country. On these three issues, the NCNC cannot accept any compromise. They are fundamental to the continued existence of our country as a nation, and we are prepared to stake everything in this political war of survival in order to vindicate our cause. If we fail, we shall be satisfied that we fell in a righteous cause, and if we succeed, it is our firm conviction that our success will save our country from humiliation and ignominy.

Let us examine these basic differences *seriatim.* Mr Obafemi Awolowo wrote a book in 1947 in which he expressed the opinion that Nigeria was not ripe for self-government. He adduced seven reasons as follows:

(1) The existence of a microscopic literary class would lead to exploitation of the great majority of illiterates by the intelligentsia.
(2) The fact that some Chiefs are oppressive and corrupt makes the idea of self-rule untenable.
(3) The plurality of societies in Nigeria is a social fact which is bound to lead to an unstable government.
(4) The heterogeneity of the Nigerian social structure makes the struggle for tribal hegemony inevitable: this must lead to civil war and/or Pakistanism.
(5) There are not sufficient leaders who are qualified or public spirited enough to make the idea of self-rule practicable.
(6) The period of tutelage has not been long enough to produce a society in Nigeria which will appreciate self-rule.
(7) Great Britain is not prepared to allow Nigeria to graduate from tutelage to home rule.

In other words, the domination of one group by another and the existence of autocratic chiefs militate against the attainment of immediate self-government for Nigeria, according to the gospel of the high priest of the Action Group. Two political beginners, in the persons of Mr A. O. Thomas and Mr S. O. Awokoya, who served on the very reactionary Drafting Committee of the Ibadan General Conference for the Revision of the Richards Constitution have also endorsed this queer idea of Mr Awolowo, and all the trio are top-ranking members of the Action Group: Awolowo is President, Thomas is Secretary and Awokoya is executive member.

To Mr Thomas belongs the distinction, in our chequered political history, of being responsible for many unprogressive measures which have ultimately led to our being denied the blessing of a democratic constitution. He advocated the merging of Lagos with the Western Region, thereby depriving Lagos of three seats at the central legislature; he supported the idea of indirect election through electoral colleges, instead of direct election by universal adult suffrage; he was in favour of the selection of ministers from among the regional or central legislature, instead of the usual method of direct election by a majority party. These inimical measures received the sanction of the tycoons of the Action Group in their mad ambition to mount the saddle of political leadership of the Western Region and to partition the country.

When Mr Thomas addressed the Ibadan General Conference on January 13, 1950, this was what he said with reference to self-government for Nigeria:

Some have urged us to say we want self-government today. Can we seriously and honestly say we want self-government today? What I am urging this house to do is to try to get together to formulate among ourselves a constitution acceptable to our people. I recommend and put before this house for serious consideration the recommendations of the Drafting Committee. I personally believe that nothing short of what the Drafting Committee has put forward will be acceptable to the great majority of the people of this country today. Nothing short of that would be worthy of the people of this country today. Anything which doesn't measure up to that will be a disgrace to the people of this country today. Anything more than that, Mr. Chairman, would be a step taken by Nigeria which would no doubt lead us to destruction, and I therefore say that nothing more nor less than what the Drafting Committee has put forward by way of political advancement is what we want in this country today.

In plain words, this politician preferred the reactionary recommendations of the Drafting Committee, of which he and many of his fellow-Groupers were members, to be accepted without amendment and gulped wholesale, and had the effrontery to label any political advancement beyond these concessions, which the Drafting Committee 'begged' for Nigeria, 'destructive'. What impudence! What chicanery! and yet this man is an important cog in the rusty machinery of intolerance and bigotry which is to run the Western Region if the Action Group secures a majority there!

Even Mr Awokoya was just as bad, in spite of his erudition. This apologist for the *status quo*, without just cause and without provocation, advocated the retention of the Governor's veto power for the next five years, in spite of opinion to the contrary! What strikes one about the tragedy of Mr Awokoya is that he had previously made out an intelligent case against the veto power, but after sipping a few cups of tea with higher-ups, he changed his mind; and, today, the new Constitution is a catalogue of veto power from the Governor down to the Lieutenant-Governors, thanks to the brigade of gradualists of the Action Group.

If the views of Messrs Awolowo, Thomas and Awokoya have stunted our growth towards political freedom, the action of the men who betrayed the National Emergency Committee was just as heinous. Here Dr Akinjola Maja, Mr F. R. A. Williams and Mr M. A. Ogun must come in for their share of blame. In February 1950, the NCNC suggested to the NEC ways for the realization of 'Self-government for Nigeria Now'—i.e. the slogan popularized by the National Emergency Committee from the tree-tops by men who later proved to be the mainsprings of the Action Group. The suggestions were as follows:

(1) formation of a provisional government, comprising equal numbers of ministers from the Nigerian Youth Movement group, and the National Council of Nigeria and the Cameroons group, with Dr Maja as Prime Minister;
(2) declaration of the independence of Nigeria;
(3) establishing of diplomatic relations with members of the family of nations.

These were shelved because they were regarded as 'extreme'. Yet one month later, the Action Group was secretly founded in order to carry out a most moderate programme which compromised the issue of self-government for one Nigeria and sought for humble pies in the form of concessions from the British Government! How can the NCNC parley with politicians who have neither the back-bone nor the moral gumption to demand their legitimate rights? How can the NCNC trust as comrades-in-arms jelly-fishes in human form, who have no faith in the capacity of the black man to rule himself in his own country? This is one reason why we are asking you, the voters of Lagos, to reject at the polls, completely and absolutely, all the candidates of the Action Group, because they do not believe in self-government for Nigeria, and because unstable people of this type can barter away our legacy of freedom for a pat on the back by the white man.

The NCNC believes in democracy. The cosmopolitan nature of our organization makes us apppreciate what Voltaire meant when he said: 'I disapprove of what you say, but I will defend to the death your right to say it.' We believe in freedom of speech and the right to opinion. We believe that our opponents have the right to exist and to express their views as they see fit, so long as they do not impinge upon the rights of others. But our opponents would deny us these basic human rights because they are Fascist-minded. They deny us the right to oppose their views; they seek by intimidation and influence, to stifle opposition from us. Clearly this is evidence of weakness. Withal, it is an unadulterated fact that throughout the electioneering campaign, since May 1951, the Action Group have done everything possible to prejudice the minds of voters by deliberate lies and perversion of the truth; they have inflicted bodily injury upon some of our men in the attempt to stifle them, and they have actually inter-fered in some of our meetings to cause disturbance. Of course, we have since enjoined upon our members to defend themselves to the best of their ability, if and when they are attacked; but the comedy of it all is that we voted a Police Department for the pur-pose of maintenance of law and order in this year's budget! How can you vote for a party which harbours political hoodlums, who pollute the air of Nigerian democracy with their crazy ideas of party politics?

Take the issue of one Nigeria. The Action Group are definite in their stand for a Pakistanized Nigeria in spite of the canards published in their newspapers to deceive the unwary. Mr Thomas made the policy of his party clear at the Ibadan General Conference when he said : 'If we bear in mind that the various peoples in this country do not belong to one race, it is for us to make provisions whereby people can live in their usual way of life and come together and work in unity.' What a bundle of contradictions! It is sheer nonsense, because as any intelligent schoolboy should know, the people of Nigeria belong to one race—the Negroid race. One does not need to have a degree in anthropology to know that, yet the Balogun of Oyo had to attend a constitutional conference at Ibadan to advertise his ignorance And that is the man who has been elected to be 'Deputy Leader' of his party in the Western House of Assembly!

Strangely, this gentleman pressed his idea of Pakistanization until some of the members allowed themselves to be misled and beguiled by him into believing that Nigerians do not belong to one race, with the result that the Northerners felt that they had nothing in common with the rest of the country. One need not be surprised that an acrimonious debate which developed as a result of this foolish talk about Pakistanism necessitated a motion in these words :

Be it resolved : That no region may in principle impose qualifications which may discriminate against the election of people born in other regions, who may for the time being be resident in the region and otherwise qualified for election to the regional house.

Believe it or not, in spite of the fact that this motion sought to preserve the political union of Nigeria, it was lost by thirty-one to fourteen votes. All the representatives from the East plus Chief Soetan of Abeokuta, Archdeacon Lennon of Ikare and Mr Ejaife of Warri supported it; Rev. Ogunbiyi of Ikeja and Chief C. D.

177

Akran of Badagry abstained from voting: whilst Messrs Bode Thomas, Timothy Odutola, Arthur Prest and S. O. Awokoya were among the thirty-one who threw the motion out in favour of a Pakistanized Nigeria. So that, whilst the NCNC believes in a common nationality for Nigeria, the Action Group prefers that each region should take care of its affairs in its own way, without any 'outside' interference—a very selfish attitude indeed, because it can only lead this country to chaos and confusion. Perhaps my referring you to this motion will enable you to appreciate why it was necessary for the Action Group clandestinely to file a petition against me in order to prevent me from voting, or being voted for, in Lagos, because I was not born in the Western Region.

In this connection, I should like to place emphasis on the belief of the NCNC in one Nigeria, especially as it affects me as a candidate for election. We of the NCNC believe that no region is socially compact enough to reserve to itself the sole right to autonomous existence politically, unless such a Region is headed towards Pakistanism. In the Western Region, we have the following linguistic groups: Yoruba, Edo, Ibo, Ijaw, Urhobo, Isoko, Itsekiri. Certainly, the evangelists of the Action Group cannot tell us that the Western Region belongs exclusively to one particular linguistic or ethnic group; and they cannot claim that because any group is numerically superior to the others therefore it can dominate the rest. Take the East for example: there you have the Ibo, Ibibio, Ijaw, Efik, Ogoja and other groups. So, too, the North: there, again, you have the Hausa, Fulani, Kanuri, Gwari, Tiv, Nupe, Idoma, Jukun, etc. So that it is not possible in the West or the East or the North to say that any particular linguistic or ethnic group can or should dominate the rest by virtue of its numerical superiority. How then can the Action Group justify the fallacious doctrine of 'West for the Westerners'? If this is not mid-day madness then I know not what it is.

From an address delivered in the Rex Cinema, Enugu, on February 14, 1953, during a rally which was convened under the auspices of the Enugu Branch of the NCNC Party.

If you knew the history of your party you would realize that it is a child of circumstance born to discharge a patriotic duty which others shirked. If you knew the philosophy which animates the various activities of this party you would appreciate the constructive role you are playing in our national history. If you knew the structure of your party you would concede the good faith of those who are working unceasingly in order to enhance efficiency in the organization and administration of your party. Armed with these incontrovertible facts, you would be mentally equipped to resist the subtle suggestion that is constantly made to the effect that the NCNC is a rabble of political adventurers, that it has no policy, that its leaders are intellectually inferior not only to the party rebels but to leaders of the Action Group, that it seeks power in order to introduce the spoils system of American politics into Nigeria.

Let me give you a gist of the historical origins of the NCNC. Unlike other political parties, the NCNC did not begin spontaneously as a political party. Early in 1942, a dozen thinkers formed themselves into what they ultimately called the Nigeria Reconstruction Group. They met every Sunday morning at 72 King George Avenue, at Yaba, which was my residence. They discussed political, social and economic problems which affected contemporary Nigeria and sought answers to them. Most of the members of this group were connected with the Yaba Higher College and its associated institutions. Their sole aim was to apply scientific methods in the solution of practical problems.

In course of their researches and discussions, they began to feel that a national front organization was necessary to act as a mouthpiece for expressing the aspirations of Nigerians in various walks of life. The aims of such a national front were stated to be the immediate improvement of social conditions and eventually the bringing about of far-reaching social progress which should include the exclusion of foreign exploitation and the establishment of self-government in Nigeria. Such aims could not be attained by only one section of the community working independently but must be faced by a front constituted of men and women who wished to see the setting up of an independent Nigeria. It was believed that only by agreement on practical measures of common action, whilst making allowance for differences of conviction, could Nigeria attain this desirable goal.

Representatives of the Nigeria Reconstruction Group then exchanged views with officials of the Nigerian Youth Movement, which was then under the leadership of Mr Ernest Ikoli. They did the same with representatives of the Nigerian National Democratic Party, under the leadership of Herbert Macaulay. The Nigerian Youth Circle was also contacted and ideas were exchanged with its leaders in the persons of Messrs H. O. Davies and J. M. Udochi. Having contacted other organizations, like the Nigeria Union of Teachers, the Union of Young Democrats, certain trade unions and tribal organizations, the NRG requested all of them to form a federation which would be an All-Nigerian National Congress.

In the meantime, a youth rally was organized to take place at the Ojukoro Farm of E. J. Alex-Taylor in November, 1943. Hundreds of youths stormed this suburban estate and a most impressive aggregation of nationalists demonstrated the possibilities of a Nigerian nationalist front. The thought was unanimous that the Nigerian Youth Movement should spearhead this front and so the NRG joined in suggesting that the Movement should summon a representative meeting of various organizations with a view to crystallizing the national front which was the dream of most nationalists. After six months of vacillation and inaction, the Nigeria Union of Students decided to assume responsibility for summoning such a meeting, which took place on August 26, 1944, in the Glover Memorial Hall, Lagos, under the chairmanship of Duse Mohamed Ali.

Subsequently, it was decided to adopt NCNC as the name of the new national front and Herbert Macaulay was elected its first President, with your humble servant as General Secretary. It is pertinent, at this stage, to give you the names of the thinkers who, without any political ambitions and without any thought of personal gain, sowed the seed which has now germinated to become the NCNC. They are as follows: T. O. Na Oruwariye, M. O. Balonwu, B. O. S. Adophy, T. E. E. Brown, S. I. Bosah, M. E. R. Okorodudu, E. E. Esua, E. C. Erokwu, Henry Collins, C. Enitan Brown, A. I. Osakwe, O. K. Ogan and Nnamdi Azikiwe.

The philosophy of the NCNC is linked with its aims and objectives. If you turn to the NCNC Constitution, which was originally framed by a committee composed of Herbert Macaulay, E. E. Esua, Dennis C. Osadebay, A. O. Omage, Glory Mordi and your humble servant, you will see that the aim is to disseminate ideas of representative democracy and parliamentary government by means of political education. Specifically, the objectives of the NCNC are political freedom, economic security, social equality and religious toleration. On attaining political freedom, the NCNC looks forward to the establishment of a socialist commonwealth.

According to the NCNC Constitution, the objects of this organization are:

1. To extend democratic principles and to advance the interests of the people of Nigeria and the Cameroons under British mandate.

2. To organize and collaborate with all its branches throughout the country.

3. To adopt suitable means for the purpose of imparting political education to the people of Nigeria with a view to achieving self-government.

4. To afford the members the advantages of a medium of expression in order to secure political freedom, economic security, social equality and religious toleration in Nigeria and the Cameroons under British Mandate as a member of the British Commonwealth of Free Nations.

Under 'Political Freedom' the NCNC hopes

5. To achieve internal self-government for Nigeria whereby the people of Nigeria and the Cameroons under British Mandate should exercise executive, legislative and judicial powers.

6. To secure freedom to think, to speak, to write, to assemble, and to trade.

The aims summarized as 'economic security' were these:

7. To secure an irrevocable acknowledgement by government of the fundamental principle upon which the land system of Nigeria is

based, namely, that the whole of the lands in all parts of Nigeria, including the colony and Protectorates (North and South), whether occupied or unoccupied, shall be declared Native Lands, and that all rights of ownership over all Native Lands shall be vested in the natives as being inalienable and untransferable to government without purchase, concession or gift.

8. To secure the control by local administrations of the means of production and distribution of the mineral resources of the country.

9. To protect Nigerian trade, products, minerals and commerce in the interests of the natives by legislating against trade monopolies so as to avoid the exploitation of the country and its people.

10. To protect the Nigerian working people by legislating for minimum wages for skilled and unskilled labour in addition to humanizing the conditions of labour in Nigeria and instituting and guaranteeing social security for the people of Nigeria.

The aims of 'social equality' were the following :

11. To secure the abolition of all forms of discrimination and segregation based on race, colour, tribe or creed in Nigeria.

12. To secure for Nigerria and the Cameroons under British Mandate the establishment of a national system of free and compulsory education for all children up to the age of sixteen.

13. To secure that a reasonable number of scholarships is awarded to Nigerians for study.

14. To secure that free medical and surgical treatment shall be provided by the central and the local governments for all the people of Nigeria who are in need of such services and to secure that there shall be no discrimination on account of race, colour, tribe or creed.

Under 'religious toleration' the NCNC aimed 'to secure for the people of Nigeria and the Cameroons under British Mandate the freedom of worship according to conscience, and for all religious organizations the freedom and right to exist in Nigeria.'

From a speech broadcast over the National Programme of the Nigerian Broadcasting Service on the eve of the Federal elections, recorded at Broadcasting House, Enugu, on November 7, 1954, at 7.30 p.m.

On the eve of the Federal elections, it has been thought fit and proper to invite political parties to clarify their points of view on certain major issues. The NCNC accepts this belated invitation in the spirit it was offered although it feels that the arrangements could have been made much earlier.

The NCNC was founded ten years ago as the harbinger of political liberty for Nigeria and the Cameroons. Because of the intrinsic value of its aims and aspirations, it aroused the interest of the masses and gained their implicit confidence as a champion and defender of Nigerian freedom. Its popular appeal is genuine and spontaneous, because neither is its leadership imposed upon the community nor is its programme bolstered by false propaganda.

In asking the voters of Nigeria to vote for NCNC candidates who are standing for election to the Federal House of Representatives, we must remind them that so far, the NCNC is the only political party in the country which is represented in all the legislatures of the land. There are NCNC members in the Northern House of Assembly, the Western House of Assembly and the Eastern House of Assembly, not to mention the dissolved House of Representatives. No other political party can match this achievement. In fact, it is a reflection of the national nature of the NCNC, which stands for the unity of Nigeria and eschews discrimination among Nigerians on grounds of tribe, language, culture or tradition.

Our main election issue is the unity of Nigeria. We do not believe in a Nigeria that is free and disunited. We do not believe in a Nigeria that is united but not politically free. We believe in a free and united Nigeria that is capable of guaranteeing to its co-ordinate units equality of opportunity, parliamentary democracy, respect for the constituted authorities, economic security, and the fundamental human rights.

A statement made after the triumph of his party (the NCNC) over the Action Group at the Federal elections, made at Benin on November 14, 1954.

Now that the people have decided in unmistakable terms to entrust the destiny of Southern Nigeria, i.e. the Eastern and Western Regions, on federal matters, into our hands, what remains for us to do is to consolidate our victory and plan for the next phase in the struggle for parliamentary control of the Federation. We shall organize ourselves and seek the co-operation of all progressive elements in the country in order to guarantee freedom and unity in Nigeria.

This is a great opportunity for the forces of progress to forge ahead and make Nigeria strong, united and prosperous. We can no longer afford to allow reactionary elements to poison the well of human relations in this country by preaching hatred and tribalism, and by stirring the emotions of the masses towards destruction of the idea of One Nigeria.

Any person or organization attempting to incite one section of the community against another should be checked according to the law of the land. Nigeria is big enough to harbour all races and nationalities within its territorial boundary, and there is no need to intensify racial or tribal bitterness. The NCNC calls on all Nigerians and apostles of human understanding to co-operate in creating a healthy climate for all sections of our communities to live in peace and harmony.

We rejoice in our victory in the Eastern and Western Regions, which was expected by us, and we are happy that, on our past performances, the voters have rejected the Action Group in our favour. With malice towards none, with charity for all, the NCNC will work hard to justify the confidence of the people.

From a presidential address delivered at the National Executive Committee of the NCNC in the Dayspring Hotel, Enugu, on December 22, 1955.

As a political party with nation-wide affiliations we are seriously concerned with the Constitutional Conference which will take place in 1956. In order to clarify the stand of the NCNC, we reiterate our policy on the political future of Nigeria.

1. *Dominion Status.* The whole of Nigeria shall no longer be a colonial territory but a completely self-governing member of the British Commonwealth of Nations.

We believe in complete self-government for Nigeria as a whole. That would be our main stand at the Constitutional Conference.

We should maintain that the next Constitution of Nigeria must enable our country, without any qualifications whatsoever, to become a full-fledged member of the British Commonwealth of Nations.

2. *Representative Democracy.* The people of Nigeria shall determine by direct and popular vote the duly accredited representatives who shall form the Government of Nigeria.

We should maintain that if Nigerians were allowed to establish a stable and democratic government, Her Majesty's Government in the United Kingdom would be able to transfer power to a responsible government which would be answerable to the sovereign people of Nigeria in accordance with the usual conventions of representative democracy.

3. *Federal Government.* A true federal government shall be created in order not only to preserve the political unity of Nigeria but also to respect its diversities in language and culture.

We should advocate the creation of a true federal form of government in Nigeria so as to strengthen the historical association of our various communities, respect their communal idiosyncrasies, preserve their political unity, and guarantee their national freedom.

4. *Common Nationality.* The goal of the Constitutional Conference shall be devoted to the preservation of the corporate existence of ONE NIGERIA in which all the citizens, bound together by common nationality, shall enjoy fundamental rights and equal opportunity for the development of their personalities and welfare.

We should emphasize our belief that the idea of ONE NIGERIA could become a reality, provided each co-ordinate unit of the Federation was allowed ample scope for local autonomy within a framework whose task would be to weld our diverse peoples into one organic whole by guaranteeing fundamental rights and by establishing common nationality.

5. *Strong Centre.* The powers to be exercised by the Federal Government shall be definitely enumerated, leaving the residual ones to the Regional Governments : this would ensure that the former was competent to discharge the responsibility of a sovereign state.

We should support the creation of a strong central authority in the Federation which would be competent to discharge the tasks of nationhood in contemporary world society. To this end, we should urge a definite enumeration of the powers to be exercised by the Federal Government, without prejudice to the right of the Regional Governments to reserve to themselves the exercise of powers not so explicitly prescribed.

6. *Parliamentary Government*. The leader of the majority party in the Lower House of the federal legislature shall be entrusted with the responsibility of forming the Government of Nigeria, and such government shall remain in office only so long as it is able to retain the confidence of that legislature.

We believe that only a cabinet system of government, modelled after Westminster, can create a healthy political atmosphere in Nigeria in which a federal form of government can function democratically, side by side with a parliamentary government that is popular and responsible. We should reiterate and amplify this view at the Constitutional Conference.

7. *Adult Suffrage*. Every person, male and female, who is not less than 21 years of age, is of sound mind, is a British subject or protected person, born of parents who are indigenous in a Region or who has been ordinarily resident in the constituency for a period of not less than six months before the closing of the electoral roll, shall be entitled to vote at elections to the federal legislatures, and shall not be disfranchised on any ground. Such person shall not be qualified to vote in more than one constituency or in more than one electoral division of any such constituency.

We agree that it is impossible to have a stable and democratic government when the sovereign people are denied the opportunity of freely exercising their will at the poll. We should hold that, in establishing a true federation that would endure, the objective should be directed towards winning the respect and recognition of the family of nations. This can be achieved if elections to the federal legislatures are conducted on the principle of a uniform electoral law which is based on adult suffrage that is direct, secret and popular.

To buttress our stand, we should refer to the experiences of India, Pakistan, the Sudan, Libya, Senegal, and Indonesia, where, in spite of diversities in religion, language and culture, not overlooking the preponderance of illiteracy, adult suffrage, which is direct, has been used successfully to ascertain the will of their sovereign peoples.

8. *Right of Self-Determination.* The majority of the diverse peoples of Nigeria shall have the right to determine whether they wish to remain in any particular Region; but in exercising this right it should be borne in mind whether such peoples can be viable to provide the revenue and raw materials which are necessary to administer a modern government and whether there is sufficient social cohesion to bind such diverse peoples together.

We should stress our sympathy with those who seek to preserve their communal identities within an over-all federation, because we realize how in practice such methods have preserved the political unity of leading nations of the world, including the federations of Australia, Austria, Brazil, Canada, Czechoslovakia, Ethiopia and Eritrea, India, Mexico, Pakistan, the United States of America, the USSR, Venezuela, Western Germany and Yugoslavia.

Since we believe in the right of self-determination for all peoples, we should support any reasonable and workable arrangement which would enable any group of majority or minority elements of our population, jointly or severally, to exercise this right. In particular, we should support the right of the Edo, Fulani, Hausa, Ibibio, Ibo, Idoma, Igbirra, Ijaw, Isoko, Itsekiri, Kanuri, Nupe, Ogoja groups, Tiv, Urhobo, Yoruba and other communities in Nigeria and the Cameroons to self-determination.

9. *Equality of States.* No Region shall be so large in area or in population as to be in a position to dominate the other regions either individually or collectively. Where a large region prefers to exist in the Federation but is unwilling to have its territory reduced, then all the Regions of the Federation shall be entitled to enjoy the right of equality of representation in the Upper and Lower Houses of the federal legislatures, irrespective of the size and population of each Region.

We should support the division of the country in such a way as to prevent any one Region or any combination of Regions from being in position to dominate the others. If this proves impracticable, then in fairness and in justice to all concerned, we should urge that the boundary of Nigeria, as officially delimited before the amalgamation of 1914, should be used for the purpose of dividing Nigeria into a true federation.

If this becomes impossible, then we should advocate that each Region should enjoy complete equality of representation in the federal legislatures, irrespective of size and population.

10. *Federal Capital.* Lagos shall continue to be the capital of Nigeria. All territories which formed the Colony Province before the promulgation of the Constitution of 1951 shall, with Lagos, form an autonomous Region within the federation, if the inhabitants thereof so desire.

With its distinguished record as our federal capital, Lagos has become the symbol of our national unity. This territory has offered equal opportunity to the people of Nigeria to reside there and develop on their own lines whilst, at the same time, it has enabled them to cultivate a sense of national one-ness. We should advocate that Lagos remain the capital of the federation. Furthermore, we should insist that if the inhabitants of the area concerned so desired, all the territories known as Colony Province before the Constitution of 1951 should be incorporated in a separate Region of the Federation.

11. *Allocation of Revenue.* All the Regions of Nigeria and the Cameroons having enjoyed economic interdependence, at least since the amalgamation, the revenue of the federation shall be allocated on the basis of National Interest, Needs, Even Development, and Derivation.

We should seek to widen the basis of revenue allocation so that it would no longer be restricted to the parochial Principle of Derivation. Bearing in mind that before 1950 certain staple products did not enjoy pre-eminence in the world market, as they do today, and that raw materials whose prices are now depreciating were then the basis of the Nigerian economy, we should

188

demand that revenue allocation be influenced by the recommendations contained in the Hicks Report.

12. *Transfer of Power.* We appeal to Her Majesty's Government in the United Kingdom to take into consideration our loyalty and comparatively peaceful association with British rule since 1866 and respect our political aspirations by transferring power to a stable and democratic government, represented by a majority Nigerian party, that is chosen by direct, popular and secret vote, and which would be responsible to the sovereign people of Nigeria.

We should pledge ourselves to demand at the Constitutional Conference the immediate attainment of complete self-government not only for those Regions that desire it, but for the whole of Nigeria within the orbit of the British Commonwealth. We should appeal to Her Majesty's Government in the United Kingdom that, in the interest of harmony and in view of our long association with British rule, our political aspirations should be respected by ensuring that power is transferred to a stable and democratic government which is represented by a duly accredited majority that is chosen by direct, popular and secret ballot, and that is responsible to the sovereign people of Nigeria.

A final appeal to the voters of the Western Region made in Lagos on May 25, 1956, on the eve of the elections to the Western House of Assembly.

Voters of the Western Region, this is the seventeenth day that I have been leading the NCNC electioneering campaign to all the Provinces of the Region. In the non-Yoruba speaking areas we were received with joy and alacrity; in the Yoruba-speaking communities we were given royal receptions and were spontaneously welcomed as redeemers of an oppressed people. Indeed, the sight of drummers manipulating their drum language and the happiness of the dancers, young and old, male and female, have been an inspiration to me. I sincerely believe that if all goes well, the wishes of the people will be gratified by an NCNC victory.

The issues at stake in this election struggle are both national and regional. We are determined to convince our people that

Nigeria is no longer a mere geographical expression but also a historical fact. In the contest that we are now embroiled in, we shall urge our people to reject the Action Group view that Nigeria cannot become a nation because of cultural and linguistic differences.

Our stand is that Nigeria is a nation in the emergence and that this political union which has been forged on the anvil of British rule is indissoluble and perpetual. We, therefore, believe in the existence of one strong and united country that is capable of commanding the respect of the family of nations.

At the forthcoming Constitutional Conference in London, the NCNC delegates will advocate the creation of a true and lasting federation which shall be divided into viable co-ordinate units, whose functions shall be clearly defined, leaving the residual powers in the centre. We shall urge that each co-ordinate unit should maintain law and order through an efficient organization of local government police, whose duties and responsibilities shall be clearly defined by law. We shall support the view that on matters concerning internal security, the subject of police should become a federal responsibility. We shall oppose the stand of the Action Group that police should be regionalized.

The NCNC delegation will insist that in order to prevent the administration of justice from being subverted for political ends, the judiciary should become a federal responsibility, whilst customary courts should continue within the framework of local government and administration.

We shall support the creation of both a Lower and Upper House in the centre. The latter should have concurrent jurisdiction with the former but should be distinguished by its delaying powers. A House of Chiefs should be established in each Region as an upper house to the popular House of Assembly.

We shall press for the incorporation of fundamental rights in the new Constitution, as the NCNC have done in the Freedom Charter of 1948, and we shall deny any Region the right to secede from the federation.

As for the allocation of revenue, we shall urge that it should be done on the basis of the Hicks Report, that is, on the Principles of

Needs, National Interest, Even Development, and Derivation; we realize that a combination of economic factors has influenced the course of our national history and we shall oppose the allocation of revenue mainly on the basis of the Principle of Derivation. In this connection, we shall spotlight the iniquity committed by Sir Louis Chick when he recommended that the revenue derived from Lagos should be regarded as revenue derived from the Western Region. We shall oppose the robbing of Lagos to buttress the revenues of the West, and we shall insist that whenever the Principle of Derivation is used to allocate revenue it should be done squarely and fairly without robbing Peter to pay Paul.

If the voters of the Western Region return the NCNC to form the next Government of the Western Region, we shall solemnly impress upon the teachers of our schools the sacredness of their trust in the education of our children. Unlike the Action Group, we shall not encourage the systematic indoctrination of our children with the ideology of hatred for any person or party or tribe or race. We shall save our teachers from becoming tools of Action Group maniacs for infusing our children with political party phobias.

We shall amend the electoral regulations to enfranchise all the male and female Nigerians who live in the Western Region on the basis of universal adult suffrage, and we shall abolish the Action Group tax suffrage which is unprogressive and inconsistent with modern democratic practice.

We shall revoke the order banishing the Alafin and we shall return this grand old ruler to Oyo with the least possible delay and we shall grant him a compassionate allowance for the rest of his life.

We shall build up the reserves of the Western Regional Production Development Board and the Government of the Western Region, unlike the Action Group, whose proclivity for squandermania has depleted the reserves of the Western Region almost to the point of bankruptcy. We shall demonstrate to the people how the Action Group failed to encourage savings so as to mobilize domestic capital during its tenure of office, and we shall rectify same.

191

We shall abolish lotteries, which were an Action Group instrument for public financing, because they are immoral and contrary to the public interest, and we shall substitute any other legitimate sources for raising funds for the Government. We shall disclose the names of all persons who have benefited from loans from public funds and we shall be fair and liberal in rendering financial assistance to trade, industry and agriculture.

We shall guarantee to the people of the Western Region, whether they are Yoruba or Edo or Uruhobo or Ibo or Ijaw or Isoko or Itsekiri or what not, freedom from fear, freedom from intimidation, freedom from victimization, freedom from persecution, freedom from ostracization, and freedom from intolerance. These weapons of the Action Group will be destroyed and the NCNC will substitute in their stead the basic human rights of free speech, free assembly and free conscience.

Finally, I wish to remind voters of the Western Region that the symbol of the NCNC is the Cock, which signalizes the dawn of a new day in Nigeria—the day of freedom, the day of unity, and the day when fair play, justice and tolerance shall pervade the atmosphere of Nigerian politics. Therefore, when you go to the polls remember that your vote can hasten or hinder the dawn of this new day. By voting for the candidates of the Cock, you will help to destroy the vestiges of Fascism in Nigeria. Vote for the NCNC! Vote for the Cock.

From a post-election speech made at the first meeting of the NCNC Parliamentary party of the Western House of Assembly, held at Ibadan on May 30, 1956, following the victory of the Action Group at the Regional Elections.

My comrades-in-arms, we are all happy because we have fought the good fight with all our might against what we believed to be an obstacle to the path of Nigerian unity. Since the electorate of the Western Region has decided by a vote of 623,826 in favour of 48 Action Group candidates, as against 584,556 for 32 NCNC candidates, that the Action Group should continue in office, we

have no choice than to accept this verdict in a spirit of sportsmanship.

I am proud that you have lived up to the highest expectations
because you have not allowed the obvious anomalies which
featured these elections to encourage you to discredit the victorious
party. I salute you for your spunk, which has enabled you to with-
stand the assault of our opponents, in spite of difficult odds and
provocations. There is no need for you to despair. You should not
feel dispirited either. As you all know, in any contest, one side is
bound to win, and which side that is depends upon the fortunes of
war. True to the worthy tradition of sportsmanship with which
your great party is identified, I did not hesitate to offer my congratulations to Chief Obafemi Awolowo on the victory of his
party at the polls. I am sure that he now realizes that both parties
have been involved in a tough fight.

The final results of the elections are as follows:

Action Group 623,826; NCNC 584,556; Nigerian People's
Party 3,029; Nigerian Commoners' Party 5,133; Nigerian Commoners' Liberal Party 5,401; Dynamic Party 4,841; Independents 64,388. The combined votes of the opposition parties total
667,348. These figures conclusively prove two things: that the
Action Group has not received the mandate of a majority of the
electorate and that the Action Group must not only reckon with
the NCNC as a serious factor in the politics of the Western
Region, but that it must expect an alert and more determined
and effective opposition in the Western House.

*From a presidential address at the Special Convention of the
NCNC which was held in the Glover Memorial Hall, Lagos,
on April 19, 1957.*

Comrades in the cause of Nigerian freedom, in the name of our
great Party I welcome you to the special convention convened to
enable you to give your mandate to the various NCNC delegates who are attending the London Constitutional Conference,
in addition to discharging other business. It is unfortunate that we
meet under abnormal conditions: there are widespread rumours

that there is a rift among your leadership and an attempt has been made on the life of your National President. Perhaps this convention will be in position to scotch the former, but the latter is an indication of the trend of our political development.

In course of this address, I will suggest ways and means of preventing misgivings in high places in this party, hoping that this will reduce the possibility of an open clash to the minimum. We know enough of political history to appreciate that these outbursts of emotion cannot always be helped, but it is also clear that a more favourable climate can be created in order to ensure mutual respect and goodwill. It is my sincerest hope that we shall bend our efforts to the accomplishment of the great task of nation-building and thereby offset any damage which a situation of mutual antagonism can cause. I am sure that wise counsel will prevail and save us from making ourselves the laughing stock of those who doubt our ability and integrity as nation-builders.

An attempt was made on my life, last Tuesday, within the precincts of the Government House. Although an alleged assailant has been apprehended, yet it is very significant that he is said to have succeeded in breaking through a crowd which milled round the entrance to the offices of the Council of Ministers in order to carry out his diabolical plot. A big stone smashed one of the window screens of my car. In fact, a split second saved my life or at least prevented the left side of my head from being permanently deformed. A very sharp and two-edged dagger was reported to have been found. An Inspector of Police and our principal organizing secretary in the Eastern Region were reported wounded. The alleged assailant has been remanded in custody.

I do not know what was the motive for this second attempt on my life. I am in a quandary to appreciate why people should conspire to take away human life in order to gratify their desires. If the motive is political, then I see no reason why I should not be told bluntly that since I have outlived my usefulness to the country I should step down. I make this statement because since December 1950 I have always requested permission to give way to those who may think that my presence on the political horizon eclipses them. It is true my request has always been treated with levity, but recent events are showing that I have been far-sighted. It would be very tragic indeed if we had to dispose of our leaders through the medium of assassination.

It grieves me that people exist in Nigeria who cannot bide their time and work their way to the top but would rather soar aloft at once and scale the heights which great men and women have reached by hard work and perseverance. Why should any person desire the life of another in order to achieve his political ambition? Why should any person prefer to have his hands stained in the blood of his compatriot so as to realize his dream? I do not believe that the way to attain personal greatness or national freedom lies in bloodshed and cold-blooded murder. History teaches mankind that those who live by the sword shall perish by the sword.

Those who conspire to destroy others must be blind to reason; otherwise, is it not a simpler process to demand abdication of powers in the normal way without taking away this precious jewel called life? Those who conspire to destroy others must be blind to their own interest; otherwise, are they incapable of foreseeing that their plans would be exposed and that they would be the most hated of men? I know that in the arena of politics the code of the jungle prevails, but I have always thought that education should differentiate human beings from the beasts of the jungle.

I must beg you to give me liberty to express my feelings the way I am doing because I have been under the stress of a great emotion and I want to get all the pent-up steam out of my system. As a student of history I know the social and psychological forces which led to certain landmarks in the evolution of the nations. Julius Caesar had his Brutus, Cassius and Casca; but he also had his Artemidorus and Mark Antony. Stalin had his Trotsky, Bukharin and Beria; but he also had his Voroshilov and Molotov. Jesus had his Pharisees and Sadducees and Judas, but he also had his Peter and John.

I do not know whether it is my destiny to drink the potion of treachery and conspiracy. I do not know whether as I speak now, my fate has been sealed. I do not know whether I am doomed to fall at the hand of a treacherous assassin. But this I know—that in this short span of fifty-two years and five months I have worked hard to raise my fellow man to a higher level of existence. In this process I have made sacrifices to enable others to enjoy the good life as much as I had done, if not better. So, if the end should come, no matter how tragic may be the method, I shall go to my maker contented that I have done my best. Let the Brutuses and the Cassiuses and the Cascas do their worst, the Artemidoruses will expose their plans and the Mark Antonys will see that retributive justice is done.

At this stage, may I thank all who have sympathized with me since this unsuccessful attempt to murder me became known. I know that they feel with me because they know what it is to embark upon a crusade for human freedom, and they appreciate what it means to be a happy warrior for twenty-three years. But every road must have an end, and coming events must cast their shadow, and only fools can fail to decipher the handwriting on the wall of destiny.

Therefore, the time has come for me to make room so that others may shine. For ten long years I have been your National President. I have said often that neither I nor any other person has a permanent lien on the National Presidentship or any national office of this great Party. We must not destroy ourselves in order to live; that would be absurd. Destruction is a form of death and death is a negation of life. We must live and we must achieve the goal that we have mapped out for our people. We must not fail them and no soldier in the rank and file of our sacred movement can be regarded as indispensable.

God knows I bear no grudge, and I have no hatred for any person, and I harbour no ill-will against any man or woman. But I know that I am staying too long as National President of this great Party, and I am bound to hurt feelings and create unnecessary complications in the relationship of those who guide and control the destiny of the NCNC. I must go and I must give way before these brave soldiers become frustrated and disillusioned. If that should happen and they are discomfited, you will have to lose not only my services but also their great contributions to the success of this great Party. These preliminary remarks are intended as an indication that I do not wish to stand for re-election when the time comes for the Party to elect its officers for the forthcoming year.

An address delivered by Dr Nnamdi Azikiwe, National President of the NCNC, at the National Executive Committee which was held at the Lagos City College on July 14, 1958.

My comrades, our great Party is passing through troublous times. The leadership is confused and the followership is very much perplexed. Tumultuous outbursts of emotions are the order of the day. Our standpats are employing destructive techniques not against a common foe but against the Party. There are conflicts which indicate that fear and uncertainties have gripped the imagination of our stalwarts. Instead of building up the Party they are wrecking it.

I have summoned this meeting by virtue of the power vested in me under the constitution, for three reasons: first, to give every one of us a fair chance to appraise the fortunes of our great Party: second, to create an atmosphere which will enable all of us to appreciate that, like lost sheep, we have forgotten our great Party and have followed the selfish desires of our own hearts; third, to forgive and forget the past and re-dedicate ourselves to the great task confronting the nation between now and 1960.

The events of the last year indicate in bold relief that we are hopelessly divided against ourselves. Some of us have become extremely chauvinistic, some have become clannish, and some have become petty, mean and vindictive. The general membership of the Party is very apprehensive and some of them have developed complexes of self-pity and despair. Whilst I do not share the views of those who point to results of recent elections to buttress their pessimism, yet I would admit that there is now a tendency for our members to become despondent.

Thus there is need for a frank exchange of views in a cordial atmosphere of self-criticism. This is not the time for bitter recriminations or the pointing of accusing fingers at one another. I have not summoned this meeting as a judicial investigation into charges and counter-charges among ourselves. What we need now is to revive the NCNC spirit of love and sympathy and human understanding, to enable us to tap our source of spiritual power and rebuild our great Party. From now on, it is not who is right but what is right for the NCNC?

Your Central Working Committee met this morning and I am authorized to announce a general amnesty for all members of our great Party who were suspended or expelled within the last year. The Committee is not concerned with the rightness or wrongness of the acts which led to the suspension or expulsion of these members, but we are firmly resolved to forgive those who have been regarded as having violated the regulations of our great Party, by the appropriate party organs, and to forget the past with all its rancour and bitterness.

I cannot disguise my feeling of disappointment at the trend of events within our Party in the face of a ruthless foe who is determined to win his engagements by foul means, so long as he wins ultimately. This negation of the elementary principles of conduct in civilized society must give us a rude shock and ginger us to positive action. Otherwise, we shall be betraying the confidence reposed in us by millions of people in this country.

Personally, I feel that just as we have risen from the depths in the past to shake off all forces which tended to keep us apart, so we can do now, especially in the face of the grave dangers that threaten to engulf this country as a result of the activities of unprincipled and power-hungry politicians whose lack of humanity and whose innate spirit of vindictiveness have become an open secret in the Western Region.

I have just returned from a courtesy visit to the Northern Region, and I am in position to say that this fair appraisal of mine regarding the tyranny and bigotry of the Action Group is equally held by the God-fearing compatriots who constitute the majority among the inhabitants of the North. My impression is that the catalogue of bad government in the Western Region is reaching a dangerous size and may endanger the unity of this country, unless all men and women of goodwill, who place the love of country above partisan politics, get together for the complete liquidation of this cancerous growth in our national organism. I am convinced that if we can establish peace and unity within our rank and file, it will enable us to marshal our forces and thus aid others to preserve the corporate existence of Nigeria.

Believe me, comrades, when I say that the Action Group is a menace to the peace and unity of Nigeria. If through pettiness and short-sightedness we dissipate our energies in fighting ourselves, then it is clear as crystal that, as soon as the British leave our shores, this country will be involved in a civil war, since it is obvious that free men will not condone the substitution for British rule of Action Group Fascism, which, as some of you already know, has to be experienced in order to be appreciated as a real danger.

As I see our internal problems as a Party, we must go back to essentials. First, we must develop a sense of humour and be wise enough to appreciate the folly of expending our energies against ourselves whilst around us lurk implacable and unprincipled enemies. Second, we must reaffirm that under a unified command our army of liberation can march forward in unity that is based on loyalty to one common ideal. Third, we must appreciate how puny we are in the cosmic scheme of things and humbly seek for divine guidance through prayer.

There are also esoteric reasons which impelled me to decide on speaking to you the way I am doing today. After reading a recent leaflet by our revered Bishop S. C. Phillips, I really felt that in our race to accomplish more than our fathers, youth seems to have overlooked the divine factor. After all, only righteousness can exalt Nigeria, and a Government which oppresses its citizens cannot be said to be righteous, because oppression is ungodly.

We need to pray to God to show us the way to a peaceful and united country. We must admit that not only our great Party, but our whole nation is engulfed in a maelstrom of discontent, indiscipline, oppression, confusion and unhappiness. This is due mainly to our failure to realize in the words of the producer of that great film, *King of Kings,* 'that the purpose of this life is understanding of the spirit and not worship before the calf of gold.'

Let us, therefore, get down on our knees and pray to God to forgive us our trespasses as we forgive those who trespass against us. This will make it clear beyond doubt that although we may have erred and strayed from the way of the Lord like lost sheep, yet through our sublime faith in God, we can always be guided to do the right thing.

In 1953, when the United States of America was overwhelmed by many problems and was gripped by the forces of confusion which were based on fear and uncertainty, President Eisenhower called upon that nation on its birthday, to develop serenity of mind by praying to God for guidance and deliverance. This produced what is now known in history as 'Uncle Sam's Prayer'. I will humbly ask you to close your eyes now and to think of your great Party and this great country of Nigeria, as I read this prayer:

Our father in heaven, we pray that You save us from ourselves. The world that You have made for us, to live in peace, we have made into an armed camp. We live in fear of war to come.

We are afraid of 'the terror that flies by night, and the arrow that flies by day, the pestilence that walks in darkness and the destruction that wastes at noonday'.

We have turned from You to go our selfish way. We have broken Your commandments and denied Your truth. We have left Your altars to serve the false gods of money and pleasure and power. Forgive us and help us.

Now, darkness gathers around us and we are confused in all our counsels. Losing faith in You, we lose faith in ourselves. Inspire us with wisdom, all of us, of every colour, race and creed, to use our wealth, our strength, to help our brother, instead of destroying him.

Help us to do Your will as it is done in heaven and to be worthy of Your promise of peace on earth. Fill us with new faith, new strength, and new courage, that we may win the battle for peace. Be swift to save us, dear God, before the darkness falls.

From a presidential address delivered by Dr Nnamdi Azikiwe, National President of the NCNC, at the Special Convention of the NCNC which was held at Enugu on October 2, 1959.

What sort of Nigeria will NCNC create? Our Manifesto shows the features of our domestic and foreign policies. They are at variance with what the Action Group preaches and practises. In our domestic policy we have promised to do the following:

1. We shall encourage the provision of essential social services to our communities in co-operation with the Regional Governments. This includes the tarring of roads, provision of pipe-borne water supply, building of hospitals and health centres, electricity, libraries, and free primary education for all, free technical secondary education for those with the aptitude, the provision of post-secondary schools in each Province, and the establishing of a university in each Region.

2. We shall adjust the tax structure so that the more one earns, the more one pays, and the less one earns, the less one pays.

3. We shall unify the judiciary and limit the scope of customary courts.

4. We shall federalize the Police including Local Government Police.

5. We shall insulate Chiefs who perform administrative or judicial functions from party politics.

6. We shall create the Mid-West State and include Warri and Akoko-Edo within its territorial jurisdiction.

7. We shall extend the boundary of the Federal territory of Lagos by 30 miles.

8. We shall enforce the fundamental freedoms and human rights and nullify any act committed under any existing Regional law which violates them.

9. We shall legislate in favour of voting by proxy to enable civil servants, police, prisoners, and other adult Nigerian nationals abroad, whether engaged in business or any other employment or studies, to exercise the right to vote.

10. We shall prescribe minimum educational standards and introduce a system of State certification at the primary, secondary and post-secondary levels.

11. We shall create uniform conditions of service for teachers and establish a National Text Books Committee in order to expurgate from the minds of our youths the inferiority complexes indoctrinated in them by certain authors.

12. We shall establish a Community Development Corps in the Armed Forces of Nigeria which will be used for public works and also to impart skill, instil discipline and stem unemployment.

13. We shall expand our Armed Forces by making full use of our man-power and equipping them with the best weapons available.

14. We shall build *Autobahns* to connect the Federal capital with the Regional capitals and other important centres.

In our foreign policy we have made our stand clear and we shall not align ourselves with any particular bloc. We shall not be partisan and we shall not be neutral; but we shall be independent in order to be in a position to maintain friendly relations with the nations of the world who are friendlily disposed towards us. We shall not be entangled in any alliance in the European or Asian theatres of military strategy and logistics; but we shall be free to decide whether perpetual or partial or benevolent neutrality will serve our national interest. We shall co-operate with the African States on the basis of equality and we shall encourage co-existence with the nations of the world, in spite of their peculiar ideological concepts.

Address delivered at the meeting of the National Executive Committee of the NCNC, which was held at the Lagos City College, Yaba, on December 22, 1959.

We have summoned the National Executive Committee in order to report to our great party the role our members and supporters played during the recent Federal elections and to thank all who co-operated in order to ensure that the NCNC and the NEPU standards were hoisted and kept flying aloft on all the battle fronts of the nation, during the most hectic election in our national history.

On behalf of our Holy Alliance, may I thank our rank and file scattered over our country for their devotion to duty. The youth and women's wings of our various branches played their parts faithfully and loyally. The Zikist National Vanguard, the Dynamic Party, the Ghana NCNC, and the NEPU youth co-operated with the Alliance in all theatres of this extensive political conflict in order to reach the voters and persuade them to vote for the NCNC-NEPU Alliance.

Our gratitude also goes to the Federal Electoral Commission for its efficiency and to the millions of men and women, young and old, throughout Nigeria, who silently and religiously supported us and prayed for our ultimate victory. Although we did not win an over-all majority as we optimistically expected, yet our

superior organization and our effective tactics baffled our perennial critics and earned the respect of the world. This has enabled
us to demonstrate convincingly the nation-wide nature of the
NCNC-NEPU Alliance.

The results of the Federal elections have been announced and
no one party has emerged with an over-all majority. The final
state of the Parties is as follows: NPC 142, NCNC-NEPU
Alliance 90, Action Group 73, Independents 7.

Analysed in detail, the NPC won 141 seats in the Northern
Region and one seat in the Eastern Region. The NCNC-
NEPU Alliance won 58 seats in the Eastern Region, 22 in the
Western Region, 8 in the Northern Region, and two in Lagos.
The Action Group won 33 seats in the Western Region, 26 in the
Northern Region, 14 in the Eastern Region, and one in Lagos.
The remaining seven seats won by the Independents are in the
Western Region, the others having declared for one or other of
the major parties.

TABLE I. *1959 Federal Elections: State of the Parties*

	NPC and Allied	NCNC-NEPU	Action Group	Inde-pendent	Totals
East	1	58	14	—	73
West	—	22	33	7	62
Lagos	—	2	1	—	3
North	141	8	26	—	174
Totals	142	90	73	7	312

Before the final position of the parties became crystal clear, the
Governor-General committed a *faux pas* by prematurely appointing the leader of the NPC Parliamentary Party to become Prime
Minister of Nigeria, apparently but wrongly assuming that his
party would win all the remaining seats. Ultimately, the Governor-
General's miscalculation created a disturbing situation which
made Nigeria's political pendulum swing from one side to another,
thus placing the whole nation in a state of suspended political
animation.

On Monday evening, December 14, an accredited spokesman
of the NPC had the courtesy to apprise me of the invitation of

the Governor-General. On Tuesday morning, December 15, three emissaries of the Action Group paid me the compliment of a visit at Zungeru Haven, where I temporarily sojourned at Onitsha.

Through its representatives, the Action Group invited the NCNC–NEPU Alliance to form a coalition Government with it. In accordance with the conventional practice in parliamentary democracies, the Alliance was offered the privilege of appointing the Prime Minister of Nigeria and the other matters discussed were postponed for determination by the Alliance.

. I thanked the Action Group emissaries and assured them that I would convey their message to the appropriate quarters of my Party to enable me to be more categorical in my reply; but I made it clear that whilst I appreciated their good intentions in offering me the Prime Ministership, that post had not necessarily been my goal in the national struggle. I emphasized that all I personally desired was to see my country free from British rule and it made no difference to me what role I might play in the future political history of Nigeria, so long as I had the spiritual satisfaction of having associated myself with others in exacting from the British our sovereignty and independence without violence. They thanked me and after cordially exchanging greetings, they returned to Ibadan.

That night, the Alliance was invited by the NPC to exchange views with its hierarchy on the possibility of our forming a coalition Government with it. I accepted the invitation and the venue was mutually agreed to be Kaduna. In the meantime, our intelligence service revealed that during the visit of the NPC leaders to Lagos, on the very Tuesday morning that the three Action Group emissaries were conferring with me at Zungeru Haven, at Onitsha, a certain leader of the Action Group was also conferring with the NPC leaders at Lagos offering to form a coalition Government with the NPC. This report was subsequently confirmed by both the AG and the NPC.

A strategic meeting of the Alliance took place at Onitsha on the same Tuesday night, and it was decided to return the courtesy of the Action Group by despatching three NCNC emissaries to Chief Obafemi Awolowo at Ibadan to convey the message that, the NCNC–NEPU Alliance was studying the proposals of the Action Group and would contact it in due course, after the Party had taken a definite stand.

On Wednesday, 16th December, the Alliance despatched its emissaries to Kaduna, where frank exchanges of views were made on the possibility of forming a coalition Government. It was agreed to defer further discussion and to reconvene on Saturday at Lagos. Our aim was to be able to report progress and give adequate consideration to the proposals placed before us.

On Friday, 18th December, I and my colleagues arrived in Lagos and all the relevant issues were given impartial analysis. Two schools of thought emerged after prolonged discussion. One school conceded that a coalition between the NCNC–NEPU Alliance and the Action Group would no doubt produce an efficient Government, but it was stressed that majority opinion in the Western Region would frown against such a coalition. Moreover, it was obvious that if the Alliance agreed to a coalition with the Action Group, then there might be a crisis within the Party with the Westerners probably breaking away and disorganizing our great Party. The other school agreed that a coalition between the Alliance with the NPC would also produce an efficient, but with it, a stable Government; yet a strong body of influential opinion severely criticized such a coalition. Warnings were given that the NEPU might feel frustrated in view of its traditional struggle with the NPC. It was feared that this might create a schism in the Alliance.

On Saturday, 19th December, the issues were carefully reviewed and it was agreed that since the fundamental human rights had been entrenched in the Constitution, its denial or contravention could lead to litigation. The final factors which outweighed all other considerations were analysed and embarrassing questions were asked the rostrum of the Alliance to answer :

Was it the NPC or the Action Group which confiscated the landed property of the National President of the NCNC and refused to pay him compensation on the pretext that a third party claimed the land, whilst in fact twelve parcels of land, formerly belonging to nine owners, were involved? Was it the NPC or the

AG who financed the lawyers who represented Mr E. O. Eyo during the Foster-Sutton tribunal? Was it the NPC or the AG who financed the lawyers who, when they advocated for the C-O-R State before the Minorities Commission, insulted the Ibo people?

What Party always gives support to those who wish to destroy the NCNC and its leadership—is it the NPC or the AG? What Party hires and employs literary hacks to attack the persons of NCNC–NEPU leaders regularly, in and out of season? When an alliance existed between the NCNC and the Action Group in 1953, did the Action Group have the courtesy to apprise the NCNC that it had planned to walk out of the Constitutional Conference, as a result of its failure to make Lagos remain part of the West, whose views were opposed to the NCNC?

Did not the Action Group unilaterally publish the text of a secret alliance which was solemnly negotiated by it and the NCNC in 1953? Did not the Action Group do the same thing in 1953 in connection with its secret correspondence with the NPC? If these are facts, what guarantee has the Alliance that, like a lame dog helped over a stile, the AG will not revert to type as soon as it suits its purpose to do so?

These suspicions and apprehensions gripped the imagination of majority opinion of the NCNC–NEPU meeting and it was thought that in view of the cordiality which exists in the personal relationship of NCNC leaders and the NPC leaders, coupled with the fact that goodwill and mutual respect are very important to the successful existence of a Cabinet, especially in a coalition Government, the NEPU leaders should be persuaded to modify their attitude and give the NCNC leaders a fair chance to work out a *modus vivendi* for the three parties, namely : NPC, NCNC and NEPU, in the interest of national solidarity. I am happy to report that the NEPU leaders gave us full co-operation in this respect.

On Sunday, 20th December, the agreement constituting the coalition Government of the Federation was signed by the leaders of the NPC and the NCNC–NEPU Alliance and the conditions are regarded by both parties as satisfactory. The coalition Government will enable Nigeria to move forward with hope and confidence towards the date fixed for our independence.

It remains for me to allay the fears of our supporters regarding my personal role in this coalition. Of my own volition, I made it clear that I did not intend to serve my country in any official capacity in this coalition Cabinet for personal reasons. I begged my colleagues to respect my feelings in this regard and not press me to change my decision on this issue, which is one of the very few irrevocable decisions in my life. They have been so understanding that they have given me full co-operation.

Every item in the Coalition Agreement was drafted and approved by all contracting parties with my full knowledge and consent. Satisfactory arrangements have been made about my present and future political status in the scheme of things, and I am quite satisfied with them. From time to time, these arrangements will unfold themselves publicly and, in my humble opinion, the people of Nigeria will have reason to be proud and not to regret. Honestly, we have done our very best in the circumstances to establish a coalition Government which is based on good faith and goodwill.

I would like to appeal to all men and women of goodwill in Nigeria to rally round this coalition Government and give it a fair chance to survive. If we believe in democracy as a way of life, then we must respect the will of the majority as collectively expressed at the polls, so long as such elections are free and fair; otherwise, our professions of belief in democracy will be a sham.

Chief Awolowo was right to say that all that was humanly possible and honourable was done by the Action Group to enter into a coalition Government with us; but our members had no faith in the leaders of this Action Group and so they opposed this coalition. May I humbly appeal to the Action Group to have second thoughts over the events of the past eight years of its existence in general, and the last three months in particular. I hope that its officers and members will agree with me that it is imperative that we give a healthy tone to the strategies and tactics of partisan politics in this country, if we are not to leave a legacy of mutual suspicion and distrust to our children. All political parties had spent large sums of money and expended a lot of energy in order not only to thrive but also to prosecute the Federal elections. In spite of this titanic effort, in spite of dissipation of our manpower and intellectual energies, no one party has emerged with an over-all majority. A coalition, therefore, becomes imperative and 'horse trading' has emerged as the order of the day, whilst the failures are consigned to the political wilderness of the 'outs'.

I do not say that it is bad to form coalitions but it is my humble view that in forming them circumstances beyond the ken of man oblige one to pick and choose his friends mainly upon the human factor.

Is it possible that learning and professional skill can be blended with the milk of human kindness? Is it possible that the instruments of public opinion can be used to build goodwill and fellowship among Nigerians, instead of their being used to exacerbate feelings and wantonly to attack the persons of our revered leaders, in our young country? Is it possible that the organs of political power may be used by our leaders to bring happiness to the inhabitants of our country, irrespective of their political affiliation or tribe or religion or station in life, instead of being used to persecute political opponents? These are the first essentials in the building of a nation. To win friends we must be friendly. To retain friendship we must demonstrate our good faith. And to prove our good faith, we must be charitable in our disposition. Bitter recrimination can only re-open old wounds. The wounds may heal but the scars will remain.

May God give Nigerian leaders the wisdom to realize the futility of pursuing a vindictive policy against their political opponents. May God give them the tact to mend their ways, so that in spite of their wealth, their knowledge and their wisdom they may be charitable to their fellow-man and win his goodwill and fellowship. This is the basis of the righteousness which should exalt our nation. May the leaders of Nigeria profit from the lessons of history.

CHAPTER 11

ZIK ON FINANCE AND BANKING

*From an address delivered during the inauguration of the African
Continental Bank Limited at the Head Office of the Bank, 76
King George Avenue, Yaba, on September 1, 1948.*

I come now to the National Bank of Nigeria Limited, which
has given hope to those who believe in the business capacity of the
Nigerian. I first saw its prospectus, which was published in the
March 25, 1933 issue of the *Nigerian Daily Times*, when I resided
in the United States. Among the first things done by me on my
return to Nigeria from the Gold Coast in 1937 was to become a
shareholder of this bank. Of course you will realize that this bank
was an offshoot of the Mercantile Bank whose fortunes I have
just described, to show the vicissitudes of Nigerian banking. Let
us go back to our National Bank.

The National Bank of Nigeria Limited was incorporated in
Nigeria on February 11, 1933, with a nominal capital of £10,000.
In its Prospectus, its Directors appealed for patronage in the fol-
lowing challenging message :

No people can be respected or regarded as a nation unless it has
its own national institutions, and the greatest of all national institutions is the financial institution in the form of a bank. This is therefore an appeal to one and all who have the interest of their country
at heart and are prepared to work for her progress.

Its first Directors were Dr Akinola Maja (medical practitioner),
Akin Adeshigbin (proprietor of Tika Tore Press), Theophilus
Adebayo Doherty (company-director), and Alfred Latunde Johnson (legal practitioner). On November 1, 1946, the National Bank
increased its capital from £10,000 to £250,000. In its prospectus,

the Directors, who had been joined by Hazart Adisa Subair, its General Manager, appealed for increased capital as follows:

With the cessation of hostilities, the post-war trade requires larger resources and the African must make sure he takes his own share of the post-war trade which will be immense. The bank, therefore, requires all the capital it can get to enable it to finance African business and enterprises. More and more foreign firms and entrepreneurs are arriving in Nigeria to take advantage of opportunities which Government development plans will provide and the African must not allow himself to be left behind in the race. With a big financial backing his chances are sure and certain.

In spite of inspired propaganda to discredit this Nigerian venture, the National Bank has come to stay. As a former shareholder of this bank, I can say that, other things being equal, it is run well and it declares ten per cent dividends regularly. Its capital is small, when compared to those of the expatriate banks, but when one takes into consideration the banking institutions in the United Kingdom which own Barclays (D. C. & O.) and the Bank of British West Africa, and bearing in mind the scarcity of money and lack of interest in investment in this part of the world, we must encourage the National Bank in its uphill struggle. I hope that if it eventually succeeds, it will also encourage the existence of other indigenous banks.

The Nigerian Farmers and Commercial Bank Limited was founded in 1947 by Mr A. S. O. Coker and his associates. In view of his previous connections with expatriate banks, it is probable that certain factors forced Mr Coker to decide on operating a bank of his own. He is working hard to make this bank a living force in our economy but the forces of monopoly are making it extremely difficult for him. He is a brave man but even the most courageous among us can be disillusioned when our own people are used against us.

The Agbon-Magbe Bank Limited was founded in 1945 by Chief M. A. Okupe, the Otunba of Iperu, in Ijebu Remo, with a head office at 1 Baddeley Avenue, Yaba. The authorized capital is £5,000 divided into 1,000 ordinary shares of £5 each. The bulk of the business done by the bank is in connection with the exchange of foodstuffs, kola nuts and cattle between petty traders in the Northern and Western Provinces. Money is usually advanced to customers at either end for these transactions. The bank relies on the interest charged, the commissions earned and the rent payable for storage space for its earnings.

There is scope in this country for small banks which should be able to specialize in certain aspects of our economy. The expatriate banks have their hands full at the moment and are not in position to handle all banking activities satisfactorily. In any case, their nature makes them incapable of appreciating the psychology of the native, hence there will always be scope for the Nigerian with the initiative and capital to find room in the banking business. The limited scope of commercial banking by expatriate banks, the paucity of branches, the need for investments on a larger scale to incorporate a wider field of Nigerian enterprises than those listed in the stock exchanges of the world, these are fields for the pioneer in banking enterprise in Nigeria. I hope that the African Continental Bank will be able to adapt itself to fill one or more of these openings in our economy.

From the circumstances surrounding the founding of the leading banks which operate in this country, it is quite evident that an element of revolt features in their emergence as a factor in the economy of Nigeria. The African Continental Bank is not an exception to this phenomenon. It was founded on a righteous revolt against palpable injustice. It was founded because prosperity had made one of the big banks so haughty and over-confident that it needed a great deal of shaking up to realize that the old order must change and yield place to new. It was founded as a challenge to those expatriate banks whose practice has been to vilify and misrepresent the African business enterpreneur whilst they wax fat by creating a virtual monopoly on the control of money in this part of the world.

You may wish to know why I founded the bank we are opening today. More than five years ago, I was invited by the British Council to visit war-time Britain in the company of seven other West African journalists. During my absence, my business as a newspaper publisher did not fare very well. On my return I decided to improve it by increasing the price of the *West African Pilot* from one penny to two pence. In the meantime, I made use of my personal resources and influence and the business was able to survive.

In the process of revitalizing my newspaper enterprise, I found myself on the short end of the bargain and my personal problems became involved and complicated. With the co-operation of some friends, I planned to acquire a rubber plantation in Benin in order to have an independent source of income, apart from my other enterprises. Since the owner required immediate cash settlement, I was obliged to seek the co-operation of a banking establishment. At that time, I was shareholder of the National Bank of Nigeria with whom I operated a personal account in addition to my business accounts. But the bulk of these accounts was handled by the Bank of British West Africa. I needed £400 to add to what savings I had effected and I was prepared to offer my building at 76 King George Avenue as a collateral. The Lagos Town Council had assessed its value at £1,450. I had valid title to the land on a lease-hold from the Crown for a period of 99 years from 1938, and the property was not encumbered.

The manager of the expatriate bank treated me shoddily. He kept me standing in his office for some minutes and he was con-descending in his attitude and demeanour. He did not make me feel that he was talking business with me. He left me under the impression that racial factors were at work, and he acted as if he was doing me a favour. After ascertaining my desires, he regretted that he could not render immediate assistance because he would have to contact London for orders, which would take some time. He advised me to make other arrangements if it was possible to do so.

Naturally, my pride was hurt and I was bitter. That a bank which had been used as a depository for my private and business funds for seven years should regard me as an extraneous factor made me ruminate on the fate of other less fortunate Africans who made use of the banking facilities made available by non-Nigerian business organizations. I felt that other things being equal, it was morally wrong for Europeans to establish banks in Nigeria and then make it difficult for Nigerians to use them to the mutual advantage of both parties. Then it dawned on me that political freedom was not enough; economic freedom must be won also.

I returned home from the bank crestfallen and I drafted a letter to the Manager, part of which read as follows:

> . . . Since 1937, I and my business establishments have patronized your bank and our turn-over is respectable. The interest which you draw from us is out of proportion to the benefit we derive from your banking facilities. . . .
>
> As long as business executives of your type are so prejudiced and unreasonable, so long will you find it impossible to have Africans of my type willing to co-operate with you, beyond the ordinary veneer of business relationship. The time will come when I, Nnamdi Azikiwe, will head a bank and face you on even terms so that you will realize that in banking, as well as in any other business activity, discretion and common sense are valuable assets in human relations. . . .
>
> I assure you of my continued co-operation, from a business point of view, but you have made it clear to me that unless Africans establish their own banks in order to call off such bluffs, the economic exploitation of Africa will continue with impunity. I will yet own a bank of my own and I am not dreaming.

In the meantime, I acquired an interest in the Tinubu Properties Limited from a Swedish realtor. Because one of the objects of the company was 'generally to act as bankers for customers and others', I changed the name of the company to Tinubu Bank Limited. Last year, we resolved to re-christen it the African Continental Bank Limited. After acquiring the business I spent four years working to organize it. In association with my parents and relatives I have been able to accumulate sufficient initial funds with which to open the doors of the bank to the public.

The background of this bank is a challenge that, in running it as a business venture, we should not be in a hurry for immediate profits; rather, we should place a premium on service, integrity and efficiency. I am not a banker by profession but I have been able to attract employees who are experienced in the law and practice of banking; it is they and not I who will operate the business. I look forward to a bright future in this business venture, but under present-day conditions, I hope that no investor in this bank will expect to reap profit by way of dividend until after the bank has existed for at least ten years.

I do not expect smooth sailing in all the activities of the bank, but I have implicit faith that if the bank is run on an efficient basis, if the employees are competent and honest, and if our patrons are men and women whose word is their bond, the bank will succeed in being a blessing to Nigerian business entrepreneurs. This is a bold attempt to do for our people what others have denied them. There is scope for expansion in Nigerian banking. I pray that with the co-operation of older banking institutions, this pioneering venture will succeed. It is a most vital phase in our struggle for economic freedom.

Excerpts from an address delivered during the debate on the Second Reading of the Appropriation Bill at the Legislative Council at Ibadan on March 16, 1949.

In a country like Nigeria, I would differentiate between productive and un-productive departments, speaking purely in terms of material economics. If a statistical study of the former is made, it will be found that the less the productive departments spend, the more the unproductive departments spend. Since there are exceptions to any rule, I will concede that certain productive departments may be obliged to spend more, whilst the unproductive ones may be obliged to spend less; this is explainable and can be adjusted without harmful effect on the tax-payer. Left to me alone, I would classify in the category of productive departments in the economy of Nigeria the following : Agriculture, Colliery, Customs and Excise, Development, Electricity, Forestry, Geological Survey, Inland Revenue, Marine, Medical, Mines, Post and Telegraphs, Public Works, Survey, and Veterinary.

I must admit that I am not happy at the way our finance is administered, not because the Honourable the Financial Secretary has not done a fine job in preparing and presenting his budget, but because, as he admits, 'Heads of departments at present carry the responsibility for the control of expenditure,' and, he continued, 'I know their difficulties in relation to staff, but I intend seeking their further co-operation in initiating this year a special drive by every officer in their departments to obtain closer control and supervision.' Very timely and well-chosen words! Had this been done in the past, the tax-payers of this country would not be in the anomalous position of having created a bureaucracy which, like Frankenstein, is now busily engaged in destroying its creator. Let us hope the Honourable the Financial Secretary will implement his promise in this respect.

I am in a quandary to appreciate the value of making a speech of a general nature at a debate on the Appropriation Bill. I know that, traditionally, after the Budget Speech, the Unofficial Members take the opportunity to survey the whole field of administration. I am not sure that this is not a dissipation of energy, because after all, participation in discussion of affairs generally is not the same as participation in the management and control of our finances. If the tax-payers of this country had management and control of their finances, they would be in position to realize that the aim of taxation is primarily to make the life of the tax-payer less irksome. Surely, inadequate water supplies, unavailability of hospital services to the great number of the people, limitation of education to a privileged few, restriction of mileage of bitumen-surfaced roads, lack of street lighting on a wide scale, virtual absence of fire protection, and a parsimonious and inefficient postal and telecommunications system, do not justify the existence of the type of bureaucracy we have in this country. It is a record of which one cannot be proud, after 83 years of Anglo-Nigerian relations. After all, students of political science agree that the criterion of good government is the ability of the government to provide the above necessities for the greatest good of the greatest number of its tax-payers.

Applying the above tests to Nigeria, I am not unmindful of possible explanations, namely: that the country is poor and incapable of financing such large-scale community enterprises and that there is shortage of staff. Granting that this is the case, are the excuses convincing? Could it not be that lack of imagination and energy are responsible?

In presenting the Appropriation Bill, the Honourable the Financial Secretary made it clear that the problem before this Honourable House was to reconcile increasing expenditure with diminishing revenue in a setting which is gloomy. For what else could he mean when in one breath he asked for £36,056,970 and in another warned us (1) that we must expect a deficit of about one million pounds, and (2) that since the prospect of the present boom in produce prices would not last long, we must anticipate increased taxation? I had expected that since our economic future was so darkened by the clouds of uncertainty a programme of positive action would have been prepared in order to save us from this prophesied maelstrom.

As I see the problems of public finance in Nigeria, I think that reliance on a few sources of revenue, exportation of Nigerian money abroad, and untrammelled bureaucracy, colonial status with implications of tutelage, and lack of zeal to industrialize Nigeria are intertwined with our economic woes. I would like to see definite planning of our public finance in the immediate future which, whilst allowing for the present political status of Nigeria, would be more energetic and adaptable in the pursuance of a more stabilized economy for the country. I would suggest the following as a way out:

1. De-nationalization of our public utilities, like Building Construction, Colliery, Electricity, Marine, Railway, Road Construction and Telecommunications. In this category, I see no reason why public corporations should not be established on purely commercial lines, to operate these utilities, as distinct from allowing them to be run under the aegis of an inefficient civil service. Perhaps a 'Cable and Wireless (Nigeria) Limited' would be an answer to the accusations of inefficiency levelled at the Posts and Telegraphs Department. Perhaps a 'Nigerian Collieries Limited' would save our Colliery Department from any financial embarrassments. Perhaps a 'Nigerian Railway Limited' would solve the adverse criticisms of our railway administration. Perhaps a 'Nigerian Shipping Limited' would be a way out of the dilemma of a Marine Department which is like Moloch in devouring the gold sacrificed to it. Who knows whether Nigerian corporations

for the construction of our roads and houses would not prove more beneficial to the tax-payers than the present system of bureaucratic control under the Public Works Department? I am informed that it is the plan to transform the government electricity undertakings into a public corporation. This is welcome. It is a step in the right direction.

2. As far as possible, Nigerian money should be kept within our territorial limits. I would rather invest surplus funds in public corporations and utilities floated in Nigeria than abroad, although I appreciate and agree with the reasons given by the Honourable the Financial Secretary for investing our money abroad in the past. I would restrict the number of non-Nigerian directors, managers and employees of companies doing business in Nigeria to a ratio of 60:60:20%, respectively, in order to benefit both the rentier and the wage and salary earning classes of Nigeria. I would cancel expatriation allowances which cost the country in the neighbourhood of half-a-million pounds annually and are a source of bad feeling between Nigerian and non-Nigerian civil servants.

3. Personal emoluments should be related to the productive capacity of our financial resources. I would trim the salary scales of the civil service and make them relate equitably with the earning capacity of Nigeria, because I am of the considered opinion that our top-flight civil servants are overpaid, if the economy of the country is used as a yardstick.

4. Interest should be charged on all public moneys advanced to individuals or groups. In this connection, I would insist that all civil servants who receive advances for any object whatsoever should pay interest on same just as one would do in a private concern, if that is not the case at present.

5. Departments which are not productive, economically, should be scrutinized thoroughly and their budget rigorously clipped and limited.

6. Plans for the industrialization of Nigeria on a large scale should be stepped up, instead of being allowed to remain in a state of doldrum, as at present. The manufacture of by-products of coal, of cement, nails, ceramics and bricks and tiles, textiles, dehydrated garri, yam and corn flour products, etc., should be

undertaken. The work that is being done by the Department of Agriculture and private enterprise in the local manufacture of citrus and other fruits can be encouraged on a wider scale : this research should help us to conserve our fruits by industrial processes, should cheapen fruit drinks and should make it possible for us to live on the products of our country. Dehydration is now a necessity, especially in our food industries. The bulk of our people live on perishable foodstuffs like garri (a product of cassava), yam and corn, together with flour obtained therefrom. Any step along these lines would be a boon to the Nigerian housekeeper.

7. Nigerianization of the civil service should be carried out at a faster tempo than at present.

From a speech delivered as leader of the Opposition in the Western House of Assembly at Ibadan on January 28, 1953, during the debate on the Appropriation Bill.

The financial policy of this Government is based on prodigality. Although our Ministers are well paid, yet one of them is paid £2,500 for the simple reason that he is the present leader of his party, and not because he does more public work or carries more official responsibility than his other colleagues with portfolios. These Ministers are also paid what the Opposition thinks is a reasonable allowance for their transport and travelling expenses, yet they have insisted successfully that the tax-payers of the Western Region should not only pay for the repairs of their cars, but, whenever necessary, they should also supply same with spare parts, tyres, oil and petrol. Mr President, this is an outrageous financial policy. Frankness demands the admission that when civil servants with official majority in the old Legislative Council controlled our finances, the tax-payers of this country did not experience such an outrage in the management of our public finance. It is true that His Honour is entitled to this privilege, but he is the head of this Government.

Another financial policy of this Government which calls for caustic comment is the entertainment allowance earmarked for our high officials. The figure of £1,440 is fair enough for the nine Ministers, but I fail to see why heads of departments and senior departmental officers should be paid 'hospitality' allowance totaling £2,000. One would have thought that the entertainment allowances of the Lieutenant-Governor and the Ministers, and the hospitality allowance of the Public Relations Officer could cover Government hospitality, especially in view of the fact that the Region is in financial distress. At this stage I would like to make it clear that the Opposition condemns the expenditure of £3,280 which was spent in order to give two Ministers and their staff a joy-ride to Asia. This is extravagance which this Region can ill afford now, what with excessive taxation bearing many aliases recurrently facing us so long as this power-drunk Government, with its Fascist tendencies, continues to remain in power. Not only has this Government used its majority strength to stifle constructive Opposition opinion in this House, particularly in matters relating to the finances of this Region, but in doing so it has proved beyond any shadow of doubt that this Government is a desecration of democracy, being a tyranny of the majority that is devoid of any scruple or scintilla of statesmanship.

A critical appraisal of the Action Group budget leads me to the following conclusions:

1. The trend of the budget is to strengthen, rather than weaken, the stranglehold of the civil service expenditures on the economy of the Region.

2. Oppressive taxation is to be used as an instrument for increasing revenue, irrespective of the canons of taxation as they relate to certainty, adequacy, an ability to pay, and elasticity.

3. Government intends to freeze certain funds of the Local Authorities, thus preventing them from enjoying reciprocity on the basis of the principle of derivation in the allocation of revenue.

4. Government has embarked upon the policy of exceeding the votes approved by this House in respect of the annual budget and has actually over-expended what it was allowed in the last year's estimates by £506,282, as supplementary expenditure.

5. The Action Group Government is worse than the previous government which was run by civil servants, in so far as the preparation of budgets its concerned.

However, I must admit that there are certain measures in the budget which should commend themselves to this House. The £100,000 voted for scholarships shows foresight and desire for progress. The earmarking of £25,000 for recreational facilities demonstrates eagerness to encourage physical education in this Region. As a member of the Nigerian Olympic Committee, I had the pleasure of attending the XVth Olympic Games at Helsinki, Finland, last July. By their prowess there, Nigerian athletes demonstrated great potentialities. A vote of this nature will hasten the time when our athletes will attract the attention of the sport-loving world. The vote of £3,000 for the Man-O'-War training scheme, the incorporation of the Social Welfare Department in our estimates, and other progressive measures of this nature, are a step in the right direction, because these are aspects of social engineering of which we are badly in need in this part of the world.

In conclusion, this budget impresses me as one which was prepared by a Government which is bent on making use of excessive taxation as the fulcrum of its financial policy. This is dangerous, because the day of reckoning is just around the corner. There are other sources of revenue to be tapped without stirring the hornet's nest; for example, earnings from Government departments can be augmented; the catering rest houses can be modernized to earn more money—telephones, loudspeakers, electric fans, etc., can be installed in each chalet at cost to the resident; the rents paid for Government property are uneconomic and in view of the all-round increase in civil service salaries, there should be corresponding increase in rents paid by them, and the maximum rent of £150 payable by certain officials can no longer be justified. Reasonable interest should be charged on all loans and advances granted to civil servants and other public officials from our funds; our surplus money invested abroad should be recalled and incorporated in the Revenue Equalization Fund; social insurance should be introduced and popularized as an incentive to savings and economic security for the workers; the suggestion of the Honourable Mover for raising a loan of £6,000,000 or more is wise and should be tackled with gusto; the idea of a co-operative bank with share capital of £1,000,000 is excellent.

In view of these observations, I cannot but feel that the defects in this budget outweigh its elements of strength. Apart from its strong civil service flavour and Fascist features, it seems to me that the slogans now adopted by the makers of this budget are: 'Soak the poor! Tax the ordinary man to the limit of his productive ability to make life less abundant for the lower-incomed group! Give freedom to the higher-incomed group to make life more abundant for them!' In the circumstances, I beg to oppose the second reading of the Appropriation Bill.

A Statement on the Economic Mission to Europe and America, made to the Parliamentary Party of the NCNC on July 31, 1954.

The Government of the Eastern Region appointed an Economic Mission to Europe and America with the following objects in view: to attract investors to Eastern Nigeria for the purpose of economic development; to make contacts for the expansion of our trade, commerce and industries; to seek co-operation in training and recruiting technicians; to make arrangements for facilitating higher vocational education in Eastern Nigeria.

The mission visited the United Kingdom, Holland, Western Germany, Austria, the United States, Sweden and Italy. The journey lasted for two months and six days, covering a distance of approximately 26,000 miles. Since the official report of the Mission will be released later by the Government of the Eastern Region, it would be highly impolitic for me to discuss its contents in detail. However, I can say at this stage that we have succeeded in attracting many investors to Eastern Nigeria; we have succeeded in making valuable contacts; we have succeeded in obtaining the necessary co-operation; we have suceeded in making arrangements for facilitating higher education.

As a result of this Mission, the economic problems of the Eastern Region will be optimistically tackled. Subject to the advice of the newly-created Economic Planning Commission, we will cultivate a variety of food and cash crops extensively; we will exploit our forest products intensively; and we shall expand our industries basically. In implementing this programme, we shall bear in mind the animal and natural resources of the Region, particularly coal, iron ore, limestone, natural gas, palm oil and kernels, rice, cocoa, sugar cane, coffee, rubber, teak, mahogany, and iroko, not to overlook our cattle, fisheries and poultry.

When we have thus diversified the pattern of our economy, it will become more balanced because more commodities will be produced. There will be increased employment, wages will be more stable, and prices will be depressed as a result of fair competition under State supervision. The result will be increased earning capacity and more purchasing power.

The economic policy of the Government of Eastern Nigeria has been officially stated to be the reduction of the cost of living and the improvement of the standard of living of the people in Eastern Nigeria. When the various industries which the Mission envisages begin to operate on a full scale, they will absorb nearly 100,000 workers. By the utilization of our indigenous raw materials and the promotion of ancillary industries, not only shall we accumulate savings in foreign exchange, but we shall develop skill and thereby contribute our fair share towards national prosperity.

Therefore, it is our duty to create a healthy atmosphere in the Eastern Region for the activities of local and foreign investors. It should be remembered that our capital investments abroad are just over £130,000 excluding the foreign investments of the statutory bodies. I mention this because certain quarters have advocated the recall of our investments abroad, which view I do not necessarily condemn.

Our Government is irrevocably committed to a policy of vigorous commercial and industrial expansion. Irrespective of prejudiced criticism and inspired opposition to this policy, we shall not only welcome foreign investors on terms which are mutually agreeable, but we shall give active encouragement to local investors as well.

From an address of welcome delivered at Enugu on April 9, 1955, in the Committee Room of the Eastern House of Assembly, at the inaugural meeting of the Plenary Session of the Economic Plan-

ning Commission, under the auspices of the Government of the Eastern Region.

On behalf of the Government of the Eastern Region I welcome you to Enugu on the occasion of the inaugural meeting of the Plenary Session of the Economic Planning Commission. You have been invited to attend this meeting because we believe that your training, academic background, skill and experience in your field of specialization will enable you, collectively, to guide the Government in formulating the economic policy of this Region.

On assumption of office, early last year, the Executive Council realized that, if the Government were to expand the social services so much desired by our people, revenues must be increased beyond their then level, which was regarded as very low. We were aware that the new fiscal arrangements coming into force with the revision of the Constitution had made regional revenues more dependent upon the economic and commercial stability of the Region. But it was also clear that the Region had neither sufficient means to finance its economic development nor had it the technical knowledge required to make such development possible.

After due consideration of the problem, Government decided that it was essential that those in other countries who had the capital and the technical 'know-how' to promote this development should be encouraged to assist in bringing it about on terms which were beneficial to both themselves and the Region. As a follow-up, it was considered that an economic mission of a sufficient status and authority should be sent to Europe and North America with the following aims and objects : (1) to attract investors to Eastern Nigeria for the purpose of economic development; (2) to make contacts for the development of trade, commerce and industries; (3) to seek co-operation *(a)* for the training and recruiting of technicians and *(b)* for facilitating higher vocational education.

In order to ensure that the Mission would be well received and that its enquiries and proposals would be accorded the respect they deserve, the Leader of the Government Business, who was at that time the Minister of Local Government, and the Honourable L. P. Ojukwu, O.B.E., were appointed its members. The Mission left Nigeria on May 8, 1954, visiting the United Kingdom, the Netherlands, Western Germany, Austria, the United States of America, Sweden and Italy, returning to Nigeria on July 10. The report of that Mission is now in the press and a copy will be placed in your possession before the next meeting of this Commission.

One of the results of the Economic Mission to Europe and North America is the establishment of the Economic Planning Commission by Government. The Executive Council held the view that, subject to a more detailed and fuller report of the recommendations of the Economic Mission, it was obvious that the future success of the Government depended basically upon its ability to increase the wealth of the Region. In the search for a solution for this problem, it was essential that the widest possible use be made of all existing sources to date.

Underlying all considerations was also the question, whether the industrial and economic development of the Eastern Region should be carried out by Government, or by Nigerian business entrepreneurs or by non-Nigerians, or by all three in combination? It was agreed that, whatever might be the answer to the above, two basic requirements must be fulfilled, namely, the provision of adequate capital and the provision of technical 'know-how' and managerial skill. Then there was the rider that these two factors were so inextricably linked that it would be most unrealistic to deny the fact that non-Nigerians control them. Hence the need either for collaboration or co-operation was clear.

On 30 July, 1954, the Executive Council decided to establish an Economic Planning Commission to advise Government on all economic matters. It voted for the provision of £2,500 in the Supplementary Estimates to meet expenses of a contingent nature pending its organization, administration and management in a permanent form. When the report of the International Bank Mission was published in December 1954, it was observed that the establishment of a National Economic Council for the country was recommended with almost identical functions with our Economic Planning Commission. In view of the detailed nature of the main recommendations of the International Bank Mission, it was thought desirable to harmonize them with the findings and recommendations of the Economic Mission to Europe and North America.

The Economic Planning Commission has been organized to function under the chairmanship of the Premier and to have eight members. The Commission will also consist of as many panels as may be expedient for the efficient discharge of its functions. For the meantime, it is thought desirable that we begin with four panels : agriculture, industries, finance, education. It is expected that trade, transport, labour and welfare will be incorporated in due course. Each panel will be under the chairmanship of the appropriate Minister, having the right to co-opt any person, whether in the civil service or not, to assist in its deliberations.

From a speech delivered whilst making a motion of adjournment in the Eastern House of Assembly on August 2, 1956, in connection with the constitutional crisis in the Eastern Region which led to the institution of a commission of inquiry into allegations of ministerial misconduct made by a former Government Chief Whip against the Premier.

The history of currency in Nigeria is a reflection of the economic policy which made this country an appanage of British financial and banking interests. Before the First World War, British silver and copper were legal tender used as ordinary currency throughout British West Africa. According to a report prepared by Lord Harlech, after his visit to West Africa, thirty years ago, when he was Parliamentary Under-Secretary of State for the Colonies, 'the coinage of this silver afforded an increasing profit to the United Kingdom, and it was felt that some part of this profit should be devoted to the revenues of the West African colonies'.

By 1911, a departmental committee of the House of Commons, 'on which the trading industries were fully represented', examined the whole question and the present scheme was evolved whereby a West African Currency Board was to be established in London. As soon as the Bank of British West Africa had acquired the undertaking known as the Bank of Nigeria and became the undisputed banking concern in the whole of British West Africa, it placed itself in position to benefit materially from any currency manipulations which are controlled from beyond the shores of this country.

In November 1912, the West African Currency Board was constituted to provide for and to control the supply of currency to the British West African territories. It was also aimed at ensuring that the currency was maintained under satisfactory conditions. The Board was required generally to watch over the currency interests of these territories. Its members are appointed by the Secretary of State for the Colonies in his absolute discretion. So far, not one Nigerian has ever been appointed to this Board, which functions on the understanding that the West African currency will always be linked to the British sterling. Through this device, British merchants in Nigeria are able to obtain coin either directly or through a bank by paying its face value in sterling to the Board in London, plus handling charges, and are then receiving the coin from the Board's agent in West Africa.

It is significant that since the establishment of the West African Currency Board, forty-four years ago, the Bank of British West Africa has always been its sole agent in West Africa. By 1952, the total currency in circulation in British West Africa zoomed to a total of £50,286,042. The House can now appreciate that the Bank of British West Africa makes quite a sizeable income from its agency commission. The House should also take note that one of the present Directors of the Bank of British West Africa was, until recently, a member of the West African Currency Board, whose signature appeared on our currency notes. As I have said earlier on, the Bank of British West Africa is the sole agent of the West African Currency Board. It is, therefore, at a vantage point since it controls our currency and makes money by controlling it. Unless the nationalists break this stranglehold by establishing a Nigerian currency in the immediate future, we shall continue to be held in leash by this minion of British banking monopoly and oligopoly.

As the sole depository of Government funds, the Bank of British West Africa held sway for many years until the Action Group and the NCNC decided to bring about a needed change in the banking policy of the Western and Eastern Regions. Instead of accepting the latest constitutional developments as a departure from the traditional pattern of Crown Colony status, the Bank of British West Africa has been unwilling to adapt itself to these changing conditions, in spite of the lip service it pays to contemporary British colonial policy. It has deliberately decided not to heed the warning sounded by Mr Duncan as far back as 1919: 'The Crown Colony system of Government is now become, speaking comparatively, in so far as these West African dependents are concerned, an effete institution, in the sense that, by reason of its autocratic character, it is unsuited to the stage of progress at which these countries have arrived.' Unless those who guide the destiny of the Bank of British West Africa decipher this handwriting on the wall, and adapt themselves accordingly, that bank is due for some thorough shaking up.

The policy formulated by this Government on investment and banking is clearly stated in the White Paper which was published last June. It is based on the following principles: to discourage monopoly on monetary transactions by any one bank; to liberalize credit facilities for Nigerian business entrepreneurs; to encourage the development of indigenous Nigerian banking; to plan for the eventual establishment of a State Bank. It will be agreed that this is a sound policy because it would enable us to enjoy political freedom *pari passu* with economic freedom.

The International Bank Mission did recommend the early creation of a bank in Nigeria, to be the principal depository for the funds of Government and semi-government organizations like statutory corporations and boards, etc., to accept deposits from local banks and to regulate their operations, to buy and sell Government securities. Later, these functions could be broadened gradually to enable the new institution to assume other functions of a central bank.

Since the Federal Government has not been very keen on establishing a State Bank or a central bank, obviously because the portfolio of finance is handled by a senior expatriate civil servant whose allegiance is primarily to the Colonial Office and not to Nigeria, this Government looks forward to the time when the

227

African Continental Bank will be transformed into a State Bank in accordance with our policy on banking. We are not prepared to wait for a slow-moving and vacillating Federal Government, which would rather perpetuate British monopoly in banking in this country than take cognisance of the warning which the International Bank Mission sounded :

The continued political and economic advancement of Nigeria is bound to lead to the establishment of a central bank. To postpone the day when the functions of currency issue and the management of foreign assets are performed in Nigeria will also postpone the day when trained Nigerians will be able to perform these functions responsibly by themselves. . . .

In the mission's view the state bank is a necessary element in the organization of the economy of a developing Nigeria, although as Mr Fisher has pointed out, its establishment would not in itself create resources for development. Its operations cannot take the place of development financing by private and government savings; they can only assist in the channelling and the most economic utilization of the country's financial resources.

Naturally, this advice has fallen on deaf ears, because Britain is not prepared to liquidate its imperial interests which must remain a cardinal point in its colonial policy. And they talk of self-government for the colonies! It is all a sham and I speak with a sense of responsibility, bearing in mind an interview I had with the Colonial Secretary last November in his office. He held out the *Report of the Economic Mission* of this Government contemptuously and told me point blank that his Government did not look with favour on the suggestions made therein for the economic rehabilitation of the Eastern Region because it was an attempt on the part of the Government of the Eastern Region to oust British trade and industry from Eastern Nigeria. When I told him that the British were not as keen in investing money and carrying out development projects in our country as the Americans, Germans, Italians, Austrians, Indians and Japanese, he replied that the demand of nationalists for self-government had scared away British investors. Not to leave me in doubt, he made it clear that he had a responsibility in British domestic politics to preserve

British colonies for the benefit of British commercial initiative and enterprise.

My honourable friend, the Minister of Industries, had identical experience in the United Kingdom, when he stopped there last November, *en route* to India and Japan. He was shocked when a responsible British official asked him : 'So you are planning to destroy British industry in the Eastern Region?' In other words, the present British Government is reverting to the 'What we have, we hold' days of that respected octogenarian, Sir Winston Churchill. The view of this Government is that economic freedom must be won side by side with political freedom; otherwise self-government becomes meaningless.

One may ask what the imperial economic policy of Britain has to do with banking monopoly in Nigeria. My answer is 'Plenty.' This Government is not prepared to abdicate the powers vested in Nigerian Ministers of this Region by the Constitution, in respect of economic and financial matters, no matter how many Orders-in-Council the Colonial Secretary promulgates from Arundel Castle to have retrospective effect. This Government is determined to root out monopoly in banking from this Region. It is an article of faith of the Government Party that control of public funds by the Government of the day also implies the right to determine where they should be banked and how they should be disbursed for the public benefit. It is an inherent right for us also to define what we mean by 'public benefit' and not necessarily to depend upon the Colonial Office, four thousand miles away, to mislead us into believing that it is in our best interest to attach our economic destiny to the apron strings of British economic imperialism.

Mr Speaker, this is the crux of the palaver between us and the Colonial Secretary who, as I have abundantly shown, is not alien either to shareholding operations or to directorates in industries keenly interested in the Nigerian market.

We believe that Nigerians must organize and administer their own banks, insurance companies and other financial institutions and enterprises. We presume that these will be organized, administered, managed honestly and efficiently for the benefit of the public. In this context, I must say without fear of contradiction that the fact that we are Africans does not necessarily imply that we run our business enterprises dishonestly; I say this because it is evident that not all British business enterprises are run honestly or efficiently. I challenge any person to say that British politicians, who may be shareholders or directors of banks and other enterprises, are more honest than their opposite numbers in this country? Any person who harbours such belief is dead from the neck up.

In other words, we are standing firm in the belief that the Government of the Eastern Region has every right to formulate its policy on banking and finance and none but the congenital idiot will dare question the integrity of NCNC Ministers in deciding to invest and disperse public funds in any particular bank, especially where it is intended that such a bank should gradually develop into a State Bank. If it were left to me alone, the African Continental Bank should be transformed overnight into a statutory corporation, if that would remove the suspicion of those who imagine that the investment of public funds in this bank was done to enable certain individuals to reap where they had not sown. I respectfully submit to the House that they should consider the advisability of urging this Government to transform the African Continental Bank into a statutory corporation with the least delay. Once this bank is nationalized, the sting in the pretext for victimizing those who criticize banking monopoly from pure motives would be gone, and it would be realized that, basically, their intention is well-meaning and sound. As this will be a death knell to the existence of banking monopoly in the Eastern Region, I will not be surprised if efforts are made to stultify the realization of this most desirable objective in our economic programme.

From an address which was broadcast over the national programme on the Nigerian Broadcasting Service on March 9, 1957, at Lagos, Enugu, Ibadan and Kaduna in connection with the general elections to the Eastern House of Assembly.

It is a fact that since assuming office, the NCNC Government has multiplied the internal revenue of Eastern Nigeria sixty times. This is most significant because the internal revenue of any Region indicates its degree of self-reliance. In January 1954, our internal revenue was £39,400. The following year we increased it to £41,000. With the excision of the Southern Cameroons from the Eastern Region, our internal revenue dropped to £36,000. Now that we have enacted the Finance Law, our internal revenue has catapulted to the enviable total of £2.5 million, compared to £900,000 for the Northern Region, and £700,000 for the Western Region. In other words, with a population of 7.3 million our internal revenue shows a per capita regional income of 6/10d., which is almost double those of the West with a population of 6.5 million (2/10d) and the North with a population of 17 million (1/-) put together. How in the world can any sane person conclude that the Eastern Region is the poorest of all the Regions in the face of these plain and unvarnished facts?

In the financial administration of Eastern Nigeria, we have been most prudent, having almost trebled our public revenue in three years to make our budget extremely buoyant. When we took office in 1954, the Eyo Ita Government left us with a measly legacy of £4.9 million as revenue. The following year we increased it to £8.3 million, but by March 1956 this had dropped to £7.4 million. By the end of this month, our estimated revenue will be £12.5 million. So that we succeeded in augmenting the revenue of Eastern Nigeria from £4.9 million in March 1954 to £12.9 million in March 1957. The most significant point to remember in our achievement is that the actual revenue of the whole of Nigeria was only £11.4 million as at March 31, 1945.

Therefore, we are proud to look back on the financial history of this Region for the last three years, because it shows a steady progress and a gradual gaining of confidence and experience in the science of public finance. When we assumed office, the surplus of revenue over expenditure was £106,000 with a general revenue balance of £623,000. In March 1955, the surplus was £2.5 million with a general revenue balance of £3.9 million. By March 1956, the surplus increased to £467,000 and the general revenue balance spiralled to an all-time high of £5.7 million. A glance at our current budget will show the very healthy state of our finances, because we have a surplus of £564,000 with a reserve of £4.4 million, having drawn £1.3 million in order to place and pay Government workers on the Gorsuch scales together with arrears retroactively from October 1, 1954. To sum up: the Eyo Ita Government left us with a revenue of £4.9 million, a surplus of £106,000 and a reserve of £623,000. That was three years ago. In that short space of time we have increased our revenue to £12.9 million, augmented our surplus to £564,000, and prudently conserved our reserve at £4.4 million. Indeed, this is clear evidence of competence and financial responsibility.

From a statement made on March 20, 1957, after the NCNC had won the general elections to the Eastern House of Assembly, following the report of the Tribunal of Inquiry into the affairs of the African Continental Bank and his conduct as a Minister of State.

The electorate of the Eastern Region has reacted without equivocation to confirm the banking policy of the NCNC Government by giving us mandate to continue in office and direct the destiny of this Region for the next five years. In spite of the studied attempt in certain circles to drag my personal reputation in the mud of public obloquy, the electorate has pronounced its verdict without ambiguity. Not only did the majority of the voters supply a categorical answer to the question whether I am a fit and proper person to hold public office, but they have consigned to the scrap heap all the vapourings of political gasbags whose stock in trade is character assassination.

Now that the electorate has spoken, one would be fair in assuming that by returning me so convincingly with such an over-whelming majority I have been given a certificate of clearance from any taint of malfeasance and a testimonial of fidelity to the cause of freedom and unity of our country. I am most grateful to those who have made this vindication a possibility and I give them assurance that I fully appreciate the importance of this credential of trustworthiness.

A speech made at the opening of Biafra House, under the auspices of the United Africa Company Limited, on September 20, 1957, at Port Harcourt.

I am very happy to be with you here today and to perform the opening ceremony of Biafra House. From time to time as I have passed through Port Harcourt I have watched these fine offices growing, and now that they are completed and fitted out it is a great pleasure to me to be asked to perform the opening ceremony.

Biafra House is another sure step along the way of progress that this Region is taking. Not only is it a worthy addition to the Garden City; it typifies the growing confidence between my Government and the great business houses.

The United Africa Company is a pioneer in the field of private investments in this country. Its role in our economic development is historic; indeed, it gives reason for pride and admiration both on the part of its Shareholders and Directors and the people of Nigeria.

There is scope for further investment in Eastern Nigeria and I assure the United Africa Company that my Government will always co-operate in stimulating investments for the expansion of our economy to our mutual advantage.

We welcome investment of this nature, we welcome co-operation for the progress and development of our country; we would welcome more Biafra Houses. Biafra House is a symbol of faith—the faith of the United Africa Company in the future stability of Eastern Nigeria.

A speech delivered on the occasion of the opening of the new six-storey building of the African Continental Bank at Ogui, Enugu, on April 30, 1959.

This occasion does not call for a long speech from me. The opening of this six-storey building is a solemn reminder to all who fight for a better standard of living for our people that banking is the sheet-anchor of contemporary society. It is also a challenge to all who love this country to appreciate that whosoever controls the banking operations of any country ultimately controls the economy of that country.

The winning of political freedom for Nigeria will be meaningless and will be lacking in reality if Nigerians are unable to win economic freedom at the same time. Any country which is free politically but whose banking operations are controlled from outside its territorial limits is not truly free.

The African Continental Bank was founded with the sole object of speeding up the economic freedom of Nigeria. In spite of the vicissitudes which have featured its chequered existence, notwithstanding the inspired campaign of vilification and denigration so actively pursued by chronic fault-finders and garrulous agents of certain vested interests, this magnificent building, which we are opening today, is a living testimony that this Bank is as solid as the Rock of Gibraltar.

When the envisaged process of nationalization of this Bank is realized, without prejudice to the continued existence of other commercial banks as products of private enterprise, the African Continental Bank will make history because it will be the first time in the economic annals of Nigeria that an indigenous banking organization has survived all attempts to destroy it and emerged to be a signpost in the struggle of our people to expand their economy by means of active Government participation in the ownership and control of this most potent medium of commerce and industry.

I salute the invitees who accepted the invitation of the Board of Directors of the Bank to be present on this historic occasion. The goodwill of the Bank has enabled it to cultivate the sympathy and support of its clientele, these eleven years of its existence. It has also attracted the attention of others who have helped the Bank in any way possible to them. By their co-operation, these genuine, whether indigenous or expatriate, supporters have demonstrated their firm belief that, in the economic development of Nigeria, the people of Nigeria must play an important role and must not be shunted to the background. It is this intangible asset of the African Continental Bank that has enabled it to survive the onslaught of the last few years.

Finally, may I offer my congratulations to the Board and Staff of the Bank, especially to my former business associate, Mr Adolphus Kofi Blankson, under whose leadership the African Continental Bank developed to its present stage. I wish the new Chairman continued success in the worthy objective of this Bank to assist in facilitating the dawn of economic freedom in Nigeria.

CHAPTER 12

ZIK ON THE PRESS
AND BROADCASTING

From an address delivered in the course of the debate on the First Reading of a Private Bill introduced by him at the Legislative Council held at Ibadan on March 10, 1949.

Your Excellency, I agree with the view that 'Liberty of the press involves the right to issue newspapers without permission of an authority.'[1] Hence it is my considered opinion that, other things being equal, Sections 3–9 of the Newspapers Ordinance, requiring recognizances and bonds for securing fines, are overdue for repeal, for the following reasons:

Firstly, it is a reactionary measure usually introduced in times when liberty of the press is restricted. This is contrary to the ideals of the United Nations, for which the flower of Nigerian manhood sacrificed their lives and limbs. Besides, Great Britain has played a positive role in connection with the Universal Declaration of Human Rights and the various conventions of the Freedom of Information and Communications. Secondly, bonds of recognizance are not incorporated in the laws of Sierra Leone, or the laws of the Gold Coast, or the laws of England. These countries enjoy with Nigeria the benefits of *pax Britannica*. Comparisons may be said to be odious, but I see no reason why what is poison for Sierra Leone and the Gold Coast, whose press laws are based on the Newspaper Libel and Registration Act of 1881, i.e. the basis of this Bill, should be meat for Nigeria. Thirdly, from all accounts, coupled with information at my disposal, Sections 3–9 of the Newspapers Ordinance, 1917, constitute a dead letter in our

[1] Cf. Rothenberg, *op. cit.*, p. 256.

statute book, so far as inability of newspaper proprietors to pay fines inflicted on them is concerned. I make bold to say, Sir, and I am open to correction by the learned Attorney-General, that there has not been one single instance in the whole history of newspaper legislation in Nigeria, where it has been necessary to invoke these objectionable sections. Fourthly, in any democratic community, due process of law is usually the instrument for the trial and punishment of those who infringe the law. There is no reason why any newspaper proprietor who fails to pay fines inflicted on him for libel should not be distressed, according to law, instead of manacling the press by bonds and recognizances which have been demonstrated to be punitive and inconsistent with the cherished traditions of the freedom of the press.

Thus, it is obvious that there is no substantial reason to continue to have in our statute book this obsolete, anachronistic, old-fashioned, reactionary and punitive provision. Surely in a democratic community or a community which professes democracy as a way of life, he who pays taxation has a right to write and to speak out his mind, whether as a proprietor or publisher or author —within the ambit of the law. In the light of these explanatory remarks, I appeal to the Government of this country to reconsider its stand on this moot issue of bond requirement and be graciously disposed to waive its application in twentieth-century Nigeria.

A speech delivered in the House of Representatives on August 23, 1954.

Mr President, this Motion seeks two things from the House : approval for the establishment of a Nigerian Broadcasting Corporation on the lines set out in the White Paper before us, and approval for the disbursement of £125,410 during the current financial year for certain capital, special and recurrent expenditure. It is based on a motion which was debated here on March 23, 1954, at the instance of the Honourable D. S. Adegbenro, who argued on the necessity for transforming the Nigerian Broadcasting Service into a statutory corporation in order to remove the impression that it is an organ of the Nigerian Government.

During the March debate, Mr Adegbenro referred to the tradition of the British Broadcasting Corporation and emphasized its freedom from political interference and control. The Honourable Michael E. Ogon expressed the opinion that whilst control of programmes by Government was not desirable, yet the fact that public funds would be employed to operate the corporation necessitated a measure of governmental supervision of how its funds were disbursed.

Mallam the Honourable Muhannadu Lapai said that whilst it was a good idea to have public corporations, yet they could only justify their existence by rendering better service at a lower rate than had previously been available. The Honourable E. U. Eronini suggested that the corporation should be completely Nigerianized within a reasonable time. The Honourable the Minister of Land and Natural Resources, speaking for the Government, accepted the Motion in principle, but warned that since statutory corporations were by nature monopolistic, they should be profit-making in order to justify the subsidy to which they owed their existence.

Bearing the above factors in mind, I endorse the Motion subject to the following reservations:

That the Nigerian Broadcasting Corporation shall be placed under the control of a Minister, preferably the Minister of Communications who, in turn, shall be responsible to the House of Representatives for the activities of this statutory body.

That the report and accounts of the Nigerian Broadcasting Corporation shall be tabled by the Minister in charge on the table of this House for debate, without prejudice to the right of the Public Accounts Committee to scrutinize them.

That whilst the Nigerian Broadcasting Corporation shall arrange its programme without political interference or control, in order to be impartial and objective, yet that should not preclude it from receiving general and specific directions from the Minister in charge for its other activities.

That Nigerianization of the staff of the Nigerian Broadcasting Corporation shall be among the directions to be given to it by the

Minister in charge, subject to the approval of the Governor-General.

That the Nigerian Broadcasting Corporation must not only render equally good (if not better) service at reasonable cost, but must also be self-supporting.

I notice from the White Paper that it is intended to model the Nigerian Broadcasting Corporation on the British Broadcasting Corporation with a national and regional organization, and 'so far as the regional organization is concerned there should, within the broad lines of the Corporation's policy, be a large measure of autonomy in deciding contents of programmes'. This view is acceptable to me because it is practical in view of the fact that, under the Revised Constitution, broadcasting and television fall within the exclusive jurisdiction of both the Federal and Regional Governments. It will be wise for the Nigerian Broadcasting Corporation, therefore, to foster consultation with the Regional Governments in respect of its policy and general activities in order to avoid embarrassment or duplications. In the planning of its operations at the national and regional levels, there should be no trace of discrimination of any sort; there should be even progress and development throughout the country.

The Rediffusion Service has come to stay. At present its over-all efficiency leaves much to be desired, even in view of the technical difficulties in this part of the world. Very few communities enjoy this aspect of radio broadcasting. In consultation with the Regional Governments, efforts should be made by the Nigerian Broadcasting Corporation to spread-eagle the country with rediffusion service, especially in the densely-populated areas. Private enterprise should be encouraged, as has been the case in the Western Region, but the granting of the franchise should be made on terms which benefit both the grantor and the grantee.

The schemes for the sale and servicing of cheap and reliable receiving sets at all rediffusion centres is welcome. I will emphasize the need for including the study of radio telegraphy in our trade centres and the Nigeria College of Arts, Science and Technology. When the implications in the White Paper under discussion are fully appreciated and implemented, it is bound to open new opportunities for our men and women to earn an honest living.

With these observations, I endorse the policy outlined in the White Paper for the establishment of the Nigerian Broadcasting Corporation, and I sanction the additional expenditure of £125,410 required for further development of broadcasting during the current financial year.

A speech delivered in the Eastern House of Assembly at Enugu on March 29, 1955, when he moved the Second Reading of a Bill for 'A law to regulate the publication and distribution of newspapers in the Eastern Region and to register newspapers and newsagents.'

Mr Speaker, I beg to move that a Bill entitled 'A Law to regulate the publication and distribution of newspapers in the Eastern Region and to register newspapers and newsagents' be read a second time. This is a complicated piece of legislation and one I think on which I must dwell at some length. Its object is twofold : firstly, to make it obligatory for newspapers and newsagents to register, and secondly, to bring up to date the law affecting libel in newspapers.

I stand behind no man in my support of the freedom of the Press and this Bill in no way seeks to curb that freedom. It is not a restrictive Bill; it is a progressive measure that goes far to preserve and secure the freedom of the Press, provided that the Press is properly conducted. It has been said that the character of a country can be observed by a study of its newspapers and it must be the desire of all of us that the standards achieved and maintained by the newspapers in our country are as high as we can make them.

We have in Nigeria a young, healthy and eager Press with a large and voracious public to satisfy. It is, I submit, our positive duty in this House to make it possible for this young personality to be assisted to reach that high standard that this country deserves. The clauses of this Bill seek to provide this assistance and I may say that not one of its clauses is new legislation. Each one has its counterpart somewhere in the Commonwealth and surely none will bring the charge that the Commonwealth restricts the freedom of the press.

This Bill is so important that I think I should take the time of the House to discuss briefly the main clauses. The first 13 of these clauses are those which enforce the registration of newspapers and newsagents together with their proprietors. These clauses are, in the main, administrative and self-explanatory. From clause 14 onwards the Bill deals with the law of libel in respect of news-papers. The origin of these clauses is clearly stated in the object and reasons of the Bill. The aim is to clarify the present somewhat obscure position. Their effect will be to provide further protection to newspapers who have made a genuine mistake. They prevent unscrupulous persons from indulging in libel actions as a per-manent source of income. Clause 19 specially prevents the multi-plicity of suits over the same libel and it gives a clear line as to what is and what is not a privileged report, details of which can be found in the second schedule of the Bill.

I have been closely associated with the newspaper world for much of my life and I know beyond all doubt that there is not an editor or a proprietor of any newspaper who will not welcome this legislation. There may be some small irritation caused by the necessity of registration, but registration itself confers benefits. As things stand today, it is not uncommon for a newspaper to lose large sums of money annually, through inefficiency or peculation by the newsagents. This Bill takes these difficulties into account and makes it obligatory for newsagents to keep accounts and to submit them regularly. By this means both inefficiency and pecula-tion will be prevented.

I have in this House regularly stressed my burning desire for the cultural development of our country, and to this end nothing can be more important than a free and enlightened and vigorous press. Government will do all in its power to promote this, and I believe this Bill represents an essential first step towards it.

CHAPTER 13

ZIK ON THE IBO PEOPLE

*From a Presidential address delivered at the Ibo State Assembly
held at Aba on Saturday, June 25, 1949.*

Harbingers of a new day for the Ibo nation, having selected
me to preside over the deliberations of this assembly of the Ibo
nation, I am conscious of the fact that you have not done so because of any extraordinary attributes in me. I realize that I am
not the oldest among you, nor the wisest, nor the wealthiest, nor
the most experienced, nor the most learned. I am therefore grateful to you for elevating me to this high pedestal.

The Ibo people have reached a cross-road and it is for us to
decide which is the right course to follow. We are confronted with
routes leading to diverse goals, but as I see it, there is only one
road that I can safely recommend for us to tread, and it is the
road to self-determination for the Ibo within the framework of a
federated commonwealth of Nigeria and the Cameroons, leading
to a United States of Africa. Other roads, in my opinion, are calculated to lead us astray from the path of national self-realization.

It would appear that God has specially created the Ibo people
to suffer persecution and be victimized because of their resolute
will to live. Since suffering is the label of our tribe, we can afford
to be sacrificed for the ultimate redemption of the children of
Africa. Is it not fortunate that the Ibo are among the few rem-
nants of indigenous African nations who are still not spoliated by
the artificial niceties of Western materialism? Is it not historically
significant that throughout the glorious history of Africa, the Ibo
is one of the select few to have escaped the humiliation of a con-
queror's sword or to be a victim of a Carthaginian treaty? Search
through the records of African history and you will fail to find an

occasion when, in any pitched battle, any African nation has either marched across Ibo territory or subjected the Ibo nation to a humiliating conquest. Instead, there is record to show that the martial prowess of the Ibo, at all stages of human history, has enabled them not only to survive persecution, but also to adapt themselves to the role thus thrust upon them by history, of preserving all that is best and most noble in African culture and tradition. Placed in this high estate, the Ibo cannot shirk the responsibility conferred on it by its manifest destiny. Having undergone a course of suffering the Ibo must therefore enter into its heritage by asserting its birthright, without apologies.

Follow me in a kaleidoscopic study of the Ibo. Four million strong in man-power! Our agricultural resources include economic and food crops which are the bases of modern civilization, not to mention fruits and vegetables which flourish in the tropics! Our mineral resources include coal, lignite, lead, antimony, iron, diatomite, clay, oil, tin! Our forest products include timber of economic value, including iroko and mahogany! Our *fauna* and *flora* are marvels of the world! Our land is blessed by waterways of world renown, including the River Niger, Imo River, Cross River! Our ports are among the best known in the continent of Africa. Yet in spite of these natural advantages, which illustrate without doubt the potential wealth of the Ibo, we are among the least developed in Nigeria, economically, and we are so ostracized socially, that we have become extraneous in the political institutions of Nigeria.

I have not come here today in order to catalogue the disabilities which the Ibo suffer, in spite of our potential wealth, in spite of our teeming man-power, in spite of our vitality as an indigenous African people; suffice it to say that it would enable you to appreciate the manifest destiny of the Ibo if I enumerated some of the acts of discrimination against us as a people. Socially, the British Press has not been sparing in describing us as 'the most hated in Nigeria'. In this unholy crusade, the *Daily Mirror, The Times, The Economist, News Review* and the *Daily Mail* have been in the forefront. In the Nigerian Press, you are living witnesses of what has happened in the last eighteen months, when Lagos,

Zaria and Calabar sections of the Nigerian Press were virtually encouraged to provoke us to tendentious propaganda. It is needless for me to tell you that today, both in England and in West Africa, the expression 'Ibo' has become a word of opprobium.

Politically, you have seen with your own eyes how four million people were disenfranchized by the British, for decades, because of our alleged backwardness. We have never been represented on the Executive Council, and not one Ibo town has had the franchise, despite the fact that our native political institutions are essentially democratic—in fact, more democratic than any other nation in Africa, in spite of our extreme individualism.

Economically, we have laboured under onerous taxation measures, without receiving sufficient social amenities to justify them. We have been taxed without representation, and our contributions in taxes have been used to develop other areas, out of proportion to the incidence of taxation in those areas. It would seem that we are becoming a victim of economic annihilation through a gradual but studied process. What are my reasons for cataloguing these disabilities and interpreting them as calculated to emasculate us, and so render us impotent to assert our right to life, liberty and the pursuit of happiness?

I shall now state the facts which should be well known to any honest student of Nigerian history. On the social plane, it will be found that outside of Government College at Umauhia, there is no other secondary school run by the British Government in Nigeria in Ibo-land. There is not one secondary school for girls run by the British Government in our part of the country. In the Northern and Western Provinces, the contrary is the case. If a survey of the hospital facilities in Ibo-land were made, embarrassing results might show some sort of discrimination. Outside of Port Harcourt, fire protection is not provided in any Ibo town. And yet we have been under the protection of Great Britain for many decades!

On the economic plane, I cannot sufficiently impress you because you are too familiar with the victimization which is our fate. Look at our roads; how many of them are tarred, compared, for example, with the roads in other parts of the country? Those of you who have travelled to this assembly by road are witnesses of the corrugated and utterly unworthy state of the roads which traverse Ibo-land, in spite of the fact that four million Ibo people pay taxes in order, among others, to have good roads. With roads must be considered the system of communications, water and electricity supplies. How many of our towns, for example, have complete postal, telegraph, telephone and wireless services, compared to towns in other areas of Nigeria? How many have pipe-borne water supplies? How many have electricity undertakings? Does not the Ibo tax-payer fulfil his civic duty? Why, then, must he be a victim of studied official victimization?

Today, these disabilities have been intensified. There is a movement to disregard traditional organization in the Ibo nation by the introduction of a specious system of a form of local government. The placing of the Ibo nation in an artificial regionalization scheme has left an unfair impression of attempted domination by minorities of the Ibo people. In the House of Assembly and the Legislative Council the electoral college system has aided in the complete disenfranchisement of the Ibo. As a climax, spurious leadership is being foisted upon us—a mis-leadership which receives official recognition, thus stultifying the legitimate aspirations of the Ibo. This leadership shows a palpable disloyalty to the Ibo and loyalty to an alien protecting power.

. . . The only worthwhile stand we can make as a nation is to assert our right to self-determination, as a unit of a prospective Federal Commonwealth of Nigeria and the Cameroons, where our rights will be respected and safeguarded. Roughly speaking, there are twenty main dialectal regions in the Ibo nation, which can be conveniently departmentalized as Provinces of an Ibo State, to wit: Mbamili in the northwest, Aniocha in the west, Anidinma and Ukwuani in the southeast, Nsukka and Udi in the north, Awgu, Awka and Onitsha in the centre, Ogbaru in the south, Abakaliki and Afikpo in the northwest, Okigwi, Orlu, Owerri and Mbaise in the east, Ngwa, Bende, Abiriba Ohafia and Etche in the southwest. These Provinces can have their territorial boundaries delimited, they can select their capitals, and then can conveniently develop their resources both for their common benefit and for those of the other nationalities who make up this great country called Nigeria and the Cameroons.

The keynote in this address is self-determination for the Ibo. Let us establish an Ibo State, based on linguistic and ethnic factors, enabling us to take our place side by side with the other linguistic and ethnic groups which make up Nigeria and the Cameroons. With the Hausa, Fulani, Kanuri, Yoruba, Ibibio (Iboku), Angus (Bi-Rom), Tiv, Ijaw, Edo, Urhobo, Itsekiri, Nupe, Igalla, Ogaja, Gwari, Duala, Bali and other nationalities asserting their right to self-determination each as separate as the fingers, but united with others as a part of the same hand, we can reclaim Nigeria and the Cameroons from this degradation which it has pleased the forces of European imperialism to impose upon us. Therefore, our meeting today is of momentous importance in the history of the Ibo, in that opportunity has been presented to us to heed the call of a despoiled race, to answer the summons to redeem a ravished continent, to rally forces to the defence of a humiliated country, and to arouse national consciousness in a demoralized but dynamic nation.

A farewell message delivered at the close of the Ibo State Assembly convened under the auspices of the Ibo State Union at Aba on June 26, 1949.

Compatriots of the Ibo nation, we have deliberated over affairs of vital importance to the Ibo nation for two days; we have listened to what the various representatives have to say, and we have contributed our quota. Now, the time has come for us to depart to the various corners of Ibo-land. As you leave this growing municipality, I have been requested to charge you with a farewell message to enable you to grasp the kernel of our deliberations, in order to explain it to those who sent you to Aba as missionaries of freedom and ambassadors of enlightenment. Go back to the folks at home, and tell them that the sons and daughters of the Ibo nation are alive to their great heritage.

Tell them that the Ibo giant is waking from his stupor and is asserting his inalienable rights in the scheme of things in this great country of Nigeria and the Cameroons. Tell them that the Ibo stands solidly behind the National Council of Nigeria and the Cameroons, and believes the NCNC is destined to weld this country into a federal commonwealth of politically free and equal nations. Tell them that in accordance with the Freedom Charter, we have answered the clarion call sounded by the NCNC for national self-determination of the various linguistic and ethnic groups of our blessed country towards the crystallization of a federal commonwealth.

Tell them that in revising the Constitution of Nigeria, and consistent with our ancestral legacy of pure democracy, the Ibo will not welcome any attempt to stultify the will of the people by subversive electoral systems, because it is undemocratic and contrary to our political institutions and traditions. Tell them that consistent with our heritage of democracy, we shall not tolerate any Constitution which disenfranchises the Ibo by the introduction of that curious political instrument of despotism known as 'The Electoral College'. Tell them that as a free people, the Ibo will not accept leadership whose choice is not of the people, but imposed from without, no matter how influential or affluent or wise or learned or diplomatic such leadership might be.

Tell them that as ethical and logical objects of creation, the Ibo will not co-operate with any leadership which treats the Ibo masses with studied contempt, and which is not responsible to the Ibo nation in its political utterances and activities, irrespective of official recognition of such spurious leadership. Tell them that as a people with a deep sense of justice, the Ibo people resent the continued employment of political officers, who are untrained in the law, in the administration of justice, thus linking the judiciary with the executive in an unholy alliance. Tell them that as Ibo-land is a protected territory and not a colonial possession, our land is our heritage and any attempt to tamper with this legacy of the centuries, no matter how subtle, will be resisted with determination.

Tell them that, consistent with our protectorate status, our mineral resources were presented to us as a blessing from the God of Africa, and that we shall oppose any unfair attempt to vest our mineral rights in any but a sovereign Ibo State, as part and parcel

247

of the Federal Commonwealth of Nigeria and the Cameroons. Tell them that since we are a law-abiding people, the taxes collected in Ibo-land constitute the result of the toil and sweat of taxable Ibo adults, and that any practice which encourages the disbursements of taxes for the improvement of other areas, to the detriment of the Ibo, will be rigorously opposed. Tell them that as progressive tax-payers, the Ibo raise serious objection to the apparent partiality and favouritism manifested in the construction of public roads and highways, the building of State schools and hospitals, the provision of public utilities—including water supplies, fire protection, electricity undertakings, postal, telegraph, telephone and wireless services—in Nigeria and the Cameroons, to the disadvantage of Ibo tax-payers.

Tell them that as a critical people, the Ibo demand, as of right, that the protecting power should prove its capacity to continue as such, by making available to us these elementary necessities of life, in the light of treaty obligations and in accordance with our protectorate status. And tell our folk throughout Ibo-land that as pure democrats, the Ibo people have expressed their resentment against the growing tendency in certain circles, in Nigeria and abroad, to regard and to treat us as an inferior people, even in our own God-given country. Tell them in all seriousness that the Ibo nation demands, as of right, equality of treatment in the appointments and promotions in the civil service of Nigeria, of which our territory is a constituent part.

Tell them that as a people who respect the pledged word, the Ibo people demand protection by their protector from *agents-provocateurs*, official and unofficial, whose tendentious propaganda tends to the branding of Ibo people as social pariahs. Tell them that as believers in righteousness and justice, the Ibo demand, as of right, equality of treatment in the award of Government scholarships, bursaries and grants which are made from the public revenue, of which the Ibo tax-payer is a contributor. And make it clear to our folk in the villages and towns in Ibo-land that as a nation with a glorious tradition and historic past, the Ibo nation demands from the protecting power freedom from persecution, freedom from ostracization, freedom from victimization, and freedom from discrimination.

These things shall be; a mighty nation shall rise again in the West of the Sudan, with love of freedom in their sinews; and it shall come to pass that the Ibo shall emerge, to suffer wrong no more, and to re-write the history written by their ancestors. It is the voice of Destiny and we must answer this call for freedom and respect in our life-time. The God of Africa has willed it. It is the handwriting on the wall. It is our manifest destiny.

Excerpts from a Presidential address to the Third Ibo State Assembly at Enugu on December 15, 1950.

Gathered here in the capital of the Eastern Provinces, where the blood of twenty-one Ibo men was shed in order to pay the price of political slavery, we owe it to our conscience as a people not to allow their sacrifice to be in vain. By laying down their lives in what is definitely a part of the common struggle for freedom in Nigeria, the twenty-one miners have bequeathed to us a legacy and it is for us to prove worthy or unworthy of the same. As a true Ibo son, I feel very bitter that twenty-one of my kith and kin should lose their lives under such tragic circumstances. Will you be good enough to stand for a few seconds in memory of these slain Ibo miners.

The Enugu tragedy is now history, but the homes of the twenty-one miners are now desolate. What do the Ibo people propose to do in order to prevent repetition of this challenge to our manhood? In 1929, Ibo women suffered like fate in Aba and Opobo areas. In 1947, Ibo men, among others, were shot at Burutu. And in 1949, Ibo men, women, and children were shot at different places. In spite of these shootings, some of which have resulted in death, and some in permanent injuries, what have the Ibo people done to show that they have been humiliated? That we have been singled out for the punitive visitations mentioned above is clearly a reflection on Ibo leadership and followership.

. . . If the lessons of history mean anything, it must be conceded that the Ibo people, though numerous, are friendly in their disposition, charitable in their relations with others, and artistic in their temperament. But they are pugnacious when aroused, and they resent injustice no matter from what quarter. They are industrious and enterprising and have powers of adaptability due to their colonizing instinct, which has led them to migrate to almost every part of West Africa. Granting that in any nation there must exist some undesirable characters, why should the Ibo nation be marked down for wholesale victimization, if the above sterling virtues are inherent in some of them?

Like the Jews of the world, the Ibo of Africa must rise to the occasion and not allow the British Press or any other institution or people to discourage them from their progressive march in concert with the other great nations of this country towards a free and independent commonwealth of Nigeria.

An address delivered to the thirteenth annual assembly of the Ibo State Union, held in the Owerri Hall, Enugu, on December 19, 1954.

Officers and members of the Ibo State Union, I welcome you to the capital of the Eastern Region on the occasion of your thirteenth annual assembly. Your Union was conceived in unity and since its founding it has dedicated itself to the worthy objective of improving the outlook and conditions of life of the Ibo-speaking peoples of this country. It is a noble ideal and it deserves support and encouragement.

According to the latest census, you represent five and a half million Nigerians scattered all over the country. There are 4,942,530 Ibo in the Eastern Region, 339,092 in the Western Region, 148,625 in the Northern Region, 31,887 in the federal capital of Lagos, and 25,794 in the trust territory of Southern Cameroons. In other words, you constitute 62 per cent of the peoples of the Eastern Region, that is, $98\frac{1}{2}$ per cent of Owerri Province, $98\frac{1}{2}$ per cent of Onitsha Province, 67 per cent of Ogoja Province, 41 per cent of Rivers Province, and 7 per cent of Calabar Province. Any people with such population figures must appreciate the supreme need for genuine co-operation with other linguistic groups in order to create a healthy social climate in our great country.

Your social institutions depict your role in the cultural development of the African peoples. The fact that you are one of the last bastions to ward off the excrescences of Western civilization has given cause for much misrepresentation about you and your culture in the literature of social anthropology. Nevertheless, the survival of your artifacts, mores and conventions, in spite of the ruthlessness of classic slavery and the clash of cultures which followed the path of European imperialism in Africa, has vindicated your social capacity.

I know that the patience of the Ibo-speaking peoples is being taxed to the limit of human endurance, not only by the irresponsible pronouncements of certain political leaders of this country and abroad, but also by the vulgar, provocative, abusive and insulting references to the Ibo in certain sections of the British and Nigerian Press; yet the law enforcement officers see no need for intervention. That was the case in 1948, when Ibo people in Lagos sought the matchet as the solution. I entreat you to be at peace with your neighbours, wherever you may live. Eschew violence, in spite of provocations. Be harmonious with those who spite you, but do not hesitate to defend your honour, if it is dragged into the mud and dirt of public obloquy.

Your reputation is your most precious possession. You must not allow it to be tarnished. It is not for me to dictate to you what steps you must take in order to protect your good name as individuals, because you are in a better position to handle this problem effectively. I can, however, offer advice to Ibo people, collectively, as one patriot to another. Obey the laws of those with whom you share the blessings of life, if fortune steers you to unknown lands for the earning of your livelihood. Respect the traditions of those in whose homeland you sojourn, but do not lose your social identity. Discharge your civic responsibilities without complaint. Exercise your political rights without apology. Never accept an inferior status in the scheme of things, be it political, social or economic. Fulfil your obligations to humanity by showing mercy

251

and consideration for the needy and the poor. Champion the cause of the oppressed. Feed mankind with the pap of human kindness. Do not seek to dominate others and do not allow others to dominate you.

The British Government, in partnership with us, is conducting a great experiment in parliamentary democracy in this country. We are completely immersed in it and are in the vanguard. The new Constitution is a visible manifestation of this acid political test of the black man's capacity for self-government. Your outlook, your attitude, and your reactions will supply the answer to those who doubt your political maturity. If those of you who listen to me happen to reside in the Eastern Region, you can make this experiment successful by being more solicitous for the welfare of your comrades than that of yourselves, and by being less ambitious to feather your own nest at the expense of your neighbour. We can make a greater success of the present Government of the Eastern Region by being more co-operative and by levelling fair and constructive criticisms than by being conscious of our pound of flesh and by denouncing imagined grievances without restraint.

I hereby exhort you, no matter where you live, to participate actively in the great movement for the emancipation of this country from the forces of reaction and conservatism. Ibo people cannot afford to be neutral, be it benevolent or malevolent, when social forces are being released day by day to redeem the lost heritage of the Negro race. Let us not be supine in the face of the events which are happening around us. We must take sides, but in doing so, let us make sure that we are tolerant and that we respect the right of others to their opinion. It is categorically imperative that Ibo people must not allow themselves to be transformed by the forces of prejudice into beasts who know only the law of the jungle, that is, might is right. Rather, let knowledge and reason prevail so that they may agree with others, when they must, and disagree when necessary, and let them do both these things without losing their bearings.

Finally, the Ibo-speaking peoples have a great role to play in the nationalist movement which is sweeping this country from

South to North, from East to West. We must co-operate energetically with other linguistic groups to make our country free and united. This must be done, without rancour and without apathy. I wish your deliberations success and trust that you will have a pleasant time at Enugu, our coal city !

CHAPTER 14

ZIK ON MORAL RE-ARMAMENT

Excerpts from a speech delivered to the teachers and students of the College of the Good Road, at Caux-sur-Montreux, Switzerland, on November 14, 1949.

It is a real privilege to address you this morning. . . . I can assure you that it has been a great honour to be here and, without flattery, I must say that I have had the most wonderful experience in my life, and I am sure that with the guidance of God it will mean a new life for me and a new life for a great number of people with whom it will be my good fortune to come into contact. I have been allowed a limited time to speak, and I understand that after speaking to you, I will be exposed to your broadsides in the form of questions; which is right, otherwise I might come here and say something not true and get away with it.

I thank you so much for your broadmindedness and indulgence in warmly receiving my colleagues and myself. These days have made us feel happy and natural, because I know that, as far as I am concerned, for the first time in my life, I am beginning to feel that I am among human beings, and I do not feel that I am only a school-mate or team-mate with a particular role to play, but I feel that I am among God's creation—people who, although come from different climes, are united in one common bond of fellowship. . . . Here we are at Caux. We have seen what Caux is like—an island of peace and harmony in a sea of discord, trying to lead humanity from the path of hatred, fear and suspicion, to one of faith and hope in the possibility of changing human nature, to enable people whose common heritage is the enjoyment of the good earth, to live like brothers and sisters.

By coming here I have also learned that it is not so much

whether the Nigerians are right or the British wrong, but the question is : What is right for Nigeria? It is a great lesson and I feel that the few days that we have spent here have actually acted like a tonic to us. We were like a run-down battery, but we have been re-charged. We shall placard the good news when we return home. Some of us have already made plans to enable our associates and friends to come and join with you in the College of the Good Road. It is our prayer that through God's guidance, the people of Nigeria shall be redeemed from the serfdom of fear, hatred, and suspicion, and that the truths of absolute honesty, absolute purity, absolute unselfishness and absolute love shall flare out anew, and presage the dawn, not only of a new Nigeria, but of a new world in the making.

An address delivered at a reception given for Nigerian students at Dr Frank Buchman's home, at Berkeley Square, London, on July 13, 1952.

Everywhere we see discord, misery and confusion, races and nations and individuals pitted against one another—people who would otherwise live in peace and enjoy the good things of the earth. Man is still a wolf to man. In spite of our scientific advances we are making no efforts to bury the hatchet, but continue to build huge scientific laboratories to enable us to destroy humanity. I do not think that God intended this beautiful world of ours to be destroyed. God is a God of love. He wants us to live in peace, to live harmoniously, so that the fruits of science and knowledge can be used in a constructive manner, and we may enjoy the bounties of the earth.

These problems confront us in Africa as well as in Europe, America, Australia, and other parts of the world. I have come here to apprise you of why I decided to pitch my tent in the ranks of Moral Re-Armament. I know it was like a bombshell when the news was given out that I was going to Caux. Accusations were levelled against me and criticisms were made, but I did not mind, because my conscience told me it was the right thing when I saw what was being done there to salvage humanity.

The reason for all the distrust and suspicion throughout the world is because of the method we employ in the quest for happiness and contentment. We all want food, clothing, shelter and the luxuries of life. These are natural things to desire, and to satisfy these desires there should be no barriers of race and nationality. They are the birthright of all human beings. When, therefore, we give the impression of being ebullient in West Africa and of taking the world to task and asking for a place in the sun, it is not because we are destructive but it is because we are human beings, and we want to share and enjoy the fruits of the earth. . . .

I am interested in politics. But I have made it clear for a long time now that I have no political ambitions, nor desire to be a politician. My supreme desire is to be a statesman, and to do something constructive in laying the foundation of a new society in my country. The foundation must be laid so that our children may enjoy it. Possibly, the structure will not be finished in our lifetime, but we must make the attempt. Otherwise, our life will have been a failure.

When, in 1949, I came here in order to attend various conferences . . . I had the opportunity to study the principles of Moral Re-Armament. What did I discover? I found that Moral Re-Armament had been able to grapple with the main problems facing humanity today. At the back of what man does is his greed for self. Everything he wants is to enable him and his kind to survive and to impose his will upon others. But I found also that Moral Re-Armament taught the doctrine of abnegation—you become impersonal in what you do so as to help your fellow man to share the benefits of the good earth.

It is not difficult to change human nature. Moral Re-Armament says it is no use waiting for the other fellow to change; you have to change yourself first. When you change, the other fellow will change. Then you have two individuals changed. Through these we can have a chain of reaction; a community can change, a nation can change, a race can change, and it is possible that we can make humanity change. We change not because we are necessarily right and the other fellow unnecessarily wrong, but because we feel that being human, we are not always right, and being humble we can bravely tell our fellow human being: 'I have wronged you. I am sorry. Let us bury the hatchet, let us live in harmony'.

Moral Re-Armament is thus based on sound ethical foundations. Whatever we do, we should not think of ourselves alone, but of others as well. The motto of my secondary school is *Non sibi sed aliis*—not for us alone but for others as well. By so doing we are able to contribute constructively to the progress of the world. The first thing I learned since my contact with Moral Re-Armament is not to point an accusing finger at the other fellow. I now realize that as one finger points at him, three fingers point back at me. So there are three chances to one I can also be wrong!

Some of us are Christians, some are Muslims, and some are Animists, but the difficulty confronting us is to have the moral courage to make the first move and take the initiative when people distrust each other. As a student of politics, I have made up my mind that I will put this idea into practice and I will not mind paying the price. I have given second thoughts to what I observed at Caux. There I heard people explain the idea of 'not who is right, but what is right'.

Indeed, this idea proved to be a pearl of great price. At the material time, we in West Africa were on the threshold of a great political awakening. I belonged to a nation-wide party. After my visit to Caux, in 1949, I made up my mind to approach my political opponents and offer them my hand of fellowship in the interests of my country and of the human race. Upon my return from Europe, I went to the house of the leader of my political opponents, and said to him: 'you want self-government for Nigeria, don't you? I and my group also want self-government for Nigeria. Why are we tearing at each other's throats? It is not who is right but what is right that matters. Is it right that we should always squabble among ourselves, because we are too proud to efface our puny selves for the common good? I am an African, and in Africa we usually respect old age. I am many years younger than you. I am sorry for what has happened between us in the past. It is not now a question of whether I am right and you are wrong; henceforth, let us concentrate on what is right for Nigeria and the Cameroons and let that be the basis of our political relationship. Here is my hand.' The old man grasped my hand and gave me an assurance of co-operation.

Naturally there was a great deal of misgiving. Many of my supporters felt I had done the wrong thing, but I told them that they were off the rails. I said: 'I don't blame you. If you had attuned yourself to the wavelength of peace and harmony in the world, you would realize that Nigeria with thirty million people is nothing but a drop in the bucket of humanity. Moral Re-Armament in the final analysis is an investment in mutual understanding that pays rich dividends.'

A short time ago, we had a conference to draw up our party programme on education. I was entrusted with that task. I felt that we placed too much emphasis on our puny selves, I thought that we should think of the future and of our children, so that they would not repeat the mistakes of the past. I was of the opinion that, in our education policy, we should make sure that our children learned to live a more ethical life. I have with me a copy of the policy which our party adopted as part of its programme. We felt that our system of education should be revolutionized so that our children would not think in terms of who is right, but what is right. Let me read it:

Education: Our educational programme shall be designed to produce citizens who are capable of adapting themselves not only to their surroundings but also to the world environment.

We shall emphasize education of the head, hand and heart, to enable our children to gain knowledge and acquire skill and to cultivate a sense of duty to the community. Whilst emphasizing the three Rs, we shall not overlook the influence of religion on character development, hence we shall encourage ethical instruction in the schools of the land with a bias on absolute moral standards of Honesty, Purity, Unselfishness and Love, not on the basis of the principle of who is right but what is right.

I want to say that I have enjoyed serenity of mind since this achievement of at-one-ness with myself, so that whatever I say to my political opponents or to my friends, I know that I am sincere and that it comes from the heart; I know that I am not playing politics, and that I do not have anything up my sleeve. Thus will the fight continue until we are able to get many more people, whether of our political faith or otherwise, to agree on what is right, and to take into account the forgotten factor, and let that change begin with themselves, for by so doing they will be able to change their nation and also change the world.

I became attracted to Moral Re-Armament because I felt that those who were preaching it were also living it. Most of us here tonight are coloured. We make no apology for being coloured people, nor for being 'under-developed' people, but may I ask : is it right for one section of humanity to be sentenced to eternal servitude—politically or economically? If it is not right, then it needs moral courage on the part of those of us who are now harbingers of a new world order, who are trying to rebuild the world, to stand firm on absolute moral standards and see that they are put into practice in our daily lives so that we do not give mere lip service to them.

We should be careful not to adopt an unnecessarily critical attitude and point accusing fingers at any particular individual or nation or race, or even ideology. I will go that far, because by not adopting a holier-than-thou attitude, we become more tolerant and less prejudiced. In all sections of the world there are many people who are yearning to mix with their fellow men. They long to interchange ideas, to be friendly, and to be befriended. We are all human beings and nobody likes to go through the streets of London trying to find comradeship or somewhere to stay, only to be snubbed and to be laughed at or to be turned to the streets. That is why this idea of change must be a two-way traffic.

We shall have to teach Britons that our coloured folk are also entitled to have life and to enjoy it as abundantly as their opposite numbers in the rest of the world, and that they must work for humanity and have no selfish ambitions for their personal aggrandisement. If we pursued this course of action, I have no doubt whatsoever in my mind that, if even it took a hundred or a thousand years to appreciate it, the life of the leading spirit whose very life epitomises Moral Re-Armament, Frank Buchman, would not have been lived in vain.

We have a war on our hands : an attempt to make life worthwhile for humanity at large, irrespective of race, or nation, or class, or caste. Once we are humble enough to appreciate that we are not necessarily always right, then we should be able to ferret out what is right and do it with moral courage, without fear or favour. I have no doubt in my mind that Moral Re-Armament will be a living force not only in the lives of a few people, but in the lives of many throughout the world.

We can start changing ourselves, on the basis of the absolute moral standards of honesty, purity, unselfishness and love. It is a herculean task, but we must be courageous, and defy convention if necessary, in order to carry forward the living spirit of this Moral Re-Armament idea. May I close with a stanza from Lowell?

> They are slaves who fear to speak
> For the fallen and the weak;
> They are slaves who will not choose
> Hatred, scoffing and abuse,
> Rather than in silence shrink
> From the truth they needs must think;
> They are slaves who dare not be
> In the right with two or three.

A Christmas message delivered at Onitsha Mansion, Ikeja, and radioed to the people of Nigeria on December 22, 1956.

The celebration of Christmas is a reminder to Christendom of the birth of the lowly Nazarene, who forged a formidable spiritual weapon with which he shook the Roman Empire.

When he lived, Jesus taught the doctrine of the irresistible might of meekness. He preached the gospel of love and lived a life of service to humanity. In spite of some of the apparent imperfections in his life, history portrays him as the nearest-to-perfect man.

The simplicity of this man's life, the depth of his knowledge of human nature, his spirit of tolerance and forgiveness are attributes of greatness which have made his life divine.

It is an irony of history that his exemplary life notwithstanding, his contemporaries denigrated his character and stultified his genuine philanthropic spirit. They broke his heart by their ingratitude and crucified him ultimately. Today, Christians worship the Nazarene and regard him as their redeemer.

I wish it were possible for Nigerians to bear these facts in mind as we celebrate the anniversary of the birth of Joshua whom the Greeks called Jesus. In this twentieth century of hydrogen bombs, when the yardstick of national greatness is reckoned in terms of military might and political duplicity, the Christmas season is a gentle reminder that 'Every generation needs a regeneration.'

It is with these humble thoughts that I wish all and sundry a happy Christmas.

From an address delivered at the Annual Convention of the NCNC, which was held at Rex Cinema, Aba, on October 28, 1957.

A great opportunity knocks at our door as a political party with an ideology of love. We should be imbued with the love of our fellow man. It is up to us to make use of this opportunity to the advantage of our country. Sacrifices have been made in the past I know, but greater sacrifices must yet be made. The sublimation of our egocentric desires for the welfare of our people is the supreme test today for Nigerian politicians. Are we prepared to diminish our ministerial emoluments? I am prepared. Are we prepared to reduce our perquisites? I am. Are we ready to take positive action so that the standard of living of the masses shall be increased? I am ready. We are in power now. Let us bring these things to pass. Are we serious in proclaiming from the housetops that we want 'One Nigeria' and 'A Strong Centre'? Let action speak louder than words. All we need to do now is to break the chains of fear, doubt, indecision and procrastination. Let us reanimate our souls and be more militant. Let us revolt against the present atmosphere of smug satisfaction with the *status quo*. Let us change our mouldy way of thinking and be more public spirited and less selfish, and Nigeria shall be reclaimed.

CHAPTER 15

ZIK ON LOCAL GOVERNMENT

From a speech delivered as Minister of Internal Affairs in the Eastern House of Assembly at Enugu on March 18, 1955, whilst moving the Second Reading of a Bill for a law to make provision for local government in the Eastern Region of Nigeria and for purposes connected therewith.

Mr Speaker, I rise to move the Second Reading of the Bill for a Law to make provision for Local Government in the Eastern Region of Nigeria and for purposes connected therewith. When the Eastern Region Local Government Ordinance 1950 was enacted, it was heralded as a great advance. That is true, but with the introduction of the new Constitution and the experience gained during nearly four years since the first application of the Eastern Region Local Government Ordinance, we have found it necessary to make a number of changes.

The object of this Bill is to give legislative sanction to this decision. The present Ordinance may appear to some Honourable Members as basically sound, but it is quite obvious that there is need for major modifications to meet the needs and conditions of the Region in its present stage of development. These changes are clearly set out in the objects and reasons of the Bill. I feel, however, that I should draw the attention of Honourable Members to certain matters of major importance to which my Ministry has directed its attention in the last four years. These changes are born out of practical experience in the application of Local Government Law.

In the first place, it is proposed to do away with the Regional Authority and to transfer the powers and responsibilities of that office to the Minister responsible for Local Government. A clause has been inserted enabling the Minister to delegate responsibility, and this delegation of powers will be amplified in the course of this debate. This envisages the appointment of Local Government Commissioners who will be charged with definite functions subject to the overall supervision of the Ministry. Then there are alterations to the structure of the present local government system. The present ordinance provides strictly for an organization which is based on the English model : that is for Local, District and County Councils. Experience has shown that such a system does not suit all areas of the Region. Provision has also been made for the establishment of municipalities. That is, single-tier all-purpose authorities whose actual or potential financial resources are adequate for the maintenance of all social services, and whose population has no true affinities with the surrounding rural areas. Port Harcourt Township might be an example of such a municipality.

Honourable Members will notice that the term 'Council' is defined to mean any local government council established by instrument under the provision of this law, and includes a municipality. The intention, as I have said, is to enable us to establish a single-tier all-purpose authority for large towns. There is provision in clause 17 for the appointment of Local Government Commissioners. Experience has shown that not a few Councils are very immature and inexperienced and there have been cases of abuse of office. The control exercised from the Ministry is too remote to be effective and it is considered that the appointment of Commissioners who exercise some of the Minister's power by delegation will provide a link between the Ministry and the Council, and will enable a stricter and closer control to be exercised by the Minister.

It is expected to appoint officers of the Administration to be Commissioners and it is planned that some powers of the Minister can conveniently be delegated, as follows : approval of certain items in the Annual Estimates, approval of certain items of supplementary expenditure, approval of appointment and dismissal of certain grades of Local Government staff, e.g. up to, and including, salary-scale D.1, writing-off arrears and deficiencies within certain limits, approval of deposit and suspense accounts,

263

approval of local council Bye-Laws, approval of certain classes of contracts—minor contracts.

It is intended in this law that the qualifications and disqualifications of Local Government Councillors should be, broadly speaking, the same as for persons seeking election to the House of Assembly and House of Representatives. It is also intended that elections to Local Government Councils shall be on the basis of direct universal adult suffrage and the Minister is empowered to make regulations to accomplish this. If Honourable Members will turn to Clause 20 of the Bill, they will notice that the disqualifications are in accordance with the Federal and Regional Electoral Regulations but with certain additions necessary for certain Local Government purposes. Police officers by the nature of their duties should not be members of Local Government Councils. Persons surcharged in sums of over £500 should be disqualified; it is clearly undesirable that such persons should be eligible for election to Councils. Persons found guilty of bribery and other serious offences in connection with Local Government elections should be disqualified. Of course, employees of Councils should not be qualified to become members of such Councils.

In connection with universal adult suffrage, Honourable Members will remember that I gave the undertaking to make a statement in this connection because it was quite clear at the time that even if we introduced local government it would be very difficult to introduce universal adult suffrage all over the Region at once for election purposes. So I promised to make a statement regarding the attitude of my Ministry and what we had in view. With your permission, Mr Speaker, I would like to make the statement at this stage.

Since the statement in the Speech from the Throne on 2nd October that it was the intention of the Regional Government to institute a single system of elections at all levels, the problem of the application of universal adult suffrage to local government elections has been under examination. The experience gained and the lessons learnt in the recent elections to the Federal House of Representatives have been of great value.

The main point that emerges clearly is the magnitude of the task.

In the Federal Elections, the average number over the Region of persons who registered to vote was not more than 30 per cent of those who, according to the census figures, were eligible to vote. The registration of this 30 per cent with the consequent compilation of the registers and the other necessary arrangements, in the period available, took up the entire time and energies of the Administration to the exclusion of all other duties. Registration was on a Divisional basis, with a more or less limited number of polling areas; there are indications that a larger number of polling areas, which means the employment of a larger staff, and additional time, would have produced a larger registration.

Local Government elections start at the village, quarter, kindred or even family level to form the Local Councils. To ensure that as many as possible of those entitled to vote do have the opportunity to register, propaganda and registration must be carried out at the lowest level. The number of these basic electoral units is enormous. For example in the Owerri Division alone there are to be over 750. In other Divisions the number varies from about a hundred to over six hundred. It is clear that to effect as full a registration as possible, and give the villagers the opportunity to exercise their right to vote, needs considerably more time and a much larger staff than was available for the Federal elections.

Then there is the question whether the District and, where necessary, the County Councils shall be directly elected. If the answer is 'yes', then there is the need to form wards of constituencies, which do not at present exist in all areas. Again, many local council areas send a multiplicity of representatives to district councils, in some parts ten or more. The difficulties of plural voting were also brought out at the Federal elections and it seems that local government councils should be formed on the basis of one-councillor wards. To achieve this will mean a complete review of the system all over the Region. The task is indeed a great one.

It is planned to bring into being on 1st April next, four or five Counties, two Urban Districts and twenty-three or twenty-four Rural Districts, as well as a large number of local councils. For the reasons already stated, it will be impossible to introduce universal adult suffrage in all these areas in the time available. The alternatives are either to defer the introduction of local government till it is possible to introduce universal adult suffrage or to bring the councils into being as promised under the old electoral system and plan for the introduction of universal adult suffrage as soon as possible for subsequent elections.

z.—18

After full consideration, I am of the opinion that it is better to introduce local government first and let the universal adult suffrage follow. It will be possible to try an experimental scheme of universal franchise in one urban district and it is is also planned to use symbols and the ballot box in village elections in one Division as a pilot scheme. From these it is hoped to learn much that will be of value in planning for the future establishment of a single system of elections at all levels, which remains the declared policy of the Regional Government.

Another innovation in this Bill is the reflection of the policy of the Ministry of Health, in which all Councils henceforth charged with the provision of health services must appoint a Health Committee, of which Committee a representative of the Ministry of Health must be a member. Municipalities and County Councils must appoint Medical Officers of Health, who may be Government officers loaned for this purpose. These officers will have the power to direct the sanitary work of the employees of Councils in the area for which they are appointed. Thus it is intended to ensure the fullest participation by Local Government Councils in the general development of urban and rural health services.

It is becoming clear that all is not well with the staff of some Councils. There have been allegations of favouritism and corruption over the making of appointments. There are cases where councils have appointed unqualified men to responsible posts and dismissed well-qualified men on the flimsiest of pretexts. The National Association of Local Government Employees has expressed the greatest concern for the future of the local government staff if steps are not taken to improve their position, their security, and the terms offered them by many Councils. To remedy the position it is proposed to make the appointment and dismissal of all local government employees subject to the approval of the Minister. This power would, in the case of lower-paid staff, be delegated to Local Government Commissioners. It may be argued that this measure would seriously interfere with the freedom of action of Councillors, but it is the object of the Government of the Eastern Region that the exercise of the Minister's powers would be little more than a formality as long as councils employed

266

suitable qualified persons and terminated appointments for good and sufficient reasons.

It is also intended to give the Minister the power of making Regulations governing the conditions of service of local government employees. Under the present Ordinance, Councils are making their own. The result of this has been either that they have not done so, or, in attempting to do so, they have brought forth protests from the National Association of Local Government Employees. There has not yet been time for the institution of any joint negotiating machinery and it is thought that the best way for the present is to permit the Ministers to make such staff regulations as will ensure uniformity of conditions of service, which all are agreed is essential. For the same reason, it is proposed that the Minister shall have power to make regulations for retiring benefits and a contributory Provident Fund scheme. It is intended to appoint a Local Government Service Board of persons of obvious integrity, to advise the Minister on appointments, dismissals, conditions of service and all matters affecting local government staff.

I come now to clause 111 of the Bill which refers to the control of expenditure of Councils. This makes it absolutely definite that any expenditure incurred by a Council, which is not in the approved estimates or sanctioned by the Minister, may be surcharged on the person responsible for such expenditure. Clause 118 of the Bill shows that it is necessary that the Minister should have this power, which at present he has not, for the purpose of ensuring proper expenditure of funds, and especially in the case of services where grants from Regional Government are concerned. Clause 120 provides for the appointment of Examiners of Accounts. At present the only way the Minister can obtain information about the conduct of a Council's finances is from the annual Audit Report, which may reveal incompetence, neglect or worse, too late for effective action, save by an inquiry, or by the use of clause 135, which empowers District Officers to have access to a Council's records of accounts, but which does not convey the power to check cash. It is proposed that the Examiners of Accounts, who will be officials of the Ministry, or District Officers, shall be able to examine the cash of Councils on the direction of the Minister or of Local Government Commissioners exercising delegated powers.

Clause 172 provides for the appointment of auditors. This is precisely the position at present. Clause 175(2) gives an opportunity for any Councillor to register his dissent in order to avoid any surcharge. Any Councillor dissenting from expenditure must cause his dissent to be recorded in the minutes to avoid surcharge. This is a most important sub-clause. It puts the onus on a Councillor to have his dissent recorded. He cannot enjoy the benefit of excessive or novel expenditure and then escape the surcharge by remaining silent. Such a clause is included in other legislation. Clause 180, sub-clause 1, makes provision for appeals against surcharge. At present there is no time limit within which persons surcharged must make their appeal, and this has led in recent cases to prevarication. A time limit of thirty days is therefore proposed.

Clause 74 deals with the granting of contracts. The Ministry appreciates how touchy this subject is, particularly to Local Government bodies, but in view of what has happened in the last four years, I am in a position to say that representations have been made to the Ministry that the methods of some Councils in making contracts is not above suspicion, and that frequently incompetent and unreliable contractors are employed. It is, therefore, proposed to give the Minister power to approve contracts which Councils are to be required to submit to him if over £500 in value. This power might conveniently be delegated to Local Government Commissioners. Clause 99 provides that any officer of a Council who is in any wise concerned or interested directly or indirectly himself or through a partner (otherwise than as a minority shareholder in a Company) in any contract for work with or executed for the Council shall be incapable of holding any office or employment under this law.

These are some of the main points to which I wish to draw the attention of Hon. Members in this Bill. Other innovations have been dictated by the practical experience of the past four years. It is hoped that, given the closest co-operation between Councils and the Ministry, the Bill will aid the development of local government in the Eastern Region under present conditions. I propose at the Committee stage to move a number of amendments, but in the meantime I commend this Bill to the favourable consideration of the House.

From a speech delivered during a debate in the Eastern House of Assembly on March 22, 1955, supporting the motion to abolish the provincial system of administration.

Mr Speaker, may I be allowed to express the view of the Government on this very important motion, which seeks to abolish the existing system of provincial administration and urges Government to set up machinery, forthwith, to administer all the Divisions in the Eastern Region directly from Enugu.

The motion is acceptable to the Government. The Government will abolish the existing system of provincial administration and set up machinery to define how the new system will work and how it will be implemented. I say this because the Government of the Region has already had under active consideration the machinery required for the future administration of the Region. It is anticipated that the form and organization of administration cannot in times of change remain unchanged. But it is also realized that so sweeping an alteration as that proposed in the motion cannot be introduced by a stroke of the pen. Careful and detailed planning is required.

Honourable Members are aware that, last week, I introduced a new Local Government Bill. Certain clauses dealing with the appointment of Local Government Commissioners will affect the workings of the administration. The Government has also in mind a Customary Courts Bill to replace the existing Native Courts Ordinance, and this will be presented at a future meeting of the House. These two Bills will result in changes in the work of the administration as it is now.

The Government also intends to introduce an Order-in-Council transferring certain powers to Ministers which hitherto had been vested in Residents and other administrative officers. As soon as this transfer has been effected, it should reduce considerably the functions and responsibilities of administrative officers in provincial administration. We hope that this will be one of the last acts before the abolition of the office of Residents. The Government has, therefore, decided that a review of the present system and organization of our administration will be undertaken, as soon as practicable, in order ultimately to replace the present provincial administration.

From a broadcast talk delivered during the 'Government Hour' over the East Regional Programme of the Nigerian Broadcasting Service, at Enugu, on April 6, 1955.

Good evening, ladies and gentlemen. Some two weeks ago I presented to the Eastern Region House of Assembly a Bill for a Local Government Law, which before the House adjourned had been debated at its second reading. It seems to me that this is an appropriate time, after the reports of that debate have appeared in the press, for me to say a little on this most important subject of local government. Why, you may ask, is this an important subject? To that question my reply is because it affects the everyday life of the people of this Region.

Your sons go off to school in the morning, you get on your bicycle and ride to work, your wife takes the baby to the dispensary to get medicine for her cough, your sister goes to market, where she rents a stall, and when she arrives she finds that the market has been cleaned and swept before it opens. If you think about these everyday things you will realize that there is an organization that does much to make them possible. And this organization is very often supplied by the local government council that is responsible for the area where you live. For example, the council may own the school to which your sons go, or it may make grants of money to assist the school to pay its teachers; the council may maintain the road along which you ride to work; it probably manages the dispensary; it has very likely built the stall where your sister sells her things and it may pay the labourers who have swept the market clean. This is what I mean when I say that local government closely affects the lives of ordinary people.

The maintenance of roads, of dispensaries, of markets, the making of grants to schools and the provision of health measures, all these are social services for the benefit of the community, and they and many others are essential, if the people are progressing, as we in this Region are determined to progress, to a decent standard of living. But you must not forget that these services cost money. The road labourers and the sanitary men must be paid; so must the teachers; the drugs you get from the dispensary have to be bought and so does the cement used to build the market stalls. Where does the money come from? This is a question that many people do not bother to answer. But it is an important question, for the answer contains one of the basic principles of local government. This is to the effect that the local services which a community enjoys must in a large degree be paid for by the community that enjoys them. That means that you must pay your share of the cost of the roads, schools, medical facilities and the rest of it, if they are to be any good to you and the others living in your area. The Government of the Region also plays its part in the maintenance of social services, and that is a matter I shall touch on in another talk later on. But the fact remains that a large part of the cost of these things that you need and use every day comes from your own pocket. It comes from the taxes and the rates you are called upon to pay.

The local government legislation makes it possible for the councils to manage many of these services. Since they are local services, it is surely better that they are managed by persons who are close to the people who have to pay for them. This brings me to a second basic principle of local government, that the services which a community enjoys should be managed by the chosen representatives of the community. This means that you are entitled to elect the councillors who will have the duty of managing the services of which you should have the benefit and for which you have, in part at least, to pay. This is often forgotten. It has only too often been said that once a man has been elected a councillor, he forgets that he is, or should be, responsible to the people who elected him and seeks nothing but his own benefit. I am afraid that this saying is not without foundation. I cannot too strongly emphasize that an elected councillor is responsible to the electors for the proper functioning of the services for which the electors pay.

If you think about this fact for a moment, you will see how much your own choice in the election of councillors can affect you and your family. If you do not trouble to cast your vote, if you do not bother to vote for a fit and proper person, if you allow your vote to be bought, then you run the risk of helping to elect a council that will not work for the good of the people, but only for their own benefit. A bad council means bad services. If the roads are not well looked after, if the market stalls are not well built, if the dispensary has no drugs, it generally means that the councillors are not doing the work which you elected them to do, and it is you and others like you who suffer. The money you pay in rates and taxes is wasted and naturally you complain that you see no result for your money. On the other hand a good council will always be seeking to improve the services; there is no doubt that improvements will mean more expense. But most people are prepared to pay for something they want and if they see good results they do not mind having to pay.

In short, then, the effect of the Local Government Ordinance on your lives is that it gives the councils the power to operate the social services which every community is beginning to expect; universal primary education, widespread health services, hospitals, maternity wards, roads and bridges, housing lay-outs, all these things are in the competence of one type of council or another. These all cost money to operate and a great part of the cost must come from the tax and rates paid by you. The councils are elected by your votes. If you elect unwisely, you will suffer because the council will not provide the good services which you are entitled to expect for your money. If you choose well, you should receive in your areas the things you need. Obviously everything will not come at once, but a good council should be able to plan to spend your money so that over a period of years there is a steady improvement of the services that affect every aspect of your life.

Yet this is perhaps the most difficult problem that our councils and our rate-payers have to solve. Everybody wants progress; but, as I have already said, more and better services cost money.

272

Though the Regional Government is prepared to assist local government councils to develop social services, much of the cost must fall on the rate-payer. And this is the problem. At what point does the cost of what the people want become greater than the people can afford? It will, of course, vary with the wealth of the community, but it seems to me that the test of a good council is that it knows just how much it can ask the community to pay for a desired service and can produce value for money. To be able to do this, a council must be in close touch with the people. I have heard it said often that councillors, once they are elected, no longer trouble to consult their electorate. This is wrong; as I have already said, councillors are responsible to the people who elected them and I would urge most strongly that councillors are always ready to consult the people about what services are most needed and to discover what they will and will not pay for.

Closely connected with this relationship of councillors and electorate, and with the levying of rates, is the problem of what is the most suitable area for the administration of social services by a particular type of council, in the conditions prevailing in this Region. The Local Ordinance provides for county, district and local councils. The intention, broadly speaking, was for the county councils to provide the services common to a fairly large area, such as the larger administrative divisions, while the district councils operated services of a more local nature, in areas of more limited size, and the local councils acted as the originators of communal and similar services at village level. It has recently been suggested that, in some parts at least, the county is too large and the council therefore too remote from the people for the best operation of services; that, in our present stage of development, the people prefer to see their money spent as close as possible to their own door-steps. I do not deny that there is substance in this argument. But I must also say that, carried too far, it will stultify the development of the more costly services that our people are rightly demanding. What I mean is this: a district council for the area of a single clan may well be able to maintain a certain number of roads, some dispensaries and maternity wards; it may be able to make grants in aid of education to a limited extent; but it might never be able alone to afford such needs as a rural hospital or a secondary school. If however it joined with one or more clans, together they could possibly manage to meet the cost, because it would be spread over a larger area and a larger population. In such a case unity is strength.

Nevertheless, I do not think that at this stage it is right to force such larger associations on people who have not yet felt the need for it. Better to let them come together of their own free will, when they see and understand the need. To this end the new Local Government Bill is designed to make for a more elastic system, so that where the peculiar conditions of a particular area are not suited to a rigid system of counties and districts, there may be only districts; the association in larger county units may come later when the districts have found that together they might afford services which alone they cannot develop.

A third problem which is engaging my attention is the supply of properly trained staff for local government councils. If councils are to provide efficient services, it is not enough only to find the money to pay for them, difficult though that may be; there must also be competent staff. Roads will not be well maintained if the overseers are not trained; there will be no bridges if there are no engineers to design and build them; so too there is a need for better qualified dispensers and midwives, if the rural health centres are to give you the attention you want. It must be admitted that at present we have not got as many trained and qualified staff as we could wish; that is unavoidable when the demand exceeds the supply; but it will be corrected as more administrative and financial staff pass through the courses held by the Extra-Mural Branch of the University College of Ibadan, as the Nigerian College of Arts, Science and Technology increases its output and as our own training schools, for example that designed by the Medical Department for the training of rural health staff, get into their stride.

There are two other aspects of this problem. Firstly, councils must realize that it is their duty to employ properly trained staff. It is no more than the truth to say that some councils have seen fit, for whatever reason, to appoint to positions of responsibility persons who are not fully qualified, though there were available more suitable candidates. Councils must be educated to employ nothing less than the best. Secondly, if the best are to be employed, they must enjoy conditions of service commensurate with their qualifications, for the labourer is worthy of his hire; they must have security both in tenure of office and for the future. My aim is to build up an efficient and contented local government service, because only if the employees of local government councils are competent and satisfied, will the councils be able to operate and develop the social services which affect so closely the daily life of the people.

From a speech delivered as Minister of Internal Affairs, in the Afikpo District Council Hall, Afikpo, on April 21, 1955, on the occasion of the inaugural meeting of the Afikpo District Council and the opening of the Council Headquarters.

May I say, Mr Chairman, that the achievement of local government is not an end in itself; it is a means to an end. It is the opportunity for the elected representatives of the people to develop the social services that the people need and rightly demand in these days of progress to nationhood. It is no light or easy task; services cost money and the Regional Government cannot provide all that is needed.

It is a principle of local government that the services enjoyed by the residents of an area must, in large measure, be paid for by those residents. But nobody likes to put his hand in his pocket for nothing; if rates must be paid, then let there be value for money. This is, I am quite sure, the most difficult, and also the most essential duty of councillors—to persuade the people to pay for the services they need and to show by performance that the money so paid is wisely and properly spent for the benefit of the people.

Councillors can never do this if, once elected, they divorce themselves from the electorate and only think of themselves. Let me be frank; in not a few places councils have shown themselves lacking in straightforwardness of purpose and in integrity; with the result that the people have lost confidence, rates have not been paid and services have stagnated or have been curtailed. One of

275

the most disturbing features of a failure to pay education rates has been that teachers have gone without salaries for considerable periods, a deplorable thing. You have given assurance in your address of welcome that this sort of thing will not happen here.

It is the declared intention of the Government of this Region to establish and maintain an honest and efficient system of local government, and to do all in its power to eradicate corruption and incompetence. I am sure that with the record and the example of good administration of the Native Authority in mind, the new council will ever strive for the good of the people of Afikpo.

Finally, Mr Chairman and Councillors, may I congratulate you on your assumption of office. I pledge the support and help of myself and of the Ministry of Internal Affairs in dealing with the problems that will undoubtedly beset you, and I offer my sincere good wishes for the future of your council and your people.

From a speech delivered in the Eastern House of Assembly on March 14, 1956, when he replied to the various criticisms levelled on 'The Speech from the Throne' outlining his government's policy for the forthcoming financial year.

As Minister responsible for local government, I can speak with a fair degree of authority on this subject. Honourable Members will recall that the experience which was gained in the practice of local self-government between 1950 and 1955 was disappointing. I refer to the sordid incidents in Port Harcourt, Aba, Onitsha, Southern Ngwa, Lower Cross River, Igbo Etiti, and other local government councils. Bribery and corruption were the order of the day. Inefficiency in administration was the rule and not the exception. Nepotism was practised under the guise of 'son of the soil' ideals. Contracts were awarded to those who could grease the palms of the councillors. Market stalls were allocated most unfairly. Taxes were assessed most incompetently and dishonestly. Several councils failed to discharge the duties imposed upon them by law, and it became necessary for the Ministry to use its good offices in order to prevent a total breakdown of our local government and administration. I am, therefore, amazed that some of my honourable colleagues could levy such criticisms on local governments.

The functions of Local Government Commissioners are clearly defined by law. They have certain delegated powers, and if there is any abuse of such powers, they can be revoked. From all reports reaching me, the Local Government Commissioners are discharging their duties most efficiently. On the question of grants, may I confess that I cannot appreciate the stand of the Opposition on this issue. A glance at the past issues of our *Hansard* will reveal the numerous pleas made by them, along with other honourable members, on behalf of their constituencies for a restitution of the practice of making grants to local government bodies in respect of grant-earning services. Now that the Government has decided to revise its previous stand, members of the Opposition are speaking in strange tongues about stifling initiative and self-reliance!

For the benefit of members of this House, may I explain that the policy of my Ministry in respect of grants to local government bodies is based on the accepted practice that such grants-in-aid are made to enable them to achieve the desired standard of efficiency in social services. Denial of such grants may mean that the councils concerned have failed to abide by the conditions stipulated for making them. Thus the withholding of a grant from a council is a reflection on that council's efficiency and competence. May I ask : does the Opposition wish that grants should not be given at all, in order that councils may exercise their initiative in poverty? If so, why did members of the Opposition criticize the old system which abolished the making of grants? I hope that my friends opposite are not playing politics, because it is a luxury which we cannot afford to play, especially when it affects millions of our poor brothers and sisters who live in the rural areas.

From a speech made in the Eastern House of Assembly on March 20, 1958.

This is a suitable moment for me to mention the changes that are proposed in the local government structure. In 1955 the Ministry of Local Government stated in a Policy Paper that the

Region, in developing its local government, was still in a period of trial and error, and that both the Government and the people would learn by experience what form of local government would suit them best.

Experience over the past three years has shown that the three-tier system of county, district and local councils has not generally been satisfactory, and that the 'district-with-county-powers' is preferred by the majority of the people. It has been said that the county is an expensive luxury, which increases overhead expenses. On more than one occasion, I have heard it called a 'waste pipe'. District councils have disliked collecting rates to meet county budgets, in the spending of which they have no say. Small districts, especially if of different linguistic groups from the majority in a county, have felt that their views can never be heeded and their requests never met.

In the face of this feeling, the Government has no alternative but to adopt the present district council areas as the units for all-purpose authorities, based on ethnic, linguistic and cultural affinities. It is proposed to substitute the name 'County' for 'District' in the rural areas. It is also the intention of this Government to use local government councils as the chief instrument of policy, and by devolving on them responsibility for the operation of social services within their competence, to avoid over-centralization. Thus the Ministries will formulate policy and will act in an advisory and supervisory capacity towards the county councils, which will be charged progressively with responsibility for the maintenance of the social services and will be assisted by means of grants-in-aid and by the advice and supervision of Government officers.

In order to ensure the proper co-ordination of the services operated by the county councils and the most effective and economical use of Government officers in their advisory and supervisory capacities, it is intended to group counties broadly, according to geography and to ethnic and linguistic affinity, in Provinces. There will be a headquarters in each Province with a senior officer of the Administration as Provincial Inspector, who will be the agent of the Government to see that the policies are carried out by the county councils. He will be assisted by County Inspectors, whose functions will be chiefly supervision of the councils and of revenue collection, and by a team of departmental officers who will provide the professional and technical supervision and advice required by the county councils in the operation of services.

I would draw the special attention of the House to the proposal to form Provincial Assemblies in each Province. Under the chairmanship of a Commissioner, they will comprise representatives of each Local Council in the Province. The aim is to secure close contact between the Government and the people and, as far as possible, to do away with the complaint that there is little or no consultation between the Government and the governed. The Assemblies will be deliberative and consultative bodies whose opinions the Government will seek on matters concerned with the progress and prosperity of the people of each Province. Thus it is my hope that Government will be brought nearer to the people.

CHAPTER 16

ZIK ON THE UNIVERSITY OF NIGERIA

A speech delivered in the Eastern House of Assembly on May 18, 1955, when seconding the motion made by the Honourable the Minister of Education that a Bill entitled 'A Law to establish a university in the Eastern Region of Nigeria, and to provide for the governance thereof and for matters incidental thereto' be read a second time.

Mr Speaker, I have the honour to second this historic motion and in doing so I wish to confine my remarks to one aspect of the speech so ably made by the Honourable the Minister of Education. I have in mind his statement about the philosophy of education which animates the introduction of this Bill. I must admit that I have been impressed by the recommendations made by the African Education Commission, which visited Nigeria in 1920 with the late Kwegyir Aggrey, under the auspices of the Phelps-Stokes Fund and the Foreign Mission Societies of North America and Europe, particularly the following :

1. That all concerned distinguish clearly the educational needs, namely, the education of the masses of the people, the training of teachers and leaders for the masses, and the preparation of professional men who must pass the conventional requirements of British universities.

2. That the education of the masses and their teachers be determined by the following elements, namely, health, ability to develop the resources of the country, household arts, sound recreation, rudiments of knowledge, character development, and community responsibility. The native teachers should also have access to the great truths of physical and social science and the inspiration of history and literature.

I make the above admission because, after 35 years, the observations and recommendations of the Commission are still timely. Indeed, I can say that this report forms a basis of the philosophy of education for Africa, not because Africans deserve a separate philosophy but, in the words of Dr Anson Phelps-Stokes, the purpose of the Commission was to help Africans 'by encouraging an education adapted to their actual needs. . . . The time has passed when the old thesis can be successfully maintained that a curriculum well suited to the needs of a group on a given scale of civilization in one country is necessarily the best for other groups on a different level of advancement in another country or section.'

But Dr Stokes did not end on a dogmatic note. After pointing out that agricultural or industrial training, under Christian auspices, proved to be the best type of education for the majority of the freed Negroes, 'at this particular time of their development', he cautioned that 'the door was and always should be kept wide open for a higher education' for those who had the ability and the character to profit by university training.

In appreciating any philosophy of education we should always find out the aims of those who postulate such ideas. As far as one can observe from a subsequent statement by the Phelps-Stokes group, the objective sought was Nigerian leadership. In one of their latest reports, it is said :

In terms of the African continent, this should clearly imply such changes as that there should be more emphasis on education for native leadership; that European officials should gradually give way to a trained native African civil service; that duly elected Africans should play a larger part in the legislative councils of the colonies; and that investments should be further controlled in the interest of better wages for native workmen, and better working and living conditions. It is believed that if such things are done the African people, and the nations in which they will form the large majority, will be happier, and will ultimately have an important contribution to make to the civilization of the world.

I believe that, side by side with higher vocational education, opportunities should be created to enable the trained individuals to play a useful role in the development of the country. Here is where I agree with the founders of Achimota College that,

The immediate aim of African education should be to develop character, initiative, and ability of the youth of the country, so that they may be reliable, useful, and intelligent in the rapidly changing life and circumstances of their own people. In other words, the aim of education is to develop the manhood and womanhood of the rising generation for the sake of their peoples. Anything narrower than this must lead to a stagnant and menacing flood of unemployed and unemployable youth.

It is important that higher educational facilities should be provided locally to enable those to be benefited to make full use of them. It is said that a fully educated person should be 'enlightened in his interests, impersonal in his judgment, ready in his sympathy for whatever is just and right, effective in the work he sets himself to do, and willing to lend a hand to anyone who is in need of it.' I strongly support the belief of the late Sir Frederick Gordon Guggisberg that 'the keystone of progress is education; but all that will be idle rhetoric if we mix the materials of the keystone badly.' In this connection, this former Governor of the Gold Coast confessed that the British would never succeed 'if the sole place in which the African can get his higher education and his professional training is Europe. Much learning, and of the best, he can get there; character-training, none. . . . We must aim at giving the whole of our education locally, and, where it is essential that an African should go to Europe for the final steps to enter a profession, we must arrange our system in such a manner that his absence will be reduced to the shortest possible time and the foundations of his character firmly laid before he goes. . . . To stand the pressure brought to bear on the Arch of Progress by the hurricane of material development, the storm of criticism, and the windy tornadoes of political agitation, the keystone must be well and truly laid and composed of strong materials.'

In order that the foundations of Nigerian leadership shall be securely laid, to the end that this country shall cease to imitate the excrescences of a civilization which is not rooted in African life, I strongly support this Bill to the effect that a full-fledged university should be established in this Region without further delay. Such a higher institution of learning should not only be cultural, according to the classical concept of universities, but it should also be vocational in its objective and Nigerian in its content. We should not offer any apologies for making such a progressive move. After all, we must do for ourselves what others hesitate to do for us. In the thoughts of a great American Negro historian, 'History shows that it does not matter who is in power or what revolutionary forces take over the government, those who have not learned to do for themselves and have to depend solely on others never obtain any more rights or privileges in the end than they had in the beginning.'

I notice that it is envisaged that the university should have six degree-conferring Faculties: Arts, Science, Law, Theology, Engineering, and Medicine. I hope that the curricula of the university will be related to the day-to-day life of our people and that they will be so organized as to relate the mission of the university to the social and economic needs of the Region. I also observe that the following twenty diploma-conferring Institutes are among those which will be established for the professional and technical education of our men and women on whom we shall have to rely heavily in the difficult years ahead: Agriculture, Architecture, Diplomacy, Domestic Science, Dramatics, Education, Finance, Fine Arts, Fishery, Forestry, Journalism, Librarianship, Music, Pharmacy, Physical Education, Public Administrations, Public Health, Secretarial Studies, Social Work, Surveying and Veterinary Science. If these Institutes are so organized as to operate *pari passu* with the Faculties, then this Region will embark upon an historic renaissance in the fields of academic, cultural, professional and technical education on the same lines as the leading countries of the world.

I wish to make it emphatic that the university should be co-educational. It will be remembered that the Cambridge Conference on African Education made reference to this subject in their report, which says:

Women and girls need an education that fits them to live in a world of social change; and they need the tools of learning to help them to understand and take a fuller part in daily life. The increasing numbers need opportunities for professional and occupational training so that they can be both economically independent and fitted to take over progressively their responsibility for educating and training their own people. The main task for education among women and girls therefore is to provide so sound a training in the techniques of living that the whole level of African life can be raised socially, intellectually, and spiritually by the full co-operation of women in the home and in the community at large. . . . We recommend that priority should now be given to providing trades and technical training for women and girls in the fields of needlecraft, catering, institutional management, and secretarial arts.

It is now accepted in progressive circles that male and female students of any modern university should be allowed to live side by side on the same campus, where residence is available; they should study together, play together, and share together the vicissitudes of the cultural atmosphere of secondary school or university life. The aim of such co-education should be to enable male and female students to engage together in academic, vocational and co-curricular activities in developing their personalities.

I feel that it is of utmost importance that we should inculcate in our university students not only the dignity of labour, but also the idea that by hard work, sacrifice and self-determination, a poor student can obtain university education. In many colleges and universities of the world today, thousands of students are demonstrating that lack of funds is not an unsurmountable barrier to higher education. The fact that students are not affluent enough to pay all their bills need not make them ashamed.

It is my earnest hope that indigent male and female students of the new university will be encouraged to work in order to be able to meet their university expenses. The experience gained thereby will stand them in good stead in the struggle for survival in life. By making sacrifices, by being thrifty, and by working hard, such students will cutivate self-reliance and confidence. As experience has shown in American and German universities, many elements which, ordinarily, would have discouraged the average student and possibly caused him to be a failure in life, are usually encountered by such working students with remarkable fortitude and determination to rely on his own resources to succeed, no matter the handicaps. Later in life, he can always recount the turning point of his life with pride.

It is my fondest wish that when the University of Nigeria ultimately becomes a reality, our young men and women will find opportunities for gaining experience in life's battle, so that lack of money will not deter them from obtaining higher vocational education in any of the faculties or institutes of the university. I hope that the training in self-help and the experience in self-reliance will make them more confident of themselves and enable them to puncture the myth of the proverbial lack of initiative and drive on the part of the Nigerian worker.

Finally, I trust that, with the establishment of this university, it will be complementary with the Ibadan University College, co-operating with it, drawing inspiration from its efforts, and gaining experience from this pioneer institution of higher education in this country.

Sir, I beg to second.

A speech delivered on April 11, 1958, moving a Motion in the Eastern House of Assembly for the Second Reading of a Bill entitled The University of Nigeria (Provisional Council) Law, 1958.

Mr Speaker, I move that a Bill for a Law to provide for the establishment of a Provisional Council to be known as the Provisional Council of the University of Nigeria and for matters ancillary thereto be read a second time.

Three years ago, this House passed the University of Nigeria Law, No. 23 of 1955, which provided for the establishment of a University of Nigeria 'so soon as may be after the commencement of the Law'. When the House discussed the provisions of the Law and finally took its decision it was the intention to start a University as soon as possible. It has now been possible for us to implement the provisions of that Law.

I have on another occasion stressed the need in this Region for a University and our determination to establish a University which, at least, we can with pride leave for posterity. I recalled that there were oppositions from various quarters to the idea but I pointed out that the opposition could only come from people who, being fully aware of the value of a University and its influence in improving the general standards of any nation, were opposing the establishment of a University in our Region in order that we might continue to remain under-developed.

Every year we vote vast sums of money for sending our children to Universities in other parts of the world. We pay highly for the cost of transport to overseas countries and we get in return education adapted to fit the ways of living of other nations. Mr Speaker, I do not mean that it is a bad thing to know how the others live nor do I say that we should not allow ourselves to be influenced by the knowledge so acquired. Indeed we must, in order to keep abreast with modern trends, adopt the techniques and borrow the experiences of other nations. It is nevertheless imperative that we must have education which is fundamentally Nigerian in content. Only in a University of our own can our culture shine forth.

As the various services in the Region expand, we need more trained people for the public services, and although we are increasing our effort to produce University trained personnel, the rate at which the services are expanding is greater than the rate at which we are producing material for filling the vacancies. Ibadan University, which serves the whole of Nigeria, turns out only a handful of graduates every year and we are forced to continue to go round the world begging for admission into Universities. This is bound to continue until we are able to establish in our own land a University which will serve our own needs, and this Government has now come to the threshold of establishment of such a University.

Under Section 7 of the University of Nigeria Law, there is provision for the establishment of a Council which will control the finances of the University and which will be the supreme governing body of the University with power to manage all matters of the University. This body, however, is not a body corporate and cannot hold land, nor can it contract.

Section 3 of the law does provide for a body corporate which shall consist of the authorities of the University and the members of the staff and students of the University for the time being. It is established to 'have entire control of and superintendence over the general policy and property of the University College and may act in such manner as appears to it to be in the best interests of the University College'. It is this body which shall have perpetual succession and common seal and may in its corporate name sue and be sued.

As we approach detailed problems of establishing a University, it has become necessary that there should be a body which will be an administrative and executive unit to deal with the preliminary work of the University. There must be a body which will undertake the detailed planning in consultation with the architects and other organizations concerned. This body will also deal with the recruitment of the initial staff of the University.

It is not considered desirable that these functions should be performed by Government since the public will thereby know less about the progress of the University, and Government is apt to move more slowly than a specially constituted Council or Board. The need to ensure the independence of the University makes it necessary that Government should, from the outset, withdraw from any act that may pull the budding University into the tentacles of slow Government machinery.

The corporate body provided under Section 3 of the University of Nigeria Law cannot come into existence until the University is itself fully established, since its members will be the authorities and members of the University. It is therefore necessary that until the University is fully established, a temporary or a provisional body should be set up to perform the preliminary duties which will precede the University and which are now pressing.

This same problem was encountered when the University College of Ibadan was established and the solution at that time was the same as we are now proposing, that is to say, the setting up of a provisional council.

Under Section 5 of the University College Ibadan (provisional

287

Council) Ordinance No. 25 of 1948, it was provided that '(1) The Council shall be a body corporate having perpetual succession and a common seal. (2) The Council shall have power to sue and to be sued, to enter into contracts, to engage staff, and to take, purchase and hold all movable and immovable property whatsoever, whether the same is situate within Nigeria or elsewhere, and to grant, demise, alienate, or otherwise dispose of the same, and to do all other things incidental or appertaining to a body corporate : Provided that the Council shall not alienate, mortgage, charge, or demise any of its immovable property without the approval in writing of the Governor in Council.'

In fact, the provision of this Provisional Council Law is not unique and is the natural step to take for building an institution such as is contemplated. It is unfortunate that this point was not taken up when the University of Nigeria Bill was passed into Law so that provision could be made for the setting up of such a temporary body to deal with the initial problems of the University.

The Bill seeks to restrict the total membership of the Provisional Council to five of which one shall be a Chairman. This is because the nature of the duties which the Council will perform requires that it must not be unwieldy. They must be able to meet as often as possible at short notice and will frequently have to take quick decisions. This cannot be achieved by a Council with many members and it will be difficult to find large numbers of able men who will be available to devote their time for such duties. For this reason the Bill also provides for a quorum of three.

As Honourable Members will observe, the Council shall be a body corporate having perpetual succession, the power to hold land and a common seal. It shall also have power to do all things which appear to it to be requisite and necessary for the establishment of the University of Nigeria in accordance with the provisions of the University of Nigeria Law, 1955.

Mr Speaker, I beg to move.

*From an address delivered by Dr Nnamdi Azikiwe at the Summer
School Convocation held in the Main Auditorium of Michigan
State University at East Lansing, Mich., U.S.A., on July 10,
1959.*

When the Government of Eastern Nigeria decided, on April 19,
1954, to send an Economic Mission to Europe and the United
States of America, of a sufficient status and authority as would
ensure that it would be well received and that its enquiries and
proposals would be accorded the respect they deserved, it made
as one of the terms of reference of this Mission the objective : 'to
make arrangements for facilitating higher vocational education in
Eastern Nigeria'.

In its report which was submitted to the Governor of Eastern
Nigeria on May 10, 1955, the Mission postulated the philosophy
of education which should animate the operation of a University
in Eastern Nigeria. It recommended that a full-fledged university
should be established without further delay. It held that such a
higher institution of learning should not only be cultural, according to the classical concept of universities, but it also should be
vocational in its objective and Nigerian in its content.

The Mission recommended that the curricula of the University
should be related to the day-to-day life of Nigerians and it should
be so organized as to relate its mission to the social and economic
needs of Eastern Nigeria. It recommended further that the University should start with six Faculties—Arts, Science, Law, Theology,
Engineering and Medicine, in addition to certain Institutes which
should be established for the professional and technical education
of men and women on whom the Government must rely heavily
as leaders in the difficult years of nation-building.

The recommendation of the Mission for the establishment of a
University was based on the philosophy which animated the
founding of Hampton and Tuskegee Institutes in America, on the
one hand, and the enactment of the Morrill Act in 1862, which
provided for the broadening of higher education by the founding
of land grant colleges in each State in the U.S.A., which would be
fully equipped to offer courses in such branches of learning as

were related to agriculture and mechanical arts, without excluding other scientific and classical studies, in order to promote the liberal and practical education of the communities as a whole.

The Economic Mission further recommended that such a university should be co-educational to enable female and male students to engage together in academic, vocational and co-curricula activities in developing their personalities, on a higher educational level, in an atmosphere which should inculcate in students not only the dignity of labour but also the idea that by hard work, sacrifice and self-determination, a poor student can obtain University education. In other words, the Economic Mission recommended that education should be employed as an instrument of social change for the building of a new society in Africa.

Later in 1955, the University of Nigeria Law was enacted by the Legislature of Eastern Nigeria. The Government immediately gave directive to one of its statutory corporations to creat a University of Nigeria Fund from December 31, 1955, by depositing £500,000 annually in it until December 31, 1964. Since then, the Eastern Regional Marketing Board has been committing £500,000 of its profit annually to create a University of Nigeria Fund which, at June 30, 1959, stood at £2,250,000. This Fund will continue to grow until December 31, 1964, when the Government will review the position, but by that time the University is expected to have the sum of £5,000,000 to its credit.

It is expected to begin construction of the main buildings of the University by the last quarter of the current year, in which case it is hoped that the first classes of the University may start their first quarter on September 12, 1960. There will be five Faculties to begin with, namely: Arts, Science, Engineering, Law and Theology. These will be supplemented by 26 Institutes or Colleges, as follows: Agriculture, Architecture, Commerce, Diplomacy, Domestic Science, Dramatics, Education, Finance, Fine Arts, Fishery, Forestry, Journalism, Languages, Librarianship, Medical Laboratory Technology, Military Studies, Music, Nursing, Pharmacy, Physical Education, Public Administration, Public Health,

Secretarial Studies, Social Work, Surveying and Veterinary Science.

The authorities of London University have given assurance of co-operation if the University of Nigeria wishes to consummate special arrangements with this world-renowned British higher institution of learning. Efforts will be made to take advantage of this generous offer, particularly in the fields of Accountancy, Banking, Estate Management, Insurance, Law, Military Studies, Music, Pharmacy and Theology, to enable graduates of the University of Nigeria to obtain qualifications which are recognizable by their opposite numbers in the United Kingdom and elsewhere in these fields.

It is also planned to contact certain professional bodies in the United Kingdom in order to come to an arrangement whereby the University can plan its curricula to enable its students to compete on the basis of equality with their counterparts in the British Isles for obtaining registrable British qualifications in the following fields: Accountancy, Architecture (including Town Planning), Banking, Dietetics, Engineering, Insurance, Librarianship, Medical Laboratory Technology, Pharmacy, Public Administration, Public Health, Secretaryship, Social Work, and Surveying (including Estate Management, Property Valuation, and Quantity Surveying).

Avenues are being explored in order to take advantage of the rich experience of Michigan State University, as the first agricultural college which set the pattern for the world-famous land grant college system in the United States of America. This system of University learning has broadened the base of higher education and spread the concept that university education is something in which all the communities concerned have a stake. The curricula of certain courses in the University of Nigeria will be based on this land-grant college idea, as practised by Michigan State University since its founding in 1855 and in other American land-grant universities. These courses will include Agriculture, Business Management, Domestic Science, Education, Engineering, Fine Arts, Fishery, Forestry, Journalism, Music, Physical Education, Social Work and Veterinary Science.

Events are moving in Africa at such a cyclonic pace that those who have been in the vanguard of the struggle for human freedom in that continent must plan for constructive leadership, otherwise the silent revolution which has gripped Africa will not bring happiness to its teeming millions. The aim of reforms should be to bring about healthy and desirable changes in society, otherwise our struggle for political freedom will be meaningless, since it would be an avenue to enable power-seekers and political opportunists to give a false impression to the outide world that Africans are incapable of making democracy work as a way of life.

It is to avoid creating a vacuum in Nigerian society, after the attainment of its independence, that the idea of a University of Nigeria was born. It was conceived that such a Temple of Knowledge should be so organized as to give physical and spiritual poise to Nigerians and facilitate the development of their personalities as free men and free women in a free world. The University should teach skills to its students, and it should challenge them to build a brave new world where man shall no longer be a wolf to his fellow man. It should imbue those who study within its portals with a sense of mission in the building of a new nation.

We are founding the University of Nigeria in order to create a glorious opportunity for ambitious men and women, young and old, who have the aptitude and the vision to prepare themselves for greater service to their communities. Through its Faculties we hope to harness our human, animal, agricultural and mineral resources in order to expand our economy by raising living standards and ushering an era of material prosperity to our people, whilst at the same time developing their mental faculties in such a way that they will guard jealously the fundamental rights of man.

Since our contact with the British, my people have passed through the crucible of tutelage in the art and practice of democracy. Those of us who were educated in this country have venerated the ideals of American democracy. In my country today, we practise the rule of law, we respect human dignity, and we guarantee the freedom of speech, freedom of peaceful assembly, freedom of movement, freedom of worship, and the right to enjoy property.

It is my fervent hope that the proposed University will also be a medium through which my people will vindicate unequivocally the soundness of democracy, not only as a way of life but as a government by discussion, based on the consent of the governed, whose will is expressed through the majority of the accredited representatives of the electorate.

A speech made as Chairman of the Provisional Council, at the inaugural meeting of the Provisional Council of the University of Nigeria, held in the Conference Room of the Premier's Lodge, at Enugu, on 3rd March, 1960.

I have laid on the table of the Provisional Council of the University of Nigeria eight official documents which expound the policy formulated by the Government of the Eastern Region in respect of the new University of Nigeria. It is now my duty to make a formal report about the progress which has been made so far before this Council assumes responsibility to discharge its functions according to law.

Like any corporate body, we are enjoined to function as a board of directors, but in our case, it is in a dual capacity, until the University Council formally assumes responsibility. In the first place, we are expected to function as a board of trustees charged with the management of the finance and properties of the University before it begins to operate. Secondly, we are charged with the duty to function as a Senate for the organization and administration of the University in all academic matters, including teaching, research and discipline.

Prior to my reporting what the Government of the Eastern Region had done in connection with the establishment of the University, before formally handing responsibility over to us, it is pertinent that I should, at this stage, remind you of four factors which lie at the background of the philosophy animating the founding of the University of Nigeria. They are as follows:

(1) Its nationalist content so as to preserve the identity of the African, as expressed by the National Congress of British West

293

Africa when the struggle for national self-determination was at its earliest beginning.[1]

(2) Its economic objective in order to provide for the requirements of industry, commerce and society.[2]

(3) Its cultural and vocational nature for community service, as analysed in the report of the Economic Mission to Europe and North Africa.[3]

(4) Its revolutionary character in attempting to blend the 'land-grant college' idea with the classical concept of universities and adapt both to the changing circumstances of contemporary Nigerian society.

The Nigerian situation has placed the founders of the University of Nigeria in a dilemma in view of the fact that the British traditional concept of University education has taken deep root in this country. With the evolution of Nigeria towards political independence, its statesmen have had to grapple with the problem of replacing expatriate executives and managerial experts in the Public Services, mercantile, transport, banking, mining, and other establishments of the country. The Government of the Eastern Region thus decided to accept the recommendations of its Economic Mission to Europe and North America by energetically making arrangements for providing professional and vocational training locally, particularly in the following fields of specialization:

(1) *Agriculture.* It was felt that this is vitally important in a country like Nigeria whose economy is basically agricultural, and it was decided that emphasis should be placed on such ancillary subjects as veterinary science, forestry, fisheries, etc.; for obvious reasons.

(2) *Engineering.* In an under-developed country like Nigeria, the dearth of engineers exposes the urgent need for locally-trained technologists to design, construct and maintain works that are

[1] See Resolution No. 2 entitled 'Education with Particular Reference to a West African University' in *Resolutions of the Conference of the Africans of British West Africa, held at Accra, Gold Coast, from 15th to 29th March, 1920.*

[2] See Chapter 1 of *Report of a Technical College Organization for Nigeria,* laid on the Table of the Legislative Council as Sessional Paper No. 11 of 1950.

[3] See *Economic Rehabilitation of Eastern Nigeria,* Sessional Paper No. 6 of 1955, laid on the Table of the Eastern House of Assembly.

needed for the expansion of the economy of the country and for raising its living standards.

(3) *Education*. With the formidable expansion of universal primary education, which has placed Nigeria at the top of the list of other countries in Africa, it was quite obvious that there is need for a continuous supply of well-qualified teachers for elementary and secondary school systems.

(4) *Commerce*. Apart from being the most populated country in the continent of Africa, Nigeria has emulated Britain by becoming a nation of shop-keepers, who in the main are ignorant of the principles of business administration, accounting and personnel management. Moreover, most of the unemployed Nigerians in the business profession are unemployable because they have not been efficiently trained to acquire skill in any of the exercises of secretarial studies.

(5) *Home Economics*. The role of home life in the development of civilized society cannot be minimized. Its functions, the nature of individuality, the beginnings of social change, problems raised in domestic relations, labour-saving machinery in the home, nutrition and dietetics, new status of women, etc.—these are among social and economic problems which confront the modern Nigerian. Higher education in Home Economics will make for a more stable and enlightened society in Nigeria.[1]

The problems of higher education which confronted the American nation in the nineteenth century and confront other emerging nations today are identical with those which face us in Nigeria. It will not be amiss if, therefore, we profit from the lessons of the more advanced countries. In formulating its policy for the establishment of the University of Nigeria, the Government of the Eastern Region was obliged to make a radical departure from the usual practice of university administration and organization and the result is the emergence of fourteen distinctive characteristics which will distinguish the University of Nigeria from others in West Africa. These characteristics are as follows :

(1) It will not be exclusively residential but it will also accommodate external students who may reside outside the precincts of the University.

[1] See Chapters I and IV in Thomas Jesse Jones, *Four Essentials of Education* (Scribner's, New York : 1926).

(2) It will not only blend professional-cum-vocational higher education, but it will create an atmosphere of social equality between the two types of students.

(3) It will adapt the 'land-grant college' philosophy of higher education with the classical tradition in an African environment.

(4) It will cater for a larger number of student members to specialize on a variety of courses, whilst maintaining the highest academic standards.

(5) It will not restrict the number of its students purely on the basis of the potential absorption of its graduates into vacant jobs within the territorial limits of Nigeria.

(6) It will spread its activities over a wide range of fields of human endeavour to enable the average student to specialize on the basis of his aptitude.

(7) Its sources of income will, in addition to the regular practice in the United Kingdom,[1] include earnings from its agricultural and commercial estates.

(8) Its curriculum will be prepared not only to measure up to the highest standards of the older universities of Europe and America, but efforts will be made to emphasize the problems created in the environments of Nigeria and Africa: e.g. Nigerian History, Nigerian Geography, Nigerian Literature, Economic History of Nigeria, African Ethnography, etc.

(9) The Foundation Loan Scholarships are a device to overcome the shortage of man-power in certain specialized fields either in the Public Services or in other spheres of employment in the country.[2]

(10) The Foundation Post-Graduate Bursaries are intended to quicken the pace of Nigerianization in the academic staff of the University.

(11) The acquisition of 1,000 acres of land for the site of the University and a further acquisition of 10,000 acres of land for agricultural and commercial estates are unique in the history of higher education in this part of the world.

(12) Competent academic staff will be recruited not exclusively from any particular country or race, but it is intended to cast the net wide over an extensive area, in all continents of the

[1] See Tables 10–11a in *Returns from Universities and University Colleges in Receipt of Treasury Grant, Academic Year 1957–58* (Cmnd. 832 of 1959).

[2] See discussion on loans to students in American universities in C. E. Lovejoy, *Complete Guide to American Colleges and Universities* (Simon and Schuster, New York: 1948), p. 11.

earth, among suitably qualified and experienced English-speaking University teachers, who will be provided with the opportunity to maintain contact with intellectual and academic life in the outside world.

(13) It will be the first time in the history of higher education in Nigeria when students will be able to study locally the ancient, modern and African languages up to degree standard.

(14) Its Stadium is intended to become a social centre where international goodwill can be fostered among athletes who represent the various universities of the African continent and other parts of the world.

With a chequered background of this nature, you will like to know what the Government of the Eastern Region has actually done in the form of a legacy which it now bequeaths to the Provisional Council. In 1955–56, the University of Nigeria Law was enacted, and in 1956 and 1958 this law was amended. On May 15, 1958, the Provisional Council Law came into operation and on June 4, 1959, an amending law also came into operation. The last two legislations created the Provisional Council, defined its functions, and clarified its relationship with the Government. Official Documents No. 2 of 1958 and No. 4 of 1958 are concerned with the preparation and publication of the Cook-Hannah-Taggert Report. Official Document No. 7 of 1959 brings the activities of the Government up to the end of 1959.

As a result of pressure brought to bear on the Government, in political as well as in other circles, it became clear as crystal that unless action was taken to provide the Region with a university, in the immediate future, it would become an election issue at any future elections. Thus an educational mission was officially sent to the United States in June 1959 under the leadership of the then Premier, and after exchanging views with the authorities of the ICA, Michigan State University and the University of New Hampshire, it was announced that the doors of the University would be officially opened on 12th September, 1960.

Not to be accused of bureaucratic inertia, which is a common disease in governmental circles, twelve definite steps have been taken in order to impress upon the legislature and the Opposition Parties that the Government was in earnest.

(1) The Ministry of Town Planning compulsorily acquired 1,000 acres of land under the relevant law for public purposes absolutely, namely, the construction of buildings, etc., in connection with the University of Nigeria.

(2) The same Ministry is further acquiring 10,000 acres of land in Nsukka Division for the purpose of agricultural and commercial estates of the University.

(3) The Ministry of Town Planning, in co-operation with the Ministry of Local Government, the Ministry of Works, and the office of the Premier, established the Nsukka Town Planning Authority not only to discourage squatters but also to ensure a rational development of the University estate and the Nsukka Township.

(4) The Hon. Premier, as Minister charged with responsibility for the University, obtained the services of Messrs James Cubitt and Partners, Architects in the United Kingdom, to advise him on the preliminary aspects of the initial problems facing higher institutions of this type. They were paid for their services.

(5) In view of the fact that the town of Nsukka will be a show piece of the Region, when the University begins to function, direction was given by the Hon. Premier, as Minister charged with responsibility for the University, to have all the streets and approach roads of Nsukka surfaced with bitumen. This involves a total of 20 miles and the work is now in hand.

(6) On November 14, 1959, a contract was negotiated for the construction of 1 Stadium to accommodate at least 30,000 spectators, 4 Association Football Fields, 12 Tennis Courts, 1 Special Tennis Court, 1 Golf Link, and the tarring of 10 miles of streets in Nsukka and 10 miles of roads within one mile approach of Nsukka Township.

(7) On December 8, 1959, a contract was negotiated for the construction of a block of flats, and bungalows to house at least 120 Professors, Lecturers, and Assistant Lecturers, in addition to six special residential quarters to house the Chancellor, Principal, Registrar, Bursar, Librarian, and Engineer of the University.

(8) On December 8, 1959, a contract was also negotiated for the construction of the following : 4 classroom blocks of buildings to house the Faculties of Arts, Science, and Engineering, in addition to an Administration Centre; 8 Halls of Residence (each to house at least 250 students), 8 offices and classrooms to house a number of Colleges, 16 offices and classrooms to house a

298

number of Colleges, 1 Library building and 60 Junior Service quarters.

(9) The Ministry of Works has contracted with the Electricity Corporation of Nigeria to supply the University with electricity, and Government has spent almost £40,000 for this project. It is expected that the University Electricity Undertaking will be in operation by July 1960.

(10) The Ministry of Works has co-operated at the initial stages of the water supply project for the University and a contract was negotiated with a British firm which sank a number of boreholes successfully. If desired by the Provisional Council, the Ministry of Works is prepared to undertake to make available sufficient water supply for the University before its formal opening.

(11) After Mr Al. Mansfield, Associate Professor at Technicon, Israel Institute of Technology, Haifa, had completed his assignment with the Government of the Eastern Region, in connection with the Independent Layout at Enugu, I, as Chairman of the Provisional Council, enlisted his co-operation in preparing a Preliminary Scheme of Lay-out for the University, which is submitted to this Council for approval, since it is the best so far in our possession.

(12) Early this year, the Honourable Minister of Agriculture instructed the Eastern Regional Marketing Board to transfer the sum of £2,500,000 to the Provisional Council to enable it to fulfil the numerous financial commitments of the University as indicated above. In a letter dated February 9, 1960, the Acting General Manager of the African Continental Bank Limited informed me of this transfer and assured me of the preparedness of the Bank to carry out the instructions of the Council.

Members of the Provisional Council, this concludes my progress report on the activities of the Government of the Eastern Region before transferring responsibility to the Provisional Council. Whilst it is true that the Council is autonomous and has its distinct function to perform according to law, nevertheless, we cannot overlook the overriding factor of ministerial control as is the case in other statutory bodies. As one who formerly exercised power of control over the University of Nigeria, before the operations of the Provisional Council, I must allay your fears that there will be any burdensome interference by officialdom in the performance of our duties, and I know that it has never been the intention of the Government either to violate academic freedom or to make the smooth functioning of its statutory bodies impossible.

By taking into consideration all that has happened in the past, before our assumption of duty, and grappling with the problem of building the University of Nigeria with a sense of mission and dedication, I implore you to join me in creating this higher institution of learning so as to implement the policy formulated by its founders. If we succeed in establishing this University we shall have done five things:

(1) We will have created an opportunity for the youth of Nigeria to give play to their talent which is latent.
(2) We will have provided skill for the clumsy hands of the unskilled.
(3) We will have enlarged the vision of those who are circumscribed by historical forces.[1]
(4) We will have restored hope to a frustrated people, who are groping in despair whilst at the threshold of political freedom.
(5) We will have answered critics who, whilst well-meaning, betray unnecessary apprehension at the speed with which the ultimate mental emancipation of a colonial territory in transition towards total political manumission is being consummated.[2]

[1] 'By all means, get a university, but get a university whose teachers are not subject to outside control and influence, and who have studied local conditions. The success of this would depend on African teachers of education and vision. First train elementary school teachers, and after such teachers show that they can succeed with the elementary grades, train next for the secondary level, and then finally university teachers.' See comments of Professor-Emeritus W. H. Kilpatrick of Teachers College, Columbia University, on the memorandum of the African Students Association of the United States and Canada to the Elliott Commission on Higher Education in West Africa in *Africa: Today and Tomorrow*, April 1945, p. 48 (published by the African Academy of Arts and Research, 55 West 42nd Street, New York).

[2] See 'Another Million Dollar Baby?' *West Africa*, No. 1996, May 28, 1955, pp. 481–82.

CHAPTER 17

ZIK ON THE DEVELOPMENT OF POLITICAL PARTIES IN NIGERIA

An address delivered at Rhodes House, Oxford University, on June 11, 1957, under the chairmanship of Sir David Keir, Master of Balliol College, Oxford.

The development of political parties in Nigeria and the Southern Cameroons cannot be divorced from the pattern which obtains in other parts of the world where parliamentary democracy has been accepted as the standard of political behaviourism. The genesis of political parties stems from the idea of majority rule which is fundamental to the ideology of democracy. Though this statement may appear rudimentary, yet it is important, for the purpose of clarity, that a careful evaluation be made of the evolution of political parties as an institution.

Aristotle did say that man is a political animal. By this statement he is usually understood in the literature of political science to mean the sociability of man as a human being. Thomas Hobbes, John Locke and Jean-Jacques Rousseau postulated the theory of the social contract to the effect that the grouping of individuals in a society implies the existence of a compact in which such individuals tacitly surrender their absolute rights to an agency known as government, which can only exist on the consent of the governed. According to Hobbes, strife motivated the need for such a compact. Locke thought that licentiousness made it imperative. Rousseau added that it was necessary for the maintenance of law and order so that the compact was by *volonté générale*.

It is not natural to expect unanimity of opinion among human beings, if we bear in mind the psychological nature of humanity. A criterion for measuring the popular will is thus a necessity. The concept of majority rule has emerged to give concrete expression to what is vaguely referred to as public opinion with which the ideology of democracy is coterminous. In the words of an American authority, 'Each individual surrendered to the community his right to execute natural law; hence the minority must be bound by the will of the majority, who might use force, if necessary.'

Lord Bryce held the view that 'The word democracy has been used ever since the time of Herodotus to denote that form of government in which the ruling power of a State is largely vested, not in any particular class or classes, but in the members of the community as a whole. . . . This means, in communities which act by voting, that rule belongs to the majority, as no other method has been found for determining peacefully and legally what is to be declared the will of a community which is not unanimous.' It is quite obvious that once we place it on record that we seek to attain the goal of political democracy in our country then we have tacitly admitted the importance of political parties as an instrument for the crystallization of public opinion. This is an expressed acceptance of the idea of majority rule.

Bearing the foregoing in mind, we can define a political party in the words of the French sociologist, Gustav Le Bon, to mean 'individuals differing greatly as to their education, their professions, and the class of society to which they belong, and with their common beliefs as the connecting link.' That is to say, a political party is an organization of voters, freely and voluntarily formed, for the attainment of common ends; there is, however, an irresistible tendency actually to control the reins of government, and in so doing, there is a concentration of power in the hands of few people who are willing and have the time and ability to practice those arts by means of which the executive control is obtained and exercised.

Since in any political society there must be conflict of views and clash of opinions on a range of issues, it is but rational that those who hold substantially similar views upon any subject should draw together into co-operative effort in order to attain these ends. Edmund Burke put it this way : 'Party is a body of men united for promoting by their joint endeavours the national interest, upon some particular principle in which they are all agreed.' It is now universally acknowledged that party control is essential to the efficient working of democracy.

The objects of political parties are *inter alia* :

(a) Disseminating of political propaganda and doctrines of the party, accomplished through the press, pulpit, radio, films, and other organs and media for the expression of public opinion; it is especially vigorous in periods preceding elections.

(b) Formulation of positive policies which find expression in party platforms or manifestoes and other official pronouncements of party leaders.

(c) Nomination of candidates for public offices, and pledging of the votes of the party for its candidates.

(d) Conducting of election campaigns involving the use of every conceivable device for convincing and persuading the electorate that the policies which its candidates represent are preferable to those of their rivals.

(e) Control, after elections, of the policy-forming organs of government so as to materialize the principles embodied in the party platform.

Professors Ogg and Ray, two American scholars, have enumerated the following among the functions of political parties :

(a) Keeping the people informed on public matters.

(b) Discussing public questions in the presence of the people.

(c) Securing not only discussion before the people but (what is quite as important) discussion by the people.

(d) Selecting and bringing forward candidates for public office.

(e) Serving in some measures as sureties for the satisfactory performance of the official duties of such persons after elections.

(f) Constituting the most important channel through which the ordinary citizen can exert a direct influence in the formulation of public policy.

Now that we have clarified the nature, objects and functions of political parties, we should as a natural corollary follow with interest the development of political parties in Nigeria and the Southern Cameroons since our historical connection with Great Britain. On this score, we must bear in mind an excellent study on the growth of political parties in Africa in which the author explained that it took three patterns : pressure groups, nationalist movements, and political parties proper.

The first category was defined as 'an organization which endeavours among other things to *influence*, but not to control government on behalf of the special interests of its members.' The second was defined as 'An organization formed to achieve self-government . . . or to secure absolute political equality within a broader Euro-African grouping . . . or within a plural society.' The third was defined as 'An organization which competes with other similar organizations in periodical elections in order to participate in formal institutions and thereby influence and control the personnel and policy of government.' [1]

Up to the year 1922, there was no well-established political party in Nigeria, if we judge by the yardstick I have outlined above. There were sporadic attempts to organize pressure groups in order to register protest against certain measures in which their sponsors had interest. These organizations had a protracted existence and some of them soon disappeared from the horizon of Nigerian politics. The amalgamation of Northern and Southern Nigeria, the enactment of the Provincial Courts Ordinance, the introduction of water rate into Lagos, the creation of paper currency for circulation in Nigeria, the agitation for recognition of the House of Docemo, these were among the political topics which commanded the attention of the Nigerian public and filled the columns of local newspapers.

Perhaps the oldest established political party in Nigeria is the Nigerian National Democratic Party (NNDP) which was founded in 1922 by the late Herbert Macaulay and supported by the leading nationalists of the day. I will say more about the NNDP in due course. It was opposed by the Peoples Union, which was said to be controlled by Dr J. K. Randle, Dr Orisadipe Obasa of Ikija, Sir Kitoyi Ajasa, Dr R. Akinwande Savage, Sir Adeyemo Alakija and others.

The policy of the Peoples Union may be said to be conservative, compared to the NNDP whose policy was radical. The political

<hr>

[1] James S. Coleman, 'The Emergence of African Political Parties', reproduced in C. Grove Haines, *Africa Today* (Baltimore: 1955), pp. 226–7.

status quo was regarded as ideal by the Peoples Union and any changes were to be gradual. This view was opposed by the NNDP which wanted complete enfranchisement of the people of Lagos and advocated a series of reforms as contained in the petition of the National Congress of British West Africa to His Majesty's Government in 1920.

The Women's Union formed a sort of counterpart of the Peoples Union and was led by Mrs Olajumoke Obasa, wife of Dr Orisadipe Obasa and a wealthy transport owner. She was a daughter of the very wealthy Nigerian merchant, F. O. Blaize, one of the original shareholders of the Bank of British West Africa.

Among the leading lights of the NNDP, besides its founder Herbert Macaulay, were Dr C. C. Adeniyi-Jones, J. Egerton Shyngle, Thomas Horatio Jackson, Karimu Kotun, J. T. White and Dr J. T. Caulcrick. The party's aims and objectives included self-government within the British Empire and 'to identify itself wholly and solely with the interests of the people; to co-operate with the important units of the majority elements of the community and to stand loyally by the people and share equally with them the vicissitudes of life under the aegis of the new Constitution.' The NNDP won all the three seats for Lagos at the elections to the Legislative Council from 1923 to 1938, and from 1943 to 1948. It also won all the seats available by election to the Lagos Town Council, from 1923 to 1953.

Today, the NNDP is an associate member of the National Council of Nigeria and the Cameroons and it restricts its activities to the contesting of the Lagos Town Council elections in alliance with NCNC, the Lagos Market Women's Association and the Labour Front. After the death of Herbert Macaulay, a schism occurred in the rank and file of the NNDP and two wings emerged. The more active wing is now in active alliance with the NCNC whilst the other wing enjoys an exiguous political existence of suspended animation.

By 1923, a young lawyer had just returned from the United Kingdom and he contacted a number of other professionals to form the Union of Young Nigerians (UYN). Chief Ayo Williams steered the fortunes of the UYN until it evanesced, following successive defeats of its candidates at elections to the Legislative Council and the Lagos Town Council. It is significant that Chief Williams joined the NNDP subsequently and became its successful candidate in one of the municipal elections. In 1938, he was instrumental in forming the Nigeria Union of Young Democrats.

Before discussing the major and minor political parties of contemporary Nigeria, I should pay attention to two youth organizations because of the impact they have had on the evolution of our country as a political entity. The first is the Nigeria Youth League Movement, which was the sole copyright of Mr Eyo Ita, who had dreamt of this semi-politico-cultural body when he was a student in New York, at the Teachers College, Columbia University. He conceived the functions of his League to be based on 'Five Fingers' which he called Health and Economicity (*sic*), Beauty, Knowledge, Patriotism, Religion. He thought that by developing certain industries he could integrate manual labour with nation-building, and he called upon Nigerian youth to come forward and save Nigerian society. Mr Ita's ideas appeared nebulous excepting for his concrete programme in building a secondary school in Calabar. These are some of his intellectual meanderings:

This is the day of Nigeria youth. It must build a new social order, for whereas yesterday belonged to our fathers and their distant future belongs to posterity, today and the immediate tomorrow are ours. We can and must shape them according to our needs and desires. . . . The time has come when the young people of Calabar must live creatively, must build new and better homes, must bring new forms to birth in literature, language, arts, music, methods and tools of industry, when they must dream of purer and juster laws and promote better health. . . .

We must secure bare living first before we can think of the luxuries of life—*Iton odu uwem okono nqua.* . . . Calabar is a land of beauty. Nigeria is a land of beauty. Our sons and daughters must reveal its concealed beauties through the use of pencil and colour. . . . Calabrian youth, like the knights of old, and like the militant youths of modern Russia, who volunteer to save their society at all cost, must pledge themselves to give themselves completely to the cause of emancipating Calabar. The love of Calabar must consume us. The zeal for her emancipation must be our food and drink. We are either Calabrians or nothing. To the degree in which Calabar is saved to that degree shall we be saved. . . .

Our God is He who cares for our homes, our womanhood, our childhood, the moral manhood of our race, our economic welfare, our health, and our political freedom, Who respects the beauty of the black man no less than He is interested in the other races of mankind. This God speaks to us through the fruits of our land, through the animals that inhabit it, through the love and fellowship of our darling mothers and friends. He is the God of Nigeria, her abiding genius, her sustaining power. The youth must realize that it is serving His cause through the activities of its movement. It must realize that the whole of Nigeria is a supreme value before God, and that its creative work is part of the vast plan of the Divine Conserver of our values.

These ideas of Mr Ita appeared to the people of Nigeria as partly utopian and partly parochial. The fact that the Nigeria Youth League Movement was dedicated to the glorification of Calabar youth and that a Calabar National Institute was founded by Mr Ita in Calabar made Nigerians question the universality of Mr Ita's conception of human brotherhood. There is no record that Mr Ita's League had popular support. It was not until twenty-five years later, when he came all out to advocate the cause of the Calabar-Ogoja-Rivers State Movement and to beat the tom-tom drums of alleged Ibo domination that Mr Ita's secret antagonism against certain tribes became obvious. These points should be borne in mind when the policy and programme of the C-O-R State Movement are subsequently examined.

Nevertheless, the desirable aspects of Mr Ita's philosophy of nationhood appeared to have influenced the thinking of Nigerians and, in 1933, the Lagos Youth Movement (LYM) was founded by Dr James Churchill Vaughan, Ernest Sissei Ikoli, Samuel A. Akin-sanya (now Odemo of Ishara) and other Nigerian nationalists resident in Lagos. Adopting a salute based on the raising of the right or left index finger above the head, in obeisance to God, the LYM attracted to its fold some of the intelligentsia of the country. By 1937, a brilliant Nigerian had returned home from the United Kingdom in the person of Hezekiah Oladipo Davies, who became the General Secretary of the Movement, and the name of the

Movement was changed from Lagos to Nigerian Youth Movement.

The NYM Charter and Constitution explains its mission as follows:

The principal aim of the NYM is the development of a united nation out of the conglomeration of peoples who inhabit Nigeria. It shall be our endeavour to encourage the fullest play of all such forces as will serve to promote complete understanding and a sense of common nationality among different elements in the country. We will combat vigorously all such tendencies as would jeopardize the unifying process. . . .

In its Political Charter, its goal was stated to be 'complete autonomy within the British Empire':

We are striving towards a position of equal partnership with other member states of the British Commonwealth of Nations, and of enjoying complete independence in the local management of our affairs. This political end of the NYM is coterminous with that repeatedly declared by His Majesty's Government as the goal of British connection with Nigeria.

The Economic Charter pledged the NYM 'to demand for our people economic opportunities equal to those enjoyed by foreigners'. It envisaged a 'First Five Years' Economic Plan', 'The Cent-a-Club', and also expressed opinion in respect of some projects devised to safeguard the economic integrity of the African. Its Cultural and Social Charter embraced the problems of education and health.

Perhaps in the most conspicuous pronouncements of the NYM, viewed in the light of contemporary affairs, is the restatement of its aims in its Constitution which reads:

The objects of the NYM are:

1. To unify the different tribes of Nigeria by adopting and encouraging means which would foster better understanding and co-operation between the tribes so that they may come to have a common ideal. . . .

4. To identify itself in a wholehearted and selfless manner with the interest of the people, irrespective of class or any other distinction, and to be always prepared to prosecute their legitimate aspirations with resolution, consistency and firmness.

308

The NYM tried to put into practice its professed policy. It contested the elections to the Legislative Council in 1938 and defeated the NNDP by winning all the three seats for Lagos. Among its leaders at this time were Dr Akinola Maja, H. S. A. Thomas, Jubril Martin and Mr (now Sir) Kofoworola Abayomi. Prominent among its back-benchers were Dr Nnamdi Azikiwe, Chief Obafemi Awolowo, Chief S. L. Akintola, J. A. Tuyo, Hamzat A. Subair, F. Ogugua-Arah, Shonibare and L. Duro Emmanuel.

When, in 1940, Dr Abayomi left Nigeria to study ophthalmology in the United Kingdom, his seat in the Legislative Council was declared vacant by the Governor. This led to what ultimately became a crisis in the party, because it split the Nigerian Youth Movement into two—one group supporting the candidature of S. A. Akinsanya, and another supporting that of Jubril Martin for the vacant seat. At a subsequent bye-election for another seat, the schism became pronounced because Akinsanya was supported by one group and Mr Ikoli was supported by another. It is significant that Mr Akinsanya's supporters held the view that an Ijebu member of a political party had as much right as any other member to stand for election and represent Lagos as a candidate of that party. Since the second split, the Nigerian Youth Movement never recovered and it ultimately degenerated into desuetude, to be succeeded by the Lagos Area Council, for purposes of municipal elections, and by the Action Group on a national scale.

By now, certain patriots were beginning to feel that whilst political parties were desirable, yet it was essential to make available to our people *facts*, in order to enable them to have an intelligent grasp of the problems confronting Nigeria and the Cameroons. It was felt that youths were not doing sufficient research work into the political, social, economic and cultural problems of Nigeria. For example, there was no need to criticize the Medical Department because of the paucity of hospitals in the country, if we were not in a position to indicate the ratio of the number of existing hospitals to the population. As a research body, to supply information to any person interested in the contemporary problems of Nigeria, especially in the post-war years, it was thought desirable to found an organization which should not necessarily be political in nature, but should be a fact-finding body to encourage research.

Founded early in 1942, this organization was christened the Nigeria Reconstruction Group. It limited its members to a select circle of intellectuals interested and willing to undertake research projects of a fact-finding nature. The members of the Nigeria Reconstruction Group, in alphabetical order, included B. O. S. Adophy, Dr Nnamdi Azikiwe, Moses O. Balonwu, S. I. Bosah, C. Enitan Brown, T. E. E. Brown, Henry Collins (a BNCO), Dr E. C. Erokwu, E. E. Esua, Dr Okoronkwo Ogan, M. E. R. Okorodudu, L. A. Onojobi, Dr T. O. na Oruwariye and Albert I. Osakwe. After having conducted research on various aspects of Nigerian life, particularly in the spheres of politics, economics, sociology and education, the Nigeria Reconstruction Group thought that the time had come for a National Front to be created in order to infuse into the people of Nigeria an idea of oneness and consciousness of kind. Once that had been done, if there were any grievances to be presented, these could be done constitutionally but with a united front, to avoid dissipation of national energy.

Again, the Nigeria Reconstruction Group thought that by the National Front enabling the various people of Nigeria and the Cameroons to present a united front, it would make easier the task of those who ruled the country, as they would be in position to know what was public opinion, at least from the majority point of view. Not to be misunderstood, the Nigeria Reconstruction Group disavowed any political ambitions; rather it decided to seek the co-operation of the Nigerian Youth Movement and to request that political body to spearhead this National Front.

The NYM was informed of the plans of the NRG; it was asked to take up the task of organizing the various political parties, tribal unions, trade unions, youth leagues, peasant organizations, professional associations, literary societies, and other social bodies, into one solid phalanx of a National Front. For six months this negotiation was carried out, but it ended abortively. As a last resort, an organization known as the Nigerian Youth Circle was contacted, through the good offices of Messrs H. O. Davies and J. M. Udochi. Both of these gentlemen attended one meeting of the NRG and some members of the NRG attended one meeting of the NYC, on the basis of reciprocity and goodwill; nevertheless, it was not possible to start a National Front, which was to be a new stage in the evolution of nationalism in Nigeria.

A Youth Rally was organized to take pace at Ojokoro, in November 1943. The Nigerian Youth Circle (NYC) and the Nigeria Union of Students played a prominent part in organizing it. At the Rally, many youths crowded this country estate of E. J. Alex-Taylor, and among those who addressed the audience were A. O. Thomas, Rotimi Williams, O. A. Alakija, H. O. Davies and Nnamdi Azikiwe. Members of the NYM, NRG, NYC, NUS and other organizations were at the head of various discussion groups, and resolutions were passed on many topics affecting the future of Nigeria. One of such resolutions was that the time had come for a National Front to be established and that the NYM should be called upon to spearhead it.

It is pertinent that I should say a few words about the Nigeria Union of Students, which was destined to make the idea of a National Front a reality. The NUS had its origin at the Abeokuta Grammar School, where it was founded in October 1939. Among its leaders were Adewale Fashanu, I. O. Dafe, Olubumi Thomas, B. B. Bamgbose and P. N. Malafa. Among its patrons were the following personalities: Rev. I. O. Ransome-Kuti, Herbert Macaulay, Dr Akinola Maja, Ernest S. Ikoli, Mrs Stella Marke, and Nnamdi Azikiwe. After waiting for almost six months, the NUS observed that no organization or individuals had been energetic in taking up the gauntlet in order to form a National Front, as was resolved at the historic Ojokoro Youth Rally.

The NUS organized mass meetings originally to start a National Education Fund and fruitlessly requested the trustees of the National School Fund to assist them. It was clear that there was vacillation on the political horizon of Nigeria, and with their youthful energy bubbling for action, the NUS issued a manifesto calling the people of Nigeria and the Cameroons to action for the establishment of a National Front. With the activities of the NUS should be studied the influence of the Resolution of the West African Students Union (WASU) in London, in 1942, calling for

311

internal self-government for British West Africa, and the memorandum issued by the West African press delegation in 1943, associating the Delegation with the demand for self-government. These ideas no doubt influenced the national consciousness already generating in Nigeria and the Cameroons.

A series of mass meetings was held in Lagos—the first two under the chairmanship of the Duse Mohamed Ali, Effendi. Many organizations were invited, including the NYM, NRG, NUS, Trades Union Congress, Nigeria Union of Teachers, and the Federal Union of Native Administrative Staffs, in addition to tribal unions, trade unions, literary societies, farmers' organizations, and professional associations (like the Bar Association and the organization of medical practitioners and dentists). Most of these responded and sent representatives.

On 26 August, 1944, the National Council of Nigeria and the Cameroons (NCNC) was born with the primary task of exerting mass pressure in order to accelerate the political development of the country. At the Third Meeting of the Inaugural Session of the NCNC, provisional officers were elected at a mass meeting assembled in the Glover Memorial Hall, as folows: President (Herbert Macaulay, G.R.I.B.A., A.M.I.C.E.), Vice President (The Venerable J. O. Lucas, M.A., D.D.), General Secretary (Nnamdi Azikiwe), Financial Secretary (Rev. A. M. Howells, M.A., B.D.), Treasurer (L. P. Ojukwu), Auditors (L. A. Onojobi and A. Ogedegbe), Legal Advisers (E. J. Alex-Taylor, J. E. C. David, the Hon., E. A. Akerele, O. A. Alakija, M.A., B.C.L., Ladipo Odunsi, and J. I. C. Taylor, M.A.).

Letters were forwarded by the Provisional General Secretary to the above gentlemen, dated 23 September, 1944. Some replied or sent messages giving reasons for their inability to accept office. Those who were willing to serve as the original officers of the NCNC included Herbert Macaulay, Nnamdi Azikiwe, L. A. Onojobi, A. Ogedegbe, E. A. Akerele, and Ladipo Odunsi. At a subsequent general meeting which was convened to confirm these elections and possibly make new ones, the acceptance or otherwise of office was announced. Mr Oyeshile Omage was elected

Financial Secretary and Dr the Honourable Abu Bakr Olorun-Nimbe, M.B., Ch.B., was elected Treasurer.

On this occasion, Herbert Macaulay delivered his inaugural address as the first National President of the NCNC, the text of which is treasured in the archives of the party as an immortal contribution to the political literature of Nigeria. This great oration, pregnant with earthly wisdom and based on experience of five decades of public life and service, has become the cornerstone which animates the philosophy of the National Council of Nigeria and the Cameroons.

After a series of constitutional conventions (whose members were Herbert Macaulay, Nnamdi Azikiwe, D. C. Osadebay, Dr A. O. Olorun-Nimbe, Prince A. Ibikunle-Akitoye, P. M. Kale, Ogunye and E. E. Esua, the NCNC Constitution was completed and subsequently adopted in 1945. Thenceforth it became the organic law of the party.

In its Constitution the objects of the NCNC were stated thus :

(1) To extend democratic principles and to advance the interests of the people of Nigeria and the Cameroons under British mandate.
(2) To organize and collaborate with all its branches throughout the country.
(3) To adopt suitable means for the purpose of imparting political education to the people of Nigeria with a view to achieving self-government.
(4) To afford the members the advantages of a medium of expression in order to secure political freedom, economic security, social equality and religious toleration in Nigeria and the Cameroons under British mandate, as a member of the British Commonwealth of Nations.

The term 'Political Freedom' was interpreted to mean the achievement of self-government whereby our people shall exercise untrammelled executive, legislative and judicial powers. It also implied freedom of speech, freedom of the press, freedom of assembly and freedom of association to enable our people to be free to think, to speak, to write, to assemble, and to trade. 'Economic Security' meant that Government shall respect the indigenous system of land tenure, and the NCNC aimed 'to secure

313

control by the local administrations of the means of production and distribution of the mineral resources of the country'. This also included protection of 'Nigerian trade, products, minerals and commerce in the interest of the natives, and legislation against trade monopolies so as to avoid the exploitation of the country and its people'. That our workers should be protected from any form of oppression or exploitation and that their conditions of work should be humanized formed the last point of this topic.

In connection with 'Social Equality', the NCNC Constitution demanded 'abolition of all forms of discrimination and segregation based on race, colour, tribe or creed in Nigeria and the Cameroons, particularly in respect of social accommodation, advantages, facilities, enjoyments, amenities, remuneration, perquisites, etc.'. It advocated 'a national system of free and compulsory education for all children up to the age of sixteen' together with the provision of 'a reasonable number of scholarships' to our people for study. It also sought 'to secure that free medical and surgical treatment shall be provided by the central and the local government' for all our people, without exception, so long as they 'are in need of such services' and that 'there shall be no discrimination and segregation in respect of hospital facilities on account of race, colour, tribe or creed'.

Religious toleration was defined as follows : 'To secure for the people of Nigeria and the Cameroons, the freedom of worship according to conscience, and for all religious organizations the freedom and right to exist'. The NCNC was not oblivious of the international aspect of our struggle towards an independent national existence, and so it incorporated the following as our goal in international relations : 'To secure for the people of Nigeria and the Cameroons an effective voice in international affairs which directly or indirectly affect them'.

In alliance with the Nigerian National Democratic Party the NCNC won all the three seats for Lagos at the 1947 elections to the Legislative Council. The same alliance won all the five seats for Lagos at the 1951 elections to the Western House of Assembly. Its Eastern section won 75 of the 83 seats at the 1951 elections to the Eastern House of Assembly, in 1953 the NCNC won 72 out of 84 seats in the Eastern House of Assembly and in 1954, 35 out of 42 seats in the East, 23 out of 42 seats in the West and one out of the two seats in Lagos, making a total of 61 out of the 184 seats in the Federal House of Representatives. In 1956 it won 32 out of the 80 seats in the Western House of Assembly and, in March 1957, 65 out of the 84 seats in the Eastern House of Assembly.

Up to 1955, the NCNC was the only nation-wide party in Nigeria since it had representatives in all the legislatures of the country, either by directly winning seats or by doing so through alliances. At present, it is the Government Party in the Eastern Region and the official Opposition in the Western House of Assembly. Together with the Northern Peoples Congress it forms a bi-partisan 'coalition' in the Federal Government. Through its allies, the Northern Elements Progressive Union, the Idoma State Union and the Moses Rwang Wing of the United Middle Belt Peoples Congress, it is part of the Opposition in the Northern House of Assembly and through its alliance with the Kamerun Peoples Party, part of the Opposition in the Southern Cameroons legislature.

The main issue which the NCNC tackled as soon as it was founded was that of self-government. At all its meetings since 1944 it has preached the doctrine that Nigeria is ready for self-government, and has spotlighted any statements which favour this point of view, whilst it attacks opposing views. In the early years of the NCNC, Mr J. V. Clinton, O.B.E., the Editor of the now defunct *Nigerian Eastern Mail*, used to gun for nationalists who demanded self-government. He claimed that Nigeria was too backward either to appreciate it or to be worthy of this political honour. This followed the forthright statement in 1944 of Mr Henry Wallace, former Vice-President of the United States, challenging Britain to indicate a time-limit for setting colonial peoples free, as an earnest of her constructive peace aims. The Labour Opposition in the House of Commons had tackled the Secretary of State for India (Leopold M. Amery) at this time and demanded the release of Mahatma Gandhi and Pandit Nehru from prison. Mr Amery prevaricated, and on being requested to state categorically what

India wanted, Mahatma Gandhi said that Indian nationalists demanded from Britain self-government for India and for the people of Africa.

Following the stand taken by WASU in London over the issue of self-government, and the views expressed by the West African Press Delegation to London, Mr Reginald Sorensen, M.P., advocated that Britain should indicate a time-limit of ten to fifteen years to enable British West Africa to be self-governing. 'I believe that if the Colonial Secretary would announce such action in our colonial empire, particularly in West Africa,' Mr Sorensen appealed, 'he would strike a stronger blow for the principles for which men are dying today than by anything which he had said before.' Not only was Mr Sorensen's plea played down by the British press, but it was suppressed by the Public Relations Department of Nigeria. It was left to the *West African Pilot* and the *Daily Service* to publicize and support Mr Sorensen's timely statement.

The local reaction to Mr Sorensen's House of Commons speech was electrifying. All over the country the issue was on every lip. At Calabar, a public debate was held under the chairmanship of Mr G. W. Clinton, father of Mr J. V. Clinton and proprietor of the *Nigerian Eastern Mail*. Dr M. A. Majekodunmi, a surgical specialist, and Mr Asuquo Nyon, a teacher in Duke Town School, debated for the affirmative, whilst Mr A. S. Evelyn-Brown, a magistrate, and Hon. E. E. E. Anwan, a lawyer, debated for the negative. It is needless to remark that the former won the debate by acclamation. This did not satisfy Mr J. V. Clinton, who did not hesitate to use the columns of his newspaper to mis-educate and confuse the public on this issue. There was widespread opposition to the effort of his press to stultify the aspirations of Nigerians and subsequently his newspaper became defunct.

On October 10, 1944, a cablegram was despatched to me from London, signed by Dr Akinola Maja, Ladipo Solanke and H. O. Davies, not only supporting the idea of immediate self-government, but suggesting that Nigerians should make a declaration asking for internal self-government and send this to the Secretary of State for the Colonies. They also advised that leaders of political thought should travel to all parts of Nigeria and secure the co-operation of the Chiefs and people. This cablegram also referred me to the WASU magazine of June 1944, which said :

The present wishes of the people of West Africa are briefly summed up as follows : That the goal of our ambition is a Dominion Status to be identically the same in nature, character and power as any of the other Dominions within the British Commonwealth. But as the appropriate and adequate preparation for this goal of our ambition, we want a substantial constitutional advancement as may practically amount to internal democratic self-government to be granted us NOW. . . .

The above constitutional grant to last for the next ten years, as from January 1, 1942, after which a complete internal self-government should, *de jure et de facto,* followed for another five years, and at the end of the latter period, a full-fledged *dominion status* should be granted. We want Mr Churchill's present government to declare the above, as soon as possible, as representing the exact and true wishes and aspirations of the people of West Africa.

Not only did the Colonial Office treat this reasonable request for constitutional reform with snobbery, but on December 6, 1944, Sir Arthur Richards (now Lord Milverton), who was then Governor of Nigeria, addressed a memorandum to the Secretary of State suggesting constitutional reforms which would enable Nigerians at all political levels 'to secure greater participation in the discussion of their own affairs'. This slap in the face was not taken lying down by the NCNC which began a nation-wide agitation against a Constitution prepared by one man without the knowledge and consent of the millions of Nigerians who were directly concerned.

Lord Milverton was not only adamant, he got his Constitution through the Legislative Council, thanks to the official and unofficial nominated members who gave it their support, with the exception of Dr N. T. Olusoga, Member for Ijebu Division, who reminded the House that they had no mandate from the people to accept a Constitution of that type. At the same meeting of the Legislative Council, the official bench introduced a number of Bills affecting the appointment and deposition of Chiefs, Crown Lands, the acquisition of public lands, and the mining of minerals. These Bills were regarded as inimical to the best interest of Nigeria

317

by the NCNC, because of their undemocratic provisions. Nevertheless, they were passed into law.

The scheme for the new Constitution which was embodied in Lord Milverton's despatch dated December 6, 1944, was laid on the table of the Legislative Council on March 5, 1945. On March 27, 1945, the NCNC submitted a memorandum to His Excellency for transmission to the Secretary of State making certain observations on the reforms suggested by the Governor. It held that the new Constitution should not only seek 'to secure greater participation by Africans in discussion of their own affairs', but it should enable them to secure 'greater participation in the *management* of their own affairs'. The NCNC opposed the linking of local government regimes with the legislature in order, as envisaged, to enable them to act as electoral colleges with majority unofficial membership, because 'it is not only inconsistent with political institutions in more progressive countries but the jurisdiction of the two are separate and distinct'. However, the NCNC accepted the view that 'Native Authorities should participate in the law-making process, due to the present stage of development of the country'.

The NCNC objected to the continued practice of nomination of members and suggested that it 'should be replaced by popular representation based on adult suffrage'. It did not accept the existence of the weighted unofficial majority with nominated members and Native Authorities, who would hold office at the pleasure of the Governor, but suggested that there should be an effective numerical majority of unofficial members. It also objected to 'vested interests' (like Mining, Banking, Shipping, Commerce and Industry) being represented as 'Unofficial Members'. Finally, it suggested the elevation of Lagos into a municipality to be presided over by a Mayor.

In spite of these considered views, the Colonial Office gave the green signal to Lord Milverton who 'railroaded' the Constitution without respecting the views of the representatives of the people, who were later described by the noble lord as 'self-appointed and self-elected' in the true fashion of the 'man on the spot'. The imperviousness of the Secretary of State to any democratic feeling for the millions of Nigerians, not to mention the lack of ordinary

318

courtesy in the public relations of the Colonial Office, so galled the NCNC that it was decided to formulate immediately a programme of positive action. In the teeth of criticism from the NYM, who scornfully described it as a globe-trotting vacation, the NCNC decided to send a delegation to the United Kingdom in order not only to discuss these constitutional and legislative measures, but also to request definite clarification of Anglo-Nigerian relations on the basis of treaty obligations and protectorate status, and to make representations on any other matters relevant to the progress and welfare of Nigeria and the Cameroons.

It was also decided to embark upon a country-wide tour in order to explain NCNC objections to the new Constitution and the offending Bills and to obtain the mandate of the Chiefs and people of Nigeria and the Cameroons in sustaining their objection to these official measures. The first step taken was to apprise the Chiefs and Native Authorities and the people of the various communities of this arrangement, and to secure their mandate to enable the delegates to act for and on their behalf. Accordingly, a circular letter was sent to almost all the natural rulers in different parts of the country, not only apprising them of the intention to send a delegation to the United Kingdom, but assuring them of our loyalty, in these words :

The object of the NCNC includes the maintenance by Nigeria, strictly and inviolate, of the connection with the British Empire; while the citizens of Nigeria enjoy unreservedly every right of free citizenship of the British Empire.

Copies of the NCNC Constitution were distributed to these natural rulers and their peoples, and the circular to the various organizations of the communities of Nigeria requested that the leading elements should use their good offices to make their communities cognizant of this impending country-wide delegation. These two circular letters were prepared and forwarded in March 1946, and it was decided to start the tour from Lagos on April 22, with the following members constituting the delegations : Messrs

319

Herbert Macaulay and Nnamdi Azikiwe, Dr the Hon. Olorun-Nimbe, Messrs. M. A. O. Imoudu and Oyeshile Omage. A reference to the NCNC Memorandum to the Secretary of State for the Colonies shows that 153 communities gave the NCNC mandate to speak and act on their behalf. These communities were widely spread over the Northern, Eastern, Western Regions, the Colony and the Trust Territory of the Northern and Southern Cameroons. These communities represented half of those visited by the NCNC tourists, and all of such places donated a sum slightly under £14,000 to finance this political venture.

The phrasing of the mandate was both specific and general because the phrasers knew that the problems of Nigeria and the Cameroons were based on more vital issues than the Richards Constitution and the four obnoxious legislations. In their opinion, the main issue in Anglo-Nigerian relations was, as it still is, self-government, in view of treaty obligations, and the protectorate and international status of Nigeria and the Cameroons respectively. The mandate each community was requested to sign was as follows :

We the people of the . . . . . . community in the Province of . . . . . . in the Protectorate or Trust Territory or Colony of . . . . . . this . . . day of . . . . . 1946, hereby give our assent to the mission of the Pan-Nigeria to London Delegation, under the auspices of the NCNC, and we hereby AUTHORIZE the officers of the said NCNC, that is, the President, the General Secretary, and the Treasurer and other accredited members of the Delegation, to be our representatives overseas, that is to say, the United Kingdom and other places, in order :

  (a) To obtain the repeal of the following ordinances which were passed in the Legislative Council of Nigeria in March 1945 : (1) Minerals Ordinance, 1945, (2) Public Lands Acquisition (Amendment) Ordinance, 1945, (3) Appointment and Deposition of Chiefs (Amendment) Ordinance, 1945, and (4) Crown Lands (Amendment) Ordinance, 1945.

  (b) To object to the principles involved in the Richards Constitution, which subverts the democratic condition of the Colony and Protectorate of Nigeria and derogates the status of the Paramount Rulers of the country.

(c) To emphasize the recognized principle of the inalienability of the communal land of the people of Nigeria and to secure the original tenure of land against exploitation, and to obtain an irrevocable acknowledgement by the British Government of the fundamental principle upon which the land system in Nigeria is erected, namely :

That the whole of the land in all parts of Nigeria, including the Colony and Protectorates, north and south, whether occupied or not occupied, shall be declared native land; and that all rights of ownership over all native lands shall be vested in the indigenous inhabitants as being inalienable and untransferable.

(d) To discuss all such OTHER MATTERS as shall be relevant to the welfare and progress of Nigeria.

On August 13, 1947, the Secretary of State (the Rt Hon. Arthur Creech Jones) received the seven delegates [1] in the Colonial Office. After listening to their representations, he advised them to return to Nigeria and co-operate in working the Constitution which they had discredited. It should be noted that throughout their stay in the United Kingdom, the main sections of the British Press viciously attacked the delegation and made a mockery of its mission. There can be no doubt that the press was inspired to take such a line, but it had adverse repercussions in Nigeria, where members and supporters of the NCNC not only resented the lack of appreciation of Nigeria's loyalty to Britain in making sacrifices and participating in the Second World War, but insisted that the NCNC should change its policy and demand self-government *outside* the British Commonwealth of Nations, no matter the nature of the sacrifice to be made.

After the return of the NCNC delegation, Chief Bode Thomas, a Lagos lawyer, began to expound a political philosophy which sought to divide Nigeria into three politically permanent regions. This novel exposition is very material to the subject of the growth of political parties in Nigeria, because it is the basis of the ideas which culminated subsequently in the formation of a new political party in Nigeria. Writing in a Lagos newspaper [2] Chief Thomas

[1] Dr Nnamdi Azikiwe, Prince Adeleke Adedoyin, Dr A. B. Olorun-Nimbe, Chief Nyong Essien, Mrs Funmilayo Ransome-Kuti, Mallam Bukar Dip-charima, and Mr P. M. Kale.

[2] *Nigerian Daily Times.*

advocated regionalization which must be based purely on political parties, whose spheres of influence would be geographically demarcated, irrespective of individual differences of opinion. He postulated his theory in the following words :

I believe that Nigeria must be better organized politically than it is today. The point is whether such organization should be based on a unilateral system or that three political bodies be set up on a regional basis to serve the needs of the East, West and North, respectively. They may be described as regional political parties and will deal exclusively with matters affecting their respective zones.

I believe that the latter suggestion, novel as it may sound, will serve the need of the country better. These three bodies may join up at the top and form a council for Nigeria which will be competent to tackle any matter that may affect the country generally. Some of the advantages of this system are :

(1) It will give to the persons directly concerned an exclusive right to determine issues which are purely their own local affairs.

(2) Leaders will be produced from each organization who will join together to accept whatever political responsibilities might be granted Nigeria in the near future.

(3) The Northerners who have always been suspicious of the Southerners will at least be satisfied that there is no intention on the part of the Southern *Kafiris* to dominate the North or to interfere in their domestic affairs.

The NCNC felt very strongly on this spurious idea of regionalization and warned the country that it was an invitation to national disaster, because it was bound to disintegrate Nigeria as a historical fact. It was thought that the idea itself was contrary to all known political ideologies because it was untenable for a political party, which was regarded as a sect, to be regionalized in the devious way suggested. It was unheard of for Socialism to be earmarked for a particular region, Oligarchy for another, and Aristocracy for yet another. During a public lecture, this issue was further developed and denounced by me from the following points of view : [1]

I concede to Mr Thomas the right to his opinion and to express same as he sees fit; naturally, he should reciprocate. There is thus no ill-feeling, other than a desire to sift the chaff from the wheat of our political crop.

[1] *West African Pilot,* December 12, 1947, p. 2.

(1) To divide the country into three exclusive units, based on political partisanship, is to stultify the corporate existence of Nigeria and the Cameroons. Rather than integrating the diverse communities of Nigeria and the Cameroons, as Mr Thomas conceives it, it would lead to disintegration.

(2) It is not consistent with the professed objectives of more experienced politicians like the Democrats and Youth Movementers who are pledged (I am reading from the Nigerian Youth Movement Constitution) 'to unify the different tribes of Nigeria by adopting and encouraging means which would foster better understanding and co-operation between the tribes so that they may come to have a common ideal'.

(3) Political parties, as sects, cannot be regionalized because, 'A sect includes individuals differing greatly as to their education, their professions, and the class of society to which they belong, and with their common beliefs as the connecting link'.

I am yet to be convinced that all Easterners must be regimented to believe in Socialism, and that all Northerners must accept Oligarchy as the best political philosophy, and all Westerners must regard Aristocracy as the best of all ideologies, and the Cameroons must believe in Communism. No person can regiment another on the basis of political parties, excepting in totalitarian states.

It is mysterious that Mr Thomas should make this ingenious suggestion to serve the need of the country better. I wonder if he had studied the NCNC Memorandum to find out how this particular issue was tackled by the introduction of a federal idea, reserving to the units concerned cultural and local autonomy, which should serve those communities better than his Pakistan idea.

Unless I have misinterpreted his views, and unless he is ignorant of what the NCNC Memorandum has to say on the point, I fail to see any point in dividing an already divided country, which made it possible for the Richards Constitution to claim to have some good points, to wit: 'In framing my proposals,' said Lord Milverton, 'I have kept three objects before me; to promote the unity of Nigeria; to provide adequately within that unity for the diverse elements which make up the country; and to secure greater participation by Africans in the discussion of their own affairs. At present no unity exists, nor does the constitution encourage its growth.'

I think I am not only justified in booting this specious idea of regionalization on the basis of political parties out of our country—lock, stock, and barrel—but also in saying that it is putting back the hands of the clock of our progress, socially and politically, thus postponing the crystallization of consciousness of kind in our blessed country. Certainly this idea would encourage separatist movements in Nigeria and the Cameroons, and destroy our corporate existence as a Commonwealth of Nations.

It should be noted down for posterity that from the time this theory of rigid regionalization was postulated, the politics of this country changed fundamentally so that by the time a Constitutional Conference took place at Ibadan, towards the end of 1949, a new Constitution confirmed the carving up of the country virtually into three constituents, as originally conceived by Chief Bode Thomas. Not only that; a new political party had arisen on the horizon of Nigerian politics, with the name of Action Group, and carrying this Thomasian banner of extreme regionalization, it won majority seats at the general election to the Western House of Assembly to form the Government of the Western Region.

I must confess that the NCNC did not give in easily to this divisive theory of regionalism. It is on record that, during the Ibadan Constitutional Conference, the late Mazi Mbonu Ojike and Mr Eyo Ita, NCNC delegates, strongly opposed the division of the country into Regions, the system of indirect election to the legislatures, the electoral college device, the creation of the House of Chiefs, and the representation of vested interests in the legislatures of the land. Not only were the NCNC objections ignored by the other delegates, but the Secretary of State paid no heed to them whatsoever. The NCNC also furiously fought for the incorporation of universal adult suffrage in the new Constitution. The two delegates submitted a minority report and advanced the argument that, 'by granting our people the ballot right, we shall be implementing the ideal that all men are born equal.' Again, their plea fell on deaf ears.

On the disenfranchisement of Nigerians who are non-Northerners resident in the Northern Region, the NCNC joined six other persons from the Eastern Region to submit a minority report. They felt unable to agree to the resolution whereby the doors of the Northern House of Assembly were closed to all persons, save only such as had Northern fathers and grandfathers. They submitted that, 'if it is the intention to have a unified Nigeria, then it must necessarily ensure that different citizenship and citizenship rights are not created within the country by the various regions for persons born in Nigeria and regarded as natives of Nigeria. Any other course will of necessity give rise to the creation of different national status among Nigerians'. Again, this minority report was absolutely ignored.

The General Conference had decided that Lagos should not become part and parcel of any Region; rather it should be preserved as the national capital. Eleven delegates, including the Oni of Ife, Messrs Akinpelu Obisesan, S. O. Awokoya, A. Soetan, M. A. Ajasin, T. A. Bankole, Ogunlana II, Bode Thomas, C. D. Akran, I. O. Ransome-Kuti, and A. E. Prest submitted a minority report and insisted that Lagos must be incorporated in the Western Region. The Secretary of State was disposed to accede to their request, and Lagos became part and parcel of the Western Region. By the time the Nigeria (Constitution) Order in Council, 1951 (otherwise known as the Macpherson Constitution), was promulgated, the Action Group had been founded virtually with the motto, 'Western Region for the Westerners, Eastern Region for the Easterners, Northern Region for the Northerners, and Nigeria for all'. This was in accordance with the gospel of extreme regionalization enunciated by Chief Bode Thomas in 1947.

The Action Group is a political protrusion of the *Egbe Omo Oduduwa*, which is a Yoruba cultural organization. Until 1955, the policy of this party had been influenced by the rigid regionalization of Chief Bode Thomas, who unfortunately died in November 1954. Since that time, pressure of public opinion has gradually forced the Action Group to modify its regional rigidity so that it has now become a nation-wide political party with membership in all the legislatures of the land, either directly or indirectly, through alliance with other parties. Today, the Action Group is the party in power in the Western House of Assembly—with a total memberhip of 48 in a House of 80. It is the recognized Opposition party in the Eastern House of Assembly—with 13 out of 84 members. It is represented in the Northern House of Assembly through alignment with the Ilorin Talaka Parapo Alliance, and it is represented in the Southern Cameroons through a loose

325

alliance with the Kamerun National Congress, which is the Government party there. It is also represented in the Federal House of Representatives by 27 members in a House of 184.

In the absence of an Action Group constitution, it is risky to chronicle accurately the aims of this party. I am however grateful to a Nigerian publication which has given what I consider to be a fair appraisal of the activities and achievements of the Action Group since its founding in 1951, in spite of certain obvious historical inaccuracies. The following[1] is the full text of this appraisal :

Of the major political parties in the South the later arrival is the Action Group. Until 1951 most of its present leaders were associated with the now defunct Nigerian Youth Movement and, later, with the Egbe Omo Oduduwa, a Yoruba cultural organization. How this party got on to the stage was dramatic, and far more dramatic is the achievement which it can claim in its five years of existence.

In the middle forties, the Nigerian Youth Movement had become the Lagos political party of Yoruba intellectuals, the Ibos having marched out of it earlier, as soon as Dr Azikiwe resigned from it. That party then degenerated and all that was left of it was to be seen on the pages of its official organ.

By 1945, however, something had happened. The creation of the NCNC had caused new political strife, and because the Yoruba intellectuals did not get as much of the control of its leadership as they desired, they returned to the fold of the Nigerian Youth Movement or whatever was left of it to continue their vocal warfare against the new organization and Dr Azikiwe, their old political foe.

At the time, in London, Chief Obafemi Awolowo, now Premier of the West, was thinking seriously of a Yoruba cultural organization. As soon as he returned to Nigeria the Egbe Omo Oduduwa (the association of the Yoruba children of Oduduwa) was formed and whipping up Yoruba nationalism as it did (it worshipped at the shrine of Oduduwa of Ife), it rapidly gained ground. But for some time the Egbe Omo Oduduwa remained just a reply to the Ibo State Union; in other words, as an assembly which catered for the social and cultural progress of the Yorubas.

On the eve of the 1951 election, the leaders of this organization dreamt new dreams. They created a political wing of the Egbe Omo Oduduwa and called it the Action Committee. A few months before

[1] *Nigeria Year Book*, 1956 (Lagos, 1956), pp. 104–7.

the elections the Committee was announced as the Action Group, and efforts were made to dissociate it from the Egbe Omo Oduduwa.

Then the party with more determination than had ever been shown in Nigerian politics, began to publish policy papers and to gain ground throughout the Western Region. Its sphere of operation was to be within the Western Region and its policy was directed at, and fed on, Yoruba nationalism. The plan worked.

When the elections were over it had won a slender majority over the less-organized mass movement of the NCNC : but in less than forty-eight hours that majority had been strengthened. Comfortably, it established itself as the Government of the West and represented the Region, under the 1951 Constitution, in the central Legislature, electing four of the twelve Ministers that constituted the Council of Ministers.

Today the Action Group is as important as any other political party in the country; it is certainly better organized than the rest.

The Action Group believes in a socialist commonwealth but also in the solidarity of the parts and the unity of all. It has asked for, and thus far won, residual powers in the Regions and advocates the regionalization of the Judiciary and the Civil Service. It believes in the country being split into more States than at present (ten it suggests) and lays emphasis on the cultural and ethnical differences which exist in the country and which, it asks, should not be overlooked in the political administration of the country.

Among the present leaders of the Action Group are Chief Obafemi Awolowo, Chief S. L. Akintola, Chief Rotimi Williams, Mr S. O. Ighodaro, Chief Dr Akinola Maja, Dr Akanni Doherty, the Oni of Ife, and the Olowo of Owo. The official address of the party is : Action Group Headquarters, Ijebu By-Pass, Ibadan.

The Northern Peoples Congress, the Government party in the Northern Region, was founded after the general elections in 1951, following the promulgation of the Macpherson Constitution. Its leader is the Sardauna of Sokoto, who is now Premier of the Northern Region. Its motto is 'One North, One People, irrespective of religion, rank or tribe'. The NPC has as its objective the attainment of self-government for Nigeria and the introduction of a permanent federal constitution. The following constitute the aims of the party :

To adopt and cultivate means that would foster better understanding and co-operation between the members and the Association and the Northern community generally, so that by such co-operation we of the North may be able to attain to that unquestionable height so desirable especially at this time of our existence and thus enabling us to have one common ideal and objective.

To study and strive to preserve the traditions which bound culture to the past, while reforming these traditions to render them capable of meeting modern conditions.

To educate Northerners for their civic and political responsibilities, to organize them to accept the leadership of the Northern Peoples Congress, and to support its candidates for elections to the Regional and Central Legislatures and to Local Councils.

To study the cultural, social, political and economic pastimes of the Northerners so that they can adjust themselves to the present changing world with the view to overcoming all the difficulties and barriers that are placed before them.

To appeal to the members to submit themselves to party discipline and loyalty; and those of them elected into the Regional Legislature shall be requested to work assiduously towards the implementation of party programmes of work for all Departments of Government.

To inculcate in the minds of the Northerners a genuine love for the Northern Region and all that is northern, and a special reverence for Religion, Laws and Order and the preservation of good customs and traditions, and the feeling that the sorrow of one northerner shall be the sorrow of all and that the happiness of one is also the happiness of all.

To make every possible effort in order to hasten the date of Self-Government for Nigeria and the consideration of introducing of a 'Permanent Federal Constitution'.

To seek for the assistance and co-operation of or to give aid to any organization or individual in or out of the Northern Region whose aims and aspirations coincide with those of the party.

Before the Constitutional Conference of 1953, the NPC suggested an eight-points programme for the virtual disintegration of Nigeria as a federal unit, but in view of the representations made to it that it would not unify the country, it withdrew its programme and agreed to the present Constitution which is now being reviewed in London. Hitherto, all the elections to the Northern House of Assembly have been won by the NPC under an electoral college system. Last year, this was modified and a tax suffrage was allowed in certain specified urban communities. It is believed that in the future the NPC will support a uniform electoral system, based on male suffrage only, since it feels that if women are allowed to vote that would be incompatible with the tenets of the religion of Islam.

The Northern Peoples Congress has earned the respect of the people of Nigeria following the initiative taken by the Sardauna to convene a Premier's Conference in Lagos, last April, which agreed that Nigeria should demand complete independence from Britain, to take effect in 1959. For this decision, its leaders have been subjected to severe strictures from certain sections of the British Press; nevertheless the Sardauna has reiterated the desire of Northerners to join with their Southern compatriots in seeking for complete freedom in 1959. The NPC and NCNC now form a bi-partisan government in the Federal Council of Ministers where they are represented, respectively, by three and six federal Ministers out of thirteen members.

The Northern Elements Progressive Union was founded in 1945 under a different name. With the coming into operation of the Macpherson Constitution in 1951, it assumed its present name. Its headquarters are at Kano. In one of its latest manifestos, the NEPU enunciated its aims and objectives as follows:

The Northern Elements Progressive Union is a Northern Nigerian Party with democratic ideals and it is absolutely divorced from tribal and religious prejudices. It stands for the welfare of the people of Northern Nigeria and to establish sound social, economic and political justice to ensure domestic tranquillity and to secure liberty of thought and expression, equality of status and opportunity for all the people of Northern Nigeria, and to promote among them all real fraternity, to the safeguarding of the individual and the unity of the people.

We the members, therefore, do hereby solemnly promise to carry out the following Economic, Social and Poitical Reforms if we are returned to power:

1. Mechanization of Agriculture and improving of Animal Husbandry to increase food production in order to raise the standard of living of the people—thus stabilizing our internal economy.

2. Reforms for a progressive system of Education; intellectual, technical and moral.

3. A scheme to dam the river Niger to provide water for drinking and irrigation, and for production of electricity.

4. Introduction of Local Government system based upon popular democratic elections—thus doing away with the autocratic Native Administration—and a sound Town and Country Planning.

5. Reform in laws relating to Transport and provision of better trunk and feeder roads.

6. A uniform judicial system throughout the Northern Region for the purpose of establishing the rule of law.

7. Development of local and secondary industries in order to provide employment—thus reducing the present high percentage of unemployment.

At the elections of 1956, the Northern Elements Progressive Union won four seats in the Northern House of Assembly and it is at present allied with the Bornu Youth Movement and the United Middle Belt Congress to form the Opposition in the Northern legislature. In 1952 and 1955, its President-General, Mallam Aminu Kano, visited London and made representations to the Colonial Office on the undemocratic system of elections in the Northern Region.

The United National Independence Party was founded in 1953, and its Constitution was adopted on August 8, 1954. It has five elected members in the Eastern House of Assembly. Its objects are :

1. To achieve complete independence for a United Nigeria.

2. To promote the political, social and economic freedom of the people of Nigeria, and more particularly to secure distribution of amenities and equal opportunities for individual and social development; mobilize the economic resources of the country in the interest of the people and on the basis of partnership between the State and the individual.

3. To promote freedom for the individual to express himself, worship, and develop his higher spiritual needs.

4. To preserve indigenous institutions and customs which are compatible with progress and the material well-being of the people.

5. To ensure that our Chiefs and Traditional Rulers participate effectively in the responsibility of Government at various levels.

6. To co-operate with other political organizations whose aims and objects are similar with a view to promoting the purposes of the party.

330

The Dynamic Party was founded in the year 1955 with its headquarters at Ibadan. Its President-General is Dr Chike Obi, who is senior Lecturer in Mathematics at the University College, Ibadan. It is a 'revolutionary dynamic organization of like-minded haters of oppression and lovers of liberty, equality and fraternity from all walks of life.' Membership of the party is restricted to Africans and the party was formed for the following objects :

(i) To raise the standard of living of Africans and thereby ensure the increase of the standard of living of mankind.

(ii) To win and maintain for Africans their self-respect in the world.

(iii) To promote the cultures and welfare of the peoples of Africa.

(iv) To do every other thing including the acquiring of power, political and otherwise, in Nigeria, the Cameroons and elsewhere in Africa which may be considered advantageous, that may be deemed essential or conducive or incidental to the attainment of the above objects or any of them.

In the pursuit of its aims the Dynamic Party is guided by the following principles :

(i) The Party shall be a rigidly disciplined body even if this means a drastic reduction in the number of the members.

(ii) When human beings form a body they surrender part of their personal freedom to the body; the bigger the body and the benefit derived from it by the individual who is a member, the greater is the apparent loss of personal freedom of the individual. The interests of the individual can only best be guaranteed by the interests of the individuals of the State taken collectively.

(iii) To guarantee the interest and security of the individuals of the State, the Party therefore believes in
(a) Public ownership of all major means of production and distribution and of the defence of the State.
(b) Making all economic and social plans from the point of view of the interests and welfare of the individuals of the State taken as a whole.
(c) The day to day control and management by the people of the means of livelihood and defence of the State.
(d) Political independence is absolutely necessary for the attainment of full freedom from cultural, intellectual and economic slavery.

(*e*) The necessity of being active, energetic and on the offensive and of using all means of persuasion at its disposal beginning from the simplest methods first and following up, when necessary, with the stronger methods.

The principle of this section may be summed up under the title 'Dynamic Collectivism'.

The symbol of the party is the ram. It contested the 1956 elections to the Western House of Assembly without winning a seat. At the 1957 elections to the Eastern House of Assembly, it joined forces with the NCNC in campaigning against the Action Group and the United National Independence Party. It has since become an affiliated member of the NCNC.

The Idoma State Union is a political party wth its headquarters at Oturkpo in Benue Province. It was founded in 1954 and its objects are as follows :

(*a*) To establish unity among all the natives of Idoma.
(*b*) To obtain and maintain just and good development educationally, socially, economically and culturally by constitutional means in Idoma-land.
(*c*) To promote and safeguard the interests of the Division.

The Union advocates the creation of a Middle Belt State. On this platform it contested the 1956 elections to the Northern House of Assembly and succeeded in gaining two seats therein. It also has two members in the House of Representatives. The Union is an offspring of the Idoma Hope Rising Union, which was formerly an associate member of the NCNC. The Union and the NCNC are in alliance.

The Conference of Chiefs of the Eastern Region is not a political party in the strict sense, but it is an organized body whose aims and objectives are directed towards the achievement of political ends. In the words of its official literature, it is 'a nonpolitical organization fully determined to fight for the recognition of Eastern Chiefs and natural rulers. Its ultimate aim is the achievement of a House of Chiefs.' It was made abundantly clear that in seeking to attain this objective the Chiefs are motivated by the idea that the only solution to the many problems thus con-

332

fronting the Conference 'is the creation of the House of Chiefs in the East, where we can take part in the legislature of our Region.'

When a Bill for the Recognition of Chiefs Law was enacted in the Eastern House of Assembly, Chiefs who are members of the Conference gave it their unqualified support. The Government of the Eastern Region allowed the Conference to nominate one of their members to attend the London Constitutional Conference as a delegate to enable the point of view of the Conference to be explained, especially in respect of the incorporation of a House of Chiefs in the next Constitution for Nigeria.

The Kamerun National Congress is in control of the Government of the Southern Cameroons. After the recent elections it was returned to power and the opposition parties are represented by the Kamerun National Democratic Party, led by J. Foncha of Bamenda; Kamerun Peoples Party led by P. M. Kale of Buea; and Kamerun United Commoners Party, led by Chief S. A. Anjeh of Mamfe.

There are many minority parties in Nigeria and the Cameroons and they help in making parliamentary government a reality in that part of the world. Among the leading ones (not already mentioned), some of which are allied to the major parties for purposes of elections in the federal or regional legislatures, are the following: Nigerian Commoners Party, Nigerian Young Democrats, Otu Edo, Middle Belt Peoples Party, United Middle Belt Congress, Bornu Youth Movement, Tiv Progressive Union, Ilorin Talaka Parapo Party, Nigerian Women's Party, and the Lagos Market Women's Association.

At present there are certain movements which are dedicated to the attainment of a particular political objective. For example, the Calabar-Ogoja-Rivers State Movement aims towards the crystallization of a union of these three provinces to form a separate state in Eastern Nigeria. The Mid-West State Movement makes propaganda for the incorporation of the Benin and Delta Provinces into a separate state in Western Nigeria. The Rivers Peoples Movement, the Rivers Peoples Congress, and the Conference of Rivers Chiefs and Peoples aim at the creation of a Rivers State in Eastern Nigeria. The United Middle Belt Congress is dedicated to the creation of a Middle Belt State in Northern Nigeria, comprising Adamawa, Benue, Ilorin, Kabba, Niger and Plateau Provinces.

CHAPTER 18

ZIK ON THE CHURCH MISSIONARY SOCIETY

A speech delivered during the Centenary Celebrations of the Niger Mission of the Church Missionary Society at the Dennis Memorial Grammar School Sports Field, Onitsha, on November 16, 1957.

Your Grace, Your Excellencies, my Lords, Sir Kenneth and Lady Grubb, Sir Francis and Lady Ibiam, Ministers in Holy Orders, Ladies and Gentlemen, the celebration of the first Centenary of the Church Missionary Society presents us with an opportunity to study how this world-renowned Christian Mission came to be founded on April 12, 1799, and how it has affected our thoughts and behaviour. Believing that the Great Commission of Jesus the Nazarene was what Dr Max A. C. Warren has called 'The Christian Imperative', the sixteen clergymen and nine laymen who founded the Society enjoined upon every Christian 'to endeavour to propagate the knowledge of the gospel . . . to the Continent of Africa'.

In two of the synoptic gospels, two fragments of the Great Commission appear. In St Matthew's gospel, Chapter XXVIII, verses 18–20, it is written : 'All power is given unto Me in heaven and in earth. Go ye therefore, and teach all nations, baptizing them in the name of the Father, and of the Son, and of the Holy Ghost : teaching them to observe all things whatsoever I have commanded you : and lo, I am with you alway, *even* unto the end of the world. Amen.' In St Mark's gospel, Chapter XVI, verse 15, it is written : 'Go ye into all the world, and preach the gospel to every creature.'

Founded upon an injunction to evangelize Africa, as a part of 'the world', the Church Missionary Society at its earliest inception appreciated that Christianity is a fellowship of the brave who live by faith. In the words of one of its contemporary standard bearers, who has the distinction to be alive and to join with us in celebrating this centenary, 'To evangelize is to proclaim good news to men in such a way as to elicit the response of acceptance. To evangelize is more than prophecy. It is even more than preaching the gospel. It is preaching the gospel *with effect,* with signs following.'

This aspect of the work of the Church Missionary Society has inspired me to speak to you today on the 'fellowship of the brave who live by faith'. In one of his Kellogg lectures at the Episcopal Theological School in Cambridge, Massachusetts, in 1955, Dr Warren made an exegesis of this fellowship of the brave by explaining the actual task confronting a preacher of the gospel. His explanation is that 'He has to be not only heard but understood. For communication . . . involves not only the transmission of the message, but also its reception in the sense of its being understood.'

After one hundred years of missionary activities in this part of Nigeria, it is a privilege for us to be living witnesses of the evangelizing work of the Society which has not only been proclaimed but has elicited response of acceptance. The good news has not only been preached but it has had effect 'with signs following'. It has not only been heard but it has been understood. From these points of view I propose now to interpret the role of pioneer missionaries and converts who laid a sure and lasting foundation for the impressive success of missionary endeavour in this diocese.

In delivering the Centenary Sermon in St Stephen's Cathedral at Bonny last Sunday, Your Grace correctly referred to our revered Bishop Crowther as the father of Nigerianization. Your Grace was then explaining how the Niger mission attempted to be self-supporting whilst at the same time appreciating the wisdom of interdependence. I submit with humility that it was this spirit that led the Rev. Henry Venn in 1864 to insist that this evangelical enterprise 'must be a purely African Mission, under an African Bishop'. It is a fact that he was criticized by some people for being optimistic, and it is equally true that the scourge of malaria had

336

caused the death of many distinguished European missionaries and had discouraged the Society from trying to 'combine Europeans and Africans in the one work of evanglization'. But then it was left to the team spirit evinced by European, West Indian, Sierra Leonean and Nigerian evangelists and converts to bring to pass the success which has attended the activities of the Society in this diocese.

When the two pioneer Sierra Leone missionaries, Bishop Samuel Adjai Crowther and Rev. John Christopher Taylor, arrived at Onitsha on July 27, 1857, they realized the need to speak to Nigerians in their own language in order to facilitate the task of evangelization. Bishop Crowther had translated a primer and part of St Matthew into Nupe, which was edited by the German linguist, Rev. Dr J. F. Schon, so Rev. Taylor, who was the first agent in charge of the CMS Compound at Onitsha, proceeded to translate Ibo reading books and portions of the Scriptures. In 1860, he succeeded in translating the four gospels, the Acts of the Apostles and St Paul's First Epistle to the Corinthians and Philemon into the Isuama (Owerri) dialect of Ibo language. He benefited a lot from his contact with Dr Schon and conducted the first baptism in Onitsha in 1862. He became very popular with the natives of Onitsha, who nicknamed him 'Eze Onowu', meaning 'Prince of Prime Ministers'. In making his translations, Rev. Taylor employed the services of some of the earliest converts.

Having laid this foundation of transmitting the message of Christianity to the people for whom it was intended, through their mother tongue, it was left for another great missionary to expand the work so well begun. This time, the lot fell to a young Oxford cleric who answered the call of the Society to serve in this part of the world. I refer to the Rev. H. H. Dobinson, whose service of seven years enabled the Society to carry out the remaining aspects of the Great Commission, that is, to heal, the others being to preach, to teach, and to baptize. In 1893, Rev. Dobinson translated the Bible into the Onitsha dialect of the Ibo language assisted by one of the most famous converts and missionary workers produced by the Society in the person of Thomas David Anyaegbunam.

Rev. Dobinson was made Archdeacon in 1896 and he died the following year. He was such a very handsome person that the natives called him 'Ekilibe ejeolu'—that is, 'His physical beauty so attracts that one is apt to forget going to work.' He was buried at the Old Cemetery at Onitsha, where his tombstone is a landmark. Through the co-operation of his sister, Miss L. M. Dobinson, a dispensary was established at Iyi Enu in 1903, named after the Archdeacon, as a tribute to his memory. Since 1907, the dispensary has developed into the Mary Elms General Hospital, and it has enabled the CMS Niger Mission to bring medical facilities to thousands.

The greatest of the translators who enabled not only a fraction of the Ibo-speaking people to understand the message of Christianity as a way of life, but whose contribution to Ibo literature made it possible for the Ibo-speaking people to be more cohesive as a unit of Nigerian society, is the man whose name honours the school whose Sports Field we are using today for this function. I refer to the Archdeacon T. J. Dennis. He was consecrated Archdeacon by Bishop Herbert Tugwell in 1905. He succeeded in translating the Bible, Hymn and Prayer Books into Ibo, but this was the Onitsha dialect out of more than a dozen dialects spoken by six million Ibo. In fact, four versions of portions of the Holy Bible existed prior to 1906, three of which were prepared by European missionaries and African clergymen of the CMS.

Archdeacon Dennis was selected as chairman of a committee to prepare a 'Union Ibo' version of the Bible, and he found in one of the members of this committee, one of the first products of the Mission, by the name of T. D. Anyaegbunam, a real team-mate. The New Testament was completed in 1908 and the following year Archdeacon Dennis settled at Egbu Owerri in order to prepare the version of the Old Testament. He is said to have regarded the extension of missionary work to Egbu Owerri as 'far and away the greatest forward movement ever made by the CMS in the evangelizing of the interior Ibo country.' Through the assistance of his committee, Archdeacon Dennis laboured diligently at his difficult task and in 1913 the complete Bible was published in the Union Ibo version.

The production of this Ibo *Esperanto* is regarded as a great legacy to Ibo-land. In 1917, when he was travelling to the United Kingdom on furlough, the *Karina* on which he was a passenger was torpedoed by a German submarine and he was drowned. Several tributes have been paid to the memory of this unforgettable missionary, but it is pertinent to say that his contributions have been valued as 'a very good example of the British and Foreign Bible Society's efforts to minimize linguistic difficulties in the mission field.' Indeed, the Union Ibo version of the Bible has provided 'a standard form of speech for all the Ibos.'

In an article written by the Rev. Frederick W. Dodds of the Primitive Methodist Nigerian Mission, which was reproduced in the *Western Equatorial Africa Church Magazine* for November 1924, and entitled 'The Union Ibo Bible and its influence', the reverend gentleman said :

'As long as Ibo remains a spoken language—and it is numbered among those along the West African coast, which seem destined to survive—the influence of that extraordinary man's work will live. Of all who have succeeded in making any impression on Ibo life and thought Archdeacon Dennis must be counted the greatest, though one is not unmindful of men like Doctor Bailie, Bishop Samuel Crowther, and Bishop Tugwell.

'Great as was their service, Archdeacon Dennis has done greater, in that, out of a very polyglot of dialects, almost as heterogeneous as the latin tongues of Europe, he has made an Esperanto of Ibo that has caught on with the masses, thereby giving to this people, the third largest of West Africa, a common vehicle of expression and a language of literature, which in turn has widened the tribal consciousness, causing it to feel the throb of its unity and to look with dim-seeing but hopeful eyes to a loftier destiny. . . . God bless the Union Ibo Bible.'

Your Grace, I feel humble in adding to this eloquent tribute paid by a contemporary missionary of another denomination, but may I say that it was a great compliment to the memory of a remarkable missionary when the CMS Niger Mission decided to dedicate the first secondary school in this diocese to the late Archdeacon T. J. Dennis. As a boy attending Christ Church School, Onitsha, I knew the Archdeacon and it was a pleasure for me, when I attended the Central School, to join my colleagues in helping to clear the bush off the site where the Dennis Memorial Grammar School now stands. Indeed, it was a joy for me to join my class-mates and school-mates in carrying stones and bricks to the site to enable the builders to erect this historic institution in his memory. I can point to some of my former chums and buddies here today who cheerfully joined in these Friday duties under the direction of our West Indian schoolmasters, T. E. Kay and J. B. Stewart. And I am not afraid to testify publicly that I and my contemporaries were choristers of the Bishop Crowther Memorial Church when the late C. A. A. Barnes, a civil engineer and architect, our talented organist, was reported to have volunteered to prepare the plans of the new Grammar School as his humble mark of respect to the memory of this great friend of Nigeria.

I have referred to the role of Reverend Taylor and Archdeacon Dobinson in preparing translations of the portions of the Holy Scriptures and the Prayer Book into certain Ibo dialects. I have also mentioned the *magnum opus* of Archdeacon Dennis and his silent and unsung collaborators, whose sacrifice and Christian fervour made the Union Ibo a possibility. But I would not be fair to the memory of another equally important authority on the Ibo language, if I failed to refer to the classic work of Rev. Julius C. Spencer of Sierra Leone. His *Ibo Grammar* enabled translators, scholars, missionaries and Government officials to appreciate the fact that the Ibo language is just as grammatical as any written language, and furthermore that it has etymology, orthography, prosody and syntax. Rev. Spencer came out to the Niger Mission from Sierra Leone and worked in the Lord's vineyard principally at Obosi. His contributions to Ibo language are equally immortal.

May I at this stage refer to the man whose untiring energy and zest for missionary work helped to make possible the achievements of Archdeacons Dobinson and Dennis in translating the Bible into Ibo. Thomas Davis Anyaegbunam was born in the village of Ogbeobi Umuaroli and was trained by the Mission partly at Onitsha and partly at the Kippo Hill Training Institute at Lokoja. He served the CMS Mission as an interpreter and translator for over thirty years, and he had the unique distinction to labour as an associate of two Archdeacons in translating the Bible, the Hymn Book and the Prayer Book.

'T.D', as he was popularly known, died in March 1917 and his last words were reported to have been : 'I have finished my work.' His funeral service was conducted by the first Ibo clergyman, the Rev. G. N. Anyaegbunam, who was ordained in 1897, that is forty years after the landing of Bishop Crowther and Rev. Taylor at Onitsha. On this occasion Rev. Anyaegbunam, who is not related to 'T.D.', took his text for the funeral sermon from 2 Samuel, Chapter III, verse 38 : 'Know ye not that there is a prince and a great man fallen this day in Israel?' His remains were interred at the Old Cemetery, Onitsha.

At the beginning of this speech, I referred to Dr Warren's 'Christian Imperative' as involving not only the transmission of the message, but also its reception in the sense of its being understood. Here allow me, my Lord Archbishop, to refer to the earliest converts to Christianity, whose reception of the gospel of Jesus Christ gave the Christian way of life a foothold in this diocese. The first and oldest Christian converts include the following names :

(1) Simon Jonas Mbanugo, Stephen Obli Nwabese, Samuel Onyejekwe Onyelo, Leah Enubuoda Onyelo, Josial Obianwu and Mrs Eliza D. Agha—all from Ogbolieke Quarter.
(2) Adam Anyaegbu, Peter Ogbolu and Samuel Osakwe from Umuasele.
(3) Andrew Nzekwu Anyogwu, Samuel Ejiofo, Simeon Emenike Nsenu and Rebecca Nzelibe from Umuaroli.
(4) Sophia Kalunkie and Onyerolu from Obikporo.
(5) Christopher Mba from Unudei.
(6) Jacob Aniegbuna Okosi, Gilbert Emesim Okosi, Obi Onije and Udeaku from Ogbembubu.

To enable the Mission to expand its valuable work it selected in 1883 a group of young men for training at the Kippo Hill Training Institution at Lokoja, and among the first batch of the would-be missionary workers were George Nicholas Anyaegbunam (later ordained as Minister in Holy Orders), Henry Venn, Gbasiuzo Okosi (later Onowu Iyase), Theophilus B. Akpom, Thomas David

341

Anyaegbunam, Ephraim I. Agha, Mark Osai Romaine, James A. Onyejekwe. These men were like the seeds of the sower which fell on fertile soil and enabled Christianity to flourish throughout the length and breadth of the area now embraced by the Niger Diocese.

The pioneer indigenous Ministers in holy orders are to be listed from 1897, when Rev. G. N. Anyaegbunam was ordained. They include Alphonso C. Onyeabo (afterwards Bishop), Hezekiah O. Nweje (now Archdeacon), Mathias C. Ogo, James E. Ibeneme, Abel N. Ekpunobi, Isaac U. Ejindu, Simon A. Okechukwu and Andrew N. Asiekwu. These men, some of whom are still alive, left their homes and kith and kin and renounced the pleasures of this material world to follow the Great Master. Their sacrifice has been a shining example and an inspiration to many.

In September 1907, the CMS Niger Mission celebrated the Jubilee of its establishment at Onitsha. It was a red-letter day in the annals of Christian evangelism in this part of the world. Walter E. Blackett, a West Indian missionary who was ordained a decade later, was then Inspector of Schools of the Mission, and he composed a song which was lustily sung in all the schools and churches of the Mission. May I, with your permission, my Lord Archbishop, read the first stanza and refrain.

> Hail the day of Jubilee, Happy day !
> Join us children as we march along the way,
> And sing the song of Jubilee, Happy day !

Refrain :

> Fifty years gone by, we have no song like this
> Then join with thankful hearts, it is our Master's choice,
> To sing the song of jubilee, Happy, Happy day !

The Jubilee Service was conducted at Christ Church, Onitsha, and the sermon was preached by Bishop Herbert Tugwell. In the afternoon, there was a public meeting which was held at the Old Compound under the tamarind tree planted by Bishop Crowther and his son Archdeacon Dandeson C. Crowther. Among those present on that occasion were Bishop A. C. Howells, Archdeacon Crowther, Rev. T. Harding, Rev. J. L. McIntyre, and Rev. H.

Proctor. That was fifty years ago, Your Grace, but today, through the tender mercies of God, we are assembled here in order to celebrate the centenary of the Mission.

One name stands out among the women pioneers of the Christian Church in this diocese and she is Mrs Fanny I. Ameh, the founder and matron of the Young Women's Christian Association at Onitsha. This woman was said to have come from Okpatu in Udi Division and after she lost her engineer husband in 1911, she decided to dedicate her life to building up the YWCA. Here, young women were taught the rudiments of domestic science in order to be well prepared to live with their husbands in homes which are saturated with Christian ideals. They were taught to read in Ibo and she laboured selflessly for over thirty years. Miss G. A. Gollock mentions her in her *Daughters of Africa* as one of the splendid examples of African womanhood.

My Lord Archbishop, may I conclude this concise survey of the activities of the Church Missionary Society in this part of Nigeria in the last hundred years. I started by referring to the founding of the Church Missionary Society in obedience to the Great Commission of our Lord and Saviour Jesus Christ to go out into the four corners of the earth to preach, to teach, to heal and to baptize. Then I demonstrated the modern interpretation of this evangelizing mission, using the thoughts of the Reverend Doctor Warren, General Secretary of the Society, to illustrate my argument. In this connection, I emphasized that in his Kellogg Lectures, the learned divine distinguished between preaching the gospel and ensuring that it is heard and understood effectively.

I proceeded to examine how this message of glad tiding was disseminated to this diocese. I referred to the fact that it had always been the aim of the Society to Nigerianize its work in this Mission and I illustrated how two Africans, in the persons of Bishop Crowther and Rev. Taylor, laid the foundations of the CMS Niger Mission at Isiokwe and then later moved to Obiofu at Onitsha. Then I pointed out that Nigerianization implied team work; and I showed how European, Sierra Leonean and Nigerian workers in Christ co-operated to make the Niger Diocese safe for Christianity through self-denial and heroic devotion to duty in translating the Bible, Hymn and Prayer Books from English into Ibo.

The imperishable legacy left to us, particularly in the fields of religious knowledge and literature, by the work of Rev. Taylor, Archdeacon Dobinson, Archdeacon Dennis, T. D. Anyaegbunam, Rev. Spencer and other unsung and almost forgotten heroes of the Christian Church of the Niger Mission were placed in their proper perspective, climaxed by the panegyric in memory of T. J. Dennis for leaving the Ibo-speaking people with a glorious heritage which now acts as a *lingua franca* in unifying them as a people. The latter part of my speech concentrated on the earliest converts of the Church, listing them and giving the names of those who were trained to carry the gospel into the innermost recesses of this part of Nigeria, together with the illustrious names of our earliest Ministers in Holy Orders.

Your Grace, my main task was to assure you and our distinguished guests that the objective of the Church Missionary Society in this diocese has been achieved. The Society has been sending evangelists, teachers and physicians to teach us, to preach to us, to heal our physical infirmities, and to baptize us so that we may experience a new life in a new society that would be Christocentric. The seed which these evangelists with a mission had sown has yielded fruits of which the Society should be proud.

Your Grace, I am happy to join in amplifying and broadcasting this historic achievement after one hundred years of sacrifice, of martyrdom, and of faith in the future of humanity. This is a modern miracle. Indeed, the Christian community is a fellowship of the brave who live by faith. Otherwise, would the sixteen clergymen and the nine laymen who founded the Church Missionary Society 158 years ago, have dreamt dreams and seen visions of a Nigeria redeemed from the thraldom of superstition and transformed into a citadel of Christendom barely a century after the landing of the *Dayspring* at Onitsha? Your Grace, 'This is the Lord's doing, and it is marvellous in our eyes.'

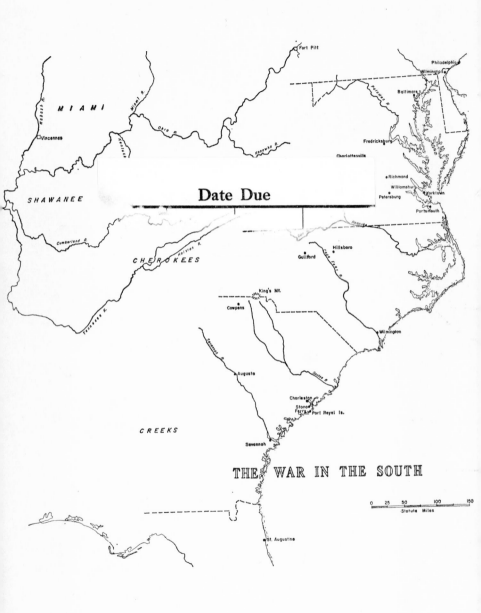

Fort Pitt

Philadelphia
Wilmington

Baltimore

MIAMI

Vincennes

Fredricksburg

Charlottesville

Richmond
Williamsburg
Petersburg
Yorktown

Portsmouth

Date Due

SHAWANEE

CHEROKEES

Hillsboro

Guilford

King's Mt.

Cowpens

Wilmington

Augusta

Charleston
Stono
Ferry
Port Royal Is.

CREEKS

Savannah

THE WAR IN THE SOUTH

0   25   50   100   150
Statute Miles

St. Augustine